GOING DEEPER WITH NEW TESTAMENT GREEK WORKBOOK

GOING DEEPER WITH NEW TESTAMENT GREEK WORKBOOK

With Exercises from Mark 8:22–10:52

John J. R. Lee and W. Tyler Sykora

Going Deeper with New Testament Greek Workbook

Published by B&H Academic®

Brentwood, Tennessee

ISBN: 978-1-4300-8834-9

Dewey Decimal Classification: 220.6

Subject Heading: BIBLE--CRITICISM \ BIBLE. NEW TESTAMENT \ GREEK LANGUAGE--GRAMMAR

All references to the textbook *Going Deeper with New Testament Greek* refer to Andreas J. Köstenberger, Benjamin L. Merkle, and Robert L. Plummer, *Going Deeper with New Testament Greek*, rev. ed. (Nashville: B&H Academic, 2020).

All Greek text is taken from Kurt Aland, Barbara Aland, Johannes Karavidopoulos, Carlo M. Martini, and Bruce M. Metzger. *Novum Testamentum Graece*. 28th ed. Stuttgart: Deutsche Bibelgesellschaft, 2012.

The web addresses referenced in this book were live and correct at the time of the book's publication but may be subject to change.

Cover design by Kristen Ingebretson. Cover images © Gregor Buir/123rf and Achim Prill/123rf.

Printed in China

30 29 28 27 26 25 RRD 1 2 3 4 5 6 7 8 9 10

CONTENTS

////////////////

(The numbers in parentheses refer to the chapters of *Going Deeper with New Testament Greek*, rev. ed.).

ABBREVIATIONS

//////////////////

MORPHOLOGICAL ABBREVIATIONS

acc	accusative
act	active
aor	aorist
chap	chapter
dat	dative
fem	feminine
fut	future
gen	genitive
impf	imperfect
impv	imperative
ind	indicative
inf	infinitive
masc	masculine
mid	middle
neut	neuter
nom	nominative
NT	New Testament
pass	passive
plur	plural
pres	present
ptc	participle
sg	singular
sub	subjunctive
voc	vocative

OTHER ABBREVIATIONS

BDAG	Bauer, Walter, Frederick Danker, William Arndt, and Wilbur Gingrich. *A Greek-English Lexicon of the New Testament and Other Early Christian Literature*, 3rd ed. Chicago: University of Chicago Press, 2000.
EDNT	Balz, H., and G Schneider. *Exegetical Dictionary of the New Testament*, 3 vols. Grand Rapids: Eerdmans, 1990–93.
Louw & Nida	Louw, Johannes P., and Eugene A. Nida. *Greek-English Lexicon of the New Testament Based on Semantic Domains.* 2 vols. New York: United Bible Societies, 1988.
LSJ	Liddell, Henry George, and Robert Scott. *A Greek-English Lexicon with a Revised Supplement*, rev. Henry Stuart Jones. Oxford: Clarendon, 1996.
NA^{28}	*Novum Testamentum Graece,* Nestle-Aland, 28th ed.
NIDNTTE	Silva, Moisés. *New International Dictionary of New Testament Theology and Exegesis*, 2nd ed. 5 vols. Grand Rapids: Zondervan, 2014.
TDNT	Kittel, G., and G. Friedrich, eds., *Theological Dictionary of the New Testament.* 10 vols. Trans. and ed. G. W. Bromiley. Grand Rapids: Eerdmans, 1964–76.
TynBul	*Tyndale Bulletin*

CHAPTER ONE

////////////////

INTRODUCTION

The late, great New Testament scholar A. T. Robertson once said, "The real New Testament is the Greek New Testament. The English is simply a translation of the New Testament, not the actual New Testament. . . . There is much that cannot be translated. It is not possible to reproduce the delicate turns of thought, the nuances of language, in translation. The freshness of the strawberry cannot be preserved in any extract."[1] Some may protest that this strong quote could instill doubt in our English translations (and we have really good English translations available today!). But since you have endeavored to read this Greek workbook, you likely already agree with him or have already begun to see the value of studying Greek so that you can read the New Testament in its original language. Our hope for this Greek workbook on the Way Discourse in Mark's Gospel is that it would further compel and equip you to keep going in your study of Greek. Studying the original languages of Scripture can be daunting at times, so our desire is to produce a helpful aid that could, Lord willing, cut through the Greek "fog" and further enable you to read the Greek New Testament proficiently.[2]

WHY THIS WORKBOOK?

In our years of studying and teaching Greek, we have noticed that there are sundry grammars available to aid the study of Koine Greek. Of late, we have especially enjoyed using Andreas J. Köstenberger, Benjamin L. Merkle, and Robert L. Plummer's *Going Deeper with New Testament Greek: An Intermediate Study of the Grammar and Syntax of the New Testament* in our classes.[3] Yet, while there are many elementary, intermediate, and advanced grammars available, there are not as many Greek workbooks on the market. Furthermore, most of the Greek workbooks that are available either work through simpler biblical texts like 1 John or are a kind of hodgepodge of passages assimilated together. While each of these approaches to a Greek workbook are, undoubtedly, helpful in their own right, we also believe readers would be served by getting into one lengthy passage of Scripture that is more difficult syntactically, but not so difficult as to prove discouraging. This was the fundamental reason we chose Mark's Way Discourse (8:22–10:52) as the text for this intermediate Greek workbook. Many have noted the genre differences between New Testament narrative—which typically tells a focused story—and epistolary literature—which typically presents a tightly woven argument. For most readers, there will be a broad familiarity with the content of Mark's Way Discourse based on an English translation. At the same time, the Greek syntax is challenging enough to force the reader to think carefully. Additionally, Mark's Way Discourse is an exegetically,

[1] A. T. Robertson, *The Minister and His Greek New Testament* (New York: George H. Doran, 1923; Birmingham: Solid Ground Christian Books, 2008), 17. Citations refer to the Solid Ground edition.

[2] William D. Mounce, *Basics of Biblical Greek Grammar*, ed. Verlyn D. Verbrugge and Christopher A. Beetham, 4th ed. (Grand Rapids: Zondervan, 2019), 47.

[3] Andreas J. Köstenberger, Benjamin L. Merkle, and Robert L. Plummer, *Going Deeper with New Testament Greek: An Intermediate Study of the Grammar and Syntax of the New Testament*, rev. ed. (Nashville: B&H Academic, 2020). Hereafter, all references are to the 2020 revised edition.

theologically, and devotionally rich passage. In fact, the (relatively) slow pace of translating the Greek may encourage the student of God's Word to dwell naturally on it in a more focused way.

WHO SHOULD USE THIS WORKBOOK?

The ideal readers for this workbook are students who are taking intermediate Greek, students who have already completed intermediate Greek, or students and pastors who want to review their intermediate Greek. It is important to know that this workbook's grammatical instruction is largely based on *Going Deeper with New Testament Greek*. In fact, the syntactical review charts come straight from that grammar. Therefore, this book will be most helpful for those who have already read *Going Deeper with New Testament Greek*. However, the workbook will still be accessible and helpful for those who have used equivalent grammars for intermediate Greek.

HOW TO USE THIS WORKBOOK

Outline

In this workbook, the syntactical topics for each chapter correspond to the contents of *Going Deeper with New Testament Greek*. However, the syntactical topics will not follow the chapter order of *Going Deeper with New Testament Greek* because they are based on the content of Mark's text. In other words, we analyzed Mark's text and discerned the syntactical topic(s) based on it. Therefore, chapter 2, on Mark 8:22–26, is focused on pronouns and adverbs given that the pericope contains a significant number of pronouns and adverbs. Below is the outline of the workbook's structure (the numbers in parentheses refer to the chapters of *Going Deeper with New Testament Greek*):

2. Mark 8:22–26: Pronouns (12) and Adverbs (12)
3. Mark 8:27–9:1: Genitives (3) and Infinitives (11)
4. Mark 9:2–13: Perfect Indicatives (9), Pluperfects Indicatives (9), and Articles (5)
5. Mark 9:14–29: Participles (10) and Vocatives (2)
6. Mark 9:30–37: Datives (4) and Accusatives (2)
7. Mark 9:38–50: Present Indicatives (8) and Sentence Structure (13)
8. Mark 10:1–16: Future Indicatives (8) and Prepositions (12)
9. Mark 10:17–31: Nominatives (2) and Adjectives (5)
10. Mark 10:32–45: Verbs (Voice, Mood, Tense, Aspect) (6, 7) and Conjunctions (12)
11. Mark 10:46–52: Aorist (9) and Imperfect Indicatives (8)
12. Textual Criticism Applied to the Way Discourse (1)
13. Diagramming Applied to Mark 8:34–38 and Mark 10:42–45 (13)

Chapter Structure

Each chapter will begin with a review of the syntactical topic(s) covered in that chapter. As mentioned earlier, we include the syntactical review charts from *Going Deeper with New Testament Greek* for your convenience and reference. Next, you will transition to a section titled "Guided Practice." In this section, you will translate the passage from Greek to English, writing your English translations between the double-spaced lines of Greek. We have provided vocabulary aids for words that occur fewer than fifty times. Then, you will enter the "Exercise" section of the chapter. In this section, you will answer exegetical questions from select verses, provide a short summary of the passage under consideration, discuss how the passage fits within its surrounding context, and parse and classify the words associated with the syntactical topic(s) for that chapter.

The answer key for each chapter will immediately follow the exercises. Our recommendation is to glance at the answer key before starting the exercises to discern the type of answers we are looking for. Once you know what to expect, however, it is strongly recommended that you think through your answers without consulting the answer key. The more you can come to your own conclusions, the better. Then, after thinking through the content yourself, consult the answer key to check your work.

Some further clarifications might be useful. The "Verse-by-Verse Questions" section in chapters 2–11 of this workbook is not limited within the given chapter's topic but instead includes various grammatical and syntactical issues related to the Markan passage discussed in the chapter. Students are therefore encouraged to consult the SUMMARY charts contained in other chapters of this workbook as needed while working through that particular section. If further assistance is needed, review the appropriate chapters in *Going Deeper with New Testament Greek*, rev. ed. Moreover, the lists of REFERENCES located at the end of the respective chapters are meant to include not only the sources cited in the footnotes but also the works consulted generally in the preparation of the pertinent chapters, which, however, did not need to be cited in the footnotes for particular points made in the main text.

As anyone familiar with intermediate Greek knows, syntactical classifications can be subjective at times. We recognize that our answers are not infallible. In fact, we are happy for students and other professors to disagree with our answers at times. You should not be discouraged if you come to a different syntactical conclusion than we do. Our hope is that you will think carefully about the possibilities and come to a reasoned conclusion.

SHORT INTRODUCTION TO MARK'S GOSPEL

Before getting into the text of Mark's Way Discourse, it will be helpful to orient you to Mark's Gospel as a whole. The more you know the context (literary, sociocultural, situational, etc.) of a given biblical book, the better you will be able to discern the intended meaning of that book. In the conclusion to this section, we will see how our understanding of the Gospel of Mark's circumstances can impact our reading, teaching, and preaching of the Way Discourse.

Authorship

Though much debate surrounds the authorship of Mark's Gospel,[4] we believe the author of the Gospel of Mark was Mark, also known as John Mark, who was a visible figure in the New Testament. The early church unanimously attributed the Gospel to Mark, and in Eusebius's *Ecclesiastical History*, we have an early account from the second-century bishop of Hierapolis, Papias, where Eusebius records Papias's testimony:

> And this presbyter used to say: "Having become the interpreter of Peter, Mark wrote accurately—not, indeed, in order—as much as he remembered of the things said or done by the Lord. For he had neither heard the Lord nor followed him, though later on, as I said, [he followed] Peter, who gave teaching in the form of *chreiai*,[5] but not making, as it were, an arrangement of the Lord's oracles, so that Mark did nothing wrong in thus writing down single points as he remembered. For to one thing he gave attention, to leave out nothing of what he had heard and to falsify nothing in them."[6]

As noted by Papias, the source for the Gospel of Mark was probably the apostle Peter. Mark was not one of the original disciples, but Scripture suggests that Mark and Peter knew one another well. In Acts 12:11–12, Peter goes to Mark's house after he escapes from prison, and we know from 1 Pet 5:13 that Mark was with Peter at the time he wrote that letter. This view is confirmed by the early church father, Irenaeus, once again captured by Eusebius in *Ecclesiastical History*:

> Matthew, indeed, . . . produced his gospel written among the Hebrews in their own dialect, while Peter and Paul proclaimed the gospel and founded the church at Rome.

---

[4] See David E. Garland, *A Theology of Mark's Gospel: Good News about Jesus the Messiah, the Son of God*, ed. Andreas J. Köstenberger, Biblical Theology of the New Testament (Grand Rapids: Zondervan, 2015), 47–67.

[5] A *chreia* is a literary form (often a narrative) that contains short, pithy statements that are frequently attributed to a well-known figure.

[6] Eusebius, *Hist. eccl.* 3.39.15. This more literal translation comes from Samuel Byrskog, *Story as History—History as Story: The Gospel Tradition in the Context of Ancient Oral History* (Leiden: Brill, 2022), 272. Note that there is also debate about Papias's account. We agree with Garland's conclusions concerning this debate: "Those who find Papias's testimony to be of no value may do so because it controverts their own theories. One can be skeptical of the skepticism of NT scholars, because if one dismisses Papias's testimony, 'then only speculation as to the geographical and authorial origin is left.'" Garland, *A Theology of Mark's Gospel,* 55.

> . . . After the departure of these, Mark, the disciple and interpreter of Peter, also transmitted to us in writing what had been preached by Peter. And Luke, the companion of Paul, committed to writing the gospel preached by him, i.e., Paul. . . . Afterwards John the disciple of our Lord, the same that lay upon his bosom, also published the gospel, while he was yet at Ephesus in Asia.[7]

Mark was from a wealthy and prominent early church family (Acts 12:12). He was the cousin of Barnabas (Col 4:10) and a younger companion of Paul and Barnabas during the first Christian missionary efforts (Acts 12:24–25; 13:5). His departure in Pamphylia during the first missionary journey (Acts 13:13) caused a rift between Paul and Barnabas (Acts 15:37–39). Despite this painful event, Paul and Mark seemed to have an intimate partnership later in their ministry (Col 4:10; Phlm v. 24; 2 Tim 4:11). Mark also served as Peter's close associate whom the apostle called ὁ υἱός μου in his first letter (1 Pet 5:13).

Provenance

Evidence points to this Gospel being written to Gentile Christians in Rome.[8] There are several reasons for this conclusion. First, there are Greek translations of Aramaic terms (e.g., 5:41; 7:34) throughout the Gospel. If Mark wrote to an audience in Galilee or Syria (the other two prominent options), there would not have been a reason to include these Greek translations, since Aramaic was spoken in both regions. Second, in Mark 7:3–4, there is an explanation of Jewish purity regulations. If Mark were writing to a group of Christians in Galilee or Syria, there would not have been a need to explain these regulations because audiences in those locations would have already been familiar with such customs.

Though not as strong as the first two on their own, the following can still be used as secondary evidence, in conjunction with the above two, for a Roman audience. Third, the presence of many Greek transliterations of Latin words (Latinisms, e.g., Mark 12:42; 15:16) gives subtle evidence for a Roman audience. Fourth, there is an emphasis in Mark's Gospel on the proclamation of the Gospel to the Gentiles (e.g., 13:10; 15:38–39; cf. 7:1–23), which seems to support a predominantly Gentile audience not near the land of Israel. Fifth and finally, in Mark 10:11–12, we see the background of the Roman law (not Jewish) in the matter of divorce. When taken collectively, these points hint at a Roman audience.

Date

The date of Mark's composition is, once again, heavily debated. Some say Mark wrote as early as the mid to late AD 40s, some say mid to late 60s, and others say post AD 70, after the destruction of Jerusalem.

It is beyond the scope of this book to deal adequately with each view under consideration.[9] We believe, however, that a mid to late 60s date is most likely for four reasons. First, the testimony of the early church seems to indicate a date right after Paul and Peter's martyrdom in the mid to late 60s. For example, Irenaeus of Lyons wrote, "After [Peter's and Paul's] departure, Mark, the disciple and interpreter of Peter, did also hand down to us in writing what had been preached by Peter."[10]

Second, within Mark's Gospel, there are warnings about followers of Jesus being rejected, mistreated, and persecuted for their faith (e.g., 4:14–19; 6:11; 8:15; 13:9–23; 14:66–72). More specifically, the call of Jesus in Mark 8:34 to "take up [one's] cross" refers to a Roman threat, since crucifixion was a Roman way of execution.[11] This likely indicates that Mark's original readers were experiencing suffering/persecution from Roman authorities. John Lee and Daniel Brueske helpfully explain the significance of this reality:

---

[7] Eusebius, *Ecclesiastical History*, 5.8.2–4.

[8] For an overview of the different options concerning the provenance of Mark's Gospel, see Garland, *A Theology of Mark's Gospel,* 67–80; more briefly, John J. R. Lee, *Christological Rereading of the Shema (Deut 6.4) in Mark's Gospel*, Wissenschaftliche Untersuchungen Zum Neuen Testament 2. Reihe 533 (Tübingen: Mohr Siebeck, 2020), 16–17.

[9] For an overview of this debate, see John J. R. Lee and Daniel Brueske, *A Ransom for Many: Mark 10:45 as a Key to the Gospel* (Bellingham, WA: Lexham Academic, 2023), 10–21.

[10] Irenaeus, *Against Heresies* (Pickerington, OH: Beloved, 2015), 3.1.1. Ellis has argued that this text from Irenaeus is actually describing the transmission of Mark's Gospel rather than the composition of it. Edward Earle Ellis, "The Date and Provenance of Mark's Gospel," *The Four Gospels*, ed. Franz van Segbroeck (Leuven, Peeters, 1992), 803, 814.

[11] Lee and Brueske, *A Ransom for Many*, 12.

> The Jewish conflict experienced by Jesus and his disciples in Mark's Gospel illustrates the hostility believers will experience or are already experiencing from various authorities as a result of their loyalty to Jesus. If Mark understands the ultimate source of opposition to Jesus as spiritual (see 3:20–27; also, 1:21–28; 5:1–20; 9:14–29), then it is not surprising that the agents of that opposition may be represented by religious leaders at one point and by Roman authorities at another. Conflict between first-century followers of Jesus and the Roman authorities varied at different times depending on the location, but the Neronian persecution of Christians in Rome in the mid-60s offers a very plausible backdrop to the warnings about suffering and persecution . . . found in Mark's Gospel. Before this time, there does not seem to be an instance of significant Roman persecution of Christians.[12]

Third, in all of Paul's writings, he never seems to refer explicitly to Mark's Gospel. Though he refers to the life of Jesus in several of his epistles, it appears that he is referring to oral tradition and not a written source.[13] This leads us to think that Paul was unaware of Mark's Gospel because it had not yet been composed, thereby making a date as early as the mid to late AD 40s unlikely.

Fourth, we believe that Mark 13 supports a date before AD 70 when Jerusalem was destroyed. Mark's details of Jesus's prediction of the destruction of Jerusalem appear to be relatively inexplicit which would support the Gospel being written before the destruction had occurred.

Though there are decent arguments for other options concerning when to date Mark's Gospel, we believe the external and internal evidence best supports a mid to late AD 60s date.[14]

Purpose

If what we have said above is correct about the provenance and date, then Mark was likely writing to Gentile believers in Rome on the brink of or in the midst of persecution by Nero. These would have been difficult times, to say the least, as the "cost of discipleship" was a daily reality (8:34–38). Therefore, Mark's primary purpose in writing seems to be pastoral rather than informational, evangelistic, or polemical. As Christopher D. Marshall writes, Mark's purpose "is to instruct and strengthen the faith of his readers by involving them in the story of Jesus in such a way that those features of his teaching and example which Mark has chosen to narrate are experienced as directly relevant to their present needs."[15] Or as Lee and Brueske state, "Mark has written a story that focuses substantially on who Jesus is and what he has done in order to motivate his audience who are facing rejection and persecution to remain loyal to Jesus."[16] In other words, to help encourage his audience to remain faithful to Jesus until the end regardless of the cost, Mark reminds his readers who Jesus is and what he had done for them (e.g., Mark 10:45). Instead of simply commanding these persecuted believers to keep going, he reminds them of the life of their Savior, and he shows them the shame and suffering that Jesus endured in an effort to encourage them to remain faithful under similar circumstances.

Overview of Mark's Narrative

German scholar Martin Kähler famously stated that New Testament Gospels are "passion narratives with extended introductions."[17] Though this hyperbolic statement presents an insightful and helpful way to look at the Gospels, it would be beneficial for us to consider how Mark's Gospel is structured specifically.

There are some who believe the Gospel follows a geographical outline:[18] Jesus's ministry in Galilee, his journey to Jerusalem, and then his suffering and passion in Jerusalem.

---

[12] Lee and Brueske, 12–13.

[13] Lee and Brueske, 13.

[14] For a response to an early date based on the end of the book of Acts and the "Synoptic Problem," see Lee and Brueske, 20.

[15] Christopher D. Marshall, *Faith as a Theme in Mark's Narrative*, Society for New Testament Studies 64 (Cambridge: Cambridge University Press, 1995), 6.

[16] Lee and Brueske, *A Ransom for Many*, 31.

[17] Martin Kähler, *The So-Called Historical Jesus and the Historic Biblical Christ*, ed. Carl E. Braaten, Fortress Texts in Modern Theology (Philadelphia: Fortress, 1988), 80n11.

[18] William L. Lane, *The Gospel According to Mark*, New International Commentary on the New Testament (Grand Rapids: Eerdmans, 1974), 29–32.

Others believe the best way to understand Mark's Gospel is through a theological structure.[19] The theological outline commonly divides the Gospel into two parts. The first part of the Gospel emphasizes Jesus's messianic authority and teaching, while the second part of the Gospel emphasizes his suffering and death, also known as his passion.

Is this two-part division warranted? Yes, in part, we believe so. However, the two parts (Messianic authority and passion) are closely connected and interwoven throughout the entire Gospel. Jesus's authority and his passion are the motifs that occur throughout the narrative of Mark, not simply one half or the other. For example, the Jewish leaders accuse Jesus of blasphemy (the reason he is put to death later in the narrative) as early as 2:7. Jesus also hints at his death in 2:20, where he depicts himself as the groom who is about to be "taken away."

We also see his authority later in the Gospel, not just in the beginning. For example, after Jesus cleanses the temple in chapter 11, the chief priests, scribes, and elders come to him and ask him by what authority he does these things (11:28). Then, as he is on trial, the chief priest asks him if he is the Messiah (14:61). He answers yes and states he is going to fulfill Psalm 110:1 and Daniel 7:13 by being seated at the right hand of power and coming with the clouds of heaven (14:62). Again, they question his authority, and he answers authoritatively. In light of this, we think there is certainly a focus throughout the Gospel both on Jesus's Messianic authority and on his passion; the two are not as segregated as some would suggest.

We can also attempt to interweave the geographical outline with the theological outline. It is hard to minimize the fact that Mark's Gospel builds and progresses as Jesus leaves Galilee, journeys on the way, and then suffers and dies in Jerusalem. The messianic authority and passion themes discussed earlier are, at times, rightly connected to geographical locations. Therefore, it may prove helpful to keep both the geographical and theological aspects in mind when outlining the structure of Mark's Gospel. Our proposed outline is as follows:

I. Preface 1:1–1:13

II. Jesus's ministry in Galilee 1:14–8:21
- A. Galilean ministry part 1: 1:16–3:6[20]
  - 1. Beginning of Jesus's public ministry: 1:16–1:45
  - 2. Series of controversies in Galilee: 2:1–3:6
- B. Galilean ministry part 2: 3:7–6:6a
- C. Galilean ministry part 3: 6:6b–8:21

III. On the way to Jerusalem 8:22–10:52
- A. Healing of a blind man at Bethsaida (two-stage healing): 8:22–26
- B. First cycle of prediction-error-teaching:[21] 8:27–9:29
- C. Second cycle of prediction-error-teaching: 9:30–10:31
- D. Third cycle of prediction-error-teaching: 10:32–45
- E. Healing of blind Bartimaeus at Jericho: 10:46–52

IV. Jesus's ministry in Jerusalem: 11:1–16:8[22]
- A. Conflicts in Jerusalem: 11:1–13:37
  - 1. Entry to Jerusalem: 11:1–11
  - 2. Jesus's prophetic action in the temple and the cursed fig tree: 11:12–25
  - 3. Series of controversies in the temple: 11:27–12:44[23]
  - 4. Jesus's prophecy concerning the fall of Jerusalem and end times: 13:1–37

---

[19] Robert A. Guelich, *Mark 1–8:26*, Word Biblical Commentary 34A (Dallas: Thomas Nelson, 1989), xxxvii–xl.

[20] The structure of 1:14–8:21 seems less clear than 8:22 through the end of the book. That is why we have decided to be satisfied with somewhat undescriptive headings such as "Galilean Ministry Part One."

[21] That is, (1) Jesus's prediction of his passion and resurrection, (2) disciples' misunderstandings and errors, and (3) Jesus's corrective teaching on discipleship.

[22] For discussion on Mark's ending and the related textual issues, see, e.g., D. A. Carson and Douglas J. Moo, *An Introduction to the New Testament*, 2nd ed. (Grand Rapids: Zondervan, 2005), 187–90. Most commentaries include some elaborations on these matters in handling Mark 16.

[23] Mark 11:27–12:44 counterbalances 2:1–3:6 in the narrative. These two sections each contain a series of Jesus's controversies with Jewish authorities.

B. Death, burial and resurrection of Jesus
 1. Death and burial: 14:1–15:47
 2. Resurrection: 16:1–8

Compared to the other Gospels (Matthew, Luke, and John), Mark's Gospel begins and progresses in a relatively quick fashion. Mark does not begin his Gospel with a birth narrative or genealogy. Instead, he starts with an Isaianic prophecy (1:2–3; more specifically, a composite quotation from Malachi 3:1 and Isaiah 40:3 [cf. Exod 23:20] under the label, "Isaiah the Prophet") and then introduces his readers to the fulfillment of that prophecy in the person of John the Baptist (1:4). John drew great attention from those in Judea and Jerusalem, yet he declared that there was someone coming who was greater than he (1:7). But who could be greater than the prophet-like figure of John the Baptist? The answer comes a couple of verses later as Jesus of Nazareth steps onto the scene. After being baptized by John, Jesus comes up out of the water, the heavens are "torn open," and a voice says, "You are my beloved Son" (1:11).

Jesus is then driven into the wilderness by the Spirit for forty days of testing (1:12). The events appear strikingly familiar to those formerly done in Israel's history. Just as Israel went through the waters of the Red Sea and then entered the wilderness for testing, so now Jesus leaves the waters of the Jordan to enter the wilderness for testing. Where Israel failed, however, Jesus succeeds. Jesus is being depicted as the true Israel, the faithful Son.

Jesus then begins his ministry in Galilee by proclaiming the good news of God: "The time is fulfilled, and the kingdom of God has come near. Repent and believe the good news!" (1:15). Mark began his Gospel by calling Jesus the Messiah or Christ (1:1), and Jesus's Messianic authority is on full display throughout the Gospel. He calls disciples to follow him, and they drop everything (1:17–20). He commands demons, and they obey (1:25, 34; 5:8). He touches the untouchable, and they are healed (1:41). He rebukes the wind and waves, and they become calm (4:39). As Jesus's authority is manifested, the crowds cannot help but be amazed. The question "Who can this be?" radiates throughout the countryside.[24]

At the same time, Jesus's authoritative deeds and teaching also cause resentment and opposition. The Jewish religious leaders are perplexed by Jesus claiming to forgive sins (2:5) and by his apparent violation of the Sabbath (2:23–27). They resolve to get rid of this blasphemer (e.g., 3:6).The truth is, many people now respected Jesus more than they did their leaders (cf. 1:22).

The climax and turning point in the narrative occurs when Jesus and his disciples are in Caesarea Philippi. Jesus asks his disciples "Who do the people say that I am?" (8:27). After a couple responses, he then asks his disciples who they think he is (8:29). Peter, perhaps speaking on behalf of the other disciples, responds, "You are the Messiah" (8:30). Jesus's true identity, already revealed by his deeds, is now confessed by his disciples. However, they still do not properly understand what it means for Jesus to be the Messiah. When Jesus begins to teach his disciples about his forthcoming suffering and death, it becomes clear that the disciples were expecting a conquering Messiah and do not leave room for a suffering one.

In the Way Discourse (8:22–10:52), Jesus predicts his suffering and death three times (8:31; 9:31; 10:33–34). Following all three passion predictions, the disciples reveal that they still don't understand what it means to follow Jesus. As they are jockeying for first place and a right-hand seat in the kingdom (10:35–45), Jesus continually corrects them on what it means to be his disciple. True discipleship involves taking up one's cross and following Jesus down a path of suffering (8:34–38). This is clearly depicted in the Gospel's theme verse, Mark 10:45: "For even the Son of Man did not come to be served, but to serve, and to give his life as a ransom for many."[25] Not only does this verse depict Jesus as *the* example to imitate; it also emphasizes his approaching substitutionary death on behalf of his followers.

Following the Way Discourse, the narrative slows its pace as Mark gives a detailed account of Jesus's final days leading up to his crucifixion and resurrection.[26] Jesus enters Jerusalem in 11:1; then Mark implements a sandwich

---

[24] See Mark L. Strauss, *Mark*, Zondervan Exegetical Commentary on the New Testament (Grand Rapids: Zondervan, 2014), 18. This question also becomes a pertinent one for Mark's readers. As Lee and Brueske state, "Mark's narration of the controversy over Jesus's authority effectively forces his audience to choose for themselves who they say Jesus is. For Mark, the answer is clear. Jesus is not some blasphemer who works by the power of Satan. Mark wants his audience to understand that Jesus is the Son of God and Son of Man who controls both the storms and the spirits and who forgives sins as only God can. This is the Jesus whom they follow." Lee and Brueske, *A Ransom for Many*, 55.

[25] For more on how this verse impacts Mark's Gospel as a whole, see Lee and Brueske, *A Ransom for Many.*

[26] One of the ways to detect the fact that the narrative slows its pace is Mark's use of εὐθύς (immediately). Mark uses εὐθύς thirty-five times in the first ten chapters and only six times in chapters 11–16.

construction where he encloses Jesus cleansing the temple with two episodes about Jesus cursing a barren fig tree (11:12–25). The cursing of the fig tree is not about the cursing of nature, but rather, he is giving a warning about the divine judgment that is looming over the temple.

Jesus then eats the Passover meal with his disciples but adds a new meaning to it. The bread represents his body that is soon to be broken, and the blood is the blood of the new covenant that is soon to be spilled (14:24; cf. Luke 22:20). Also, during the Passover Jesus predicts both Judas's betrayal (14:18, 20) and the disciples' desertion of him (14:27). Even though the disciples respond strongly that they would never do such a thing, it would not be long before Jesus would be standing alone before a mob with swords and clubs (14:43). Jesus is then arrested, condemned, and handed over to the Romans to be crucified. Mark's depiction of the crucifixion scene is somber and mixed with great irony. Those passing by Jesus's crucifixion hurl insults at him, saying, "He saved others, but he cannot save himself! Let the Messiah, the King of Israel, come down now from the cross, so that we may see and believe" (15:31–32). The very converse is true; he saves others by not saving himself. Perhaps the greatest irony comes in the fact that the first person to realize Jesus's true identity in his suffering is a pagan Roman centurion. Mark began his Gospel with the heavens being "torn apart" (1:10) and a voice declaring, "You are my beloved Son" (1:11), and now the Gospel is coming to its climax with the temple curtain being "torn in two" (15:38) and the centurion exclaiming, "Truly this man was the Son of God" (15:39).[27]

Jesus is then buried, and his body is in the tomb for three days. But on the first day of the week, some of the women who saw where Jesus was buried go to the tomb to anoint his body (16:1–3). What they find is not a corpse; instead, they see the stone rolled away and a man in white clothes telling them that Jesus has risen (16:6). What Jesus predicted numerous times has come true; he is risen from the dead! The Gospel concludes in a somewhat strange manner. The women are informed about Jesus's resurrection and then commanded to go and tell the other disciples. But they are overwhelmed with fear and don't tell anyone anything. Why would Mark end his Gospel this way? There has been much speculation about the answer to this question, but for our purposes here, it seems that Mark wants to challenge his readers with what they just read. Jesus is risen from the dead. His messianic claim has been vindicated. Now, what are you going to do about it? Mark is calling his readers to believe it and to endure suffering and shame on behalf of this great truth. Not only that, but Mark is also calling his readers to share this good news. Will you be like the women and keep it to yourself in fear? Or will you be bold with this good news and share it with others regardless of the cost? This question is a perennial one for every follower of Christ.

A WORD OF EXHORTATION

After reading this brief introduction, you are now ready to dive into Mark's Way Discourse. As you do, remember the great privilege it is to study God's Word at this depth. Whether you are a student who has been assigned this workbook for a class, a pastor who wants to keep up your Greek, or simply a lover of Greek seeking a new challenge, we encourage you to work through this resource with a devotional spirit. There is a real temptation to turn the study of God's Word into mere academic exercise. When this happens, one's soul begins to dry up and languish. Instead, approach each chapter with prayer asking God to help you not only to understand what the text means but also to apply its truth to your heart. It is our prayer that this book will further challenge every reader and equip each one to follow Jesus on the way of cross-bearing discipleship (Mark 8:34; 10:42–45).

---

[27] Joel Marcus, *Mark 8–16: A New Translation with Introduction and Commentary*, The Anchor Yale Bible 27A (New Haven, CT: Yale University Press, 2009), 1067–68. See also Strauss, *Mark*, 19.

CHAPTER TWO

////////////////

MARK 8:22–26

WITH ATTENTION TO PRONOUNS AND ADVERBS

GRAMMAR REVIEW:

Pronouns

Definition and Description

Pronouns are words that replace nouns or ideas. They provide a shorthand way of mentioning something without specifically naming or repeating it. So, though small, they carry a lot of weight. The NT has over 16,000 pronouns, and they show up in four-fifths of its verses. Usually, a pronoun will follow the word to which it is referring, called its *antecedent*. Sometimes, the pronoun precedes the word, in which case the referent is a *postcedent*.[1]

Pronouns can be classified into seven categories, some of which have subcategories. When encountering a pronoun in a text, the most important task is to identify the antecedent or postcedent, if it has one. While usually individual words, they can also be clauses or entire passages. Ambiguities in determining a referent can have exegetical significance.

> Consider Eph 2:8: Τῇ γὰρ χάριτί ἐστε σεσῳσμένοι διὰ πίστεως· καὶ **τοῦτο** οὐκ ἐξ ὑμῶν, θεοῦ τὸ δῶρον.

If τοῦτο has an antecedent (and some argue that it does not),[2] to what does it refer? It could possibly refer to πίστεως, the closest substantive, or possibly to χάριτί or σεσῳσμένοι—or it could even refer to the entire preceding clause. Since pronouns usually match their referents in number and gender, τοῦτο (sg, neut) would most likely reference the entire clause, rather than χάριτί (sg, fem), πίστεως (sg, fem), or σεσῳσμένοι (plur, masc). There are, however, many exceptions to this "rule," and, thus, the debate continues.[3]

---

[1] Cf. Steven E. Runge, *Discourse Grammar of the Greek New Testament: A Practical Introduction for Teaching and Exegesis* (Peabody, MA: Hendrickson, 2010), 66–68.

[2] See this discussion in Daniel B. Wallace, *Greek Grammar Beyond the Basics: An Exegetical Syntax of the New Testament* (Grand Rapids: Zondervan, 1996), 334–35.

[3] Harold W. Hoehner, *Ephesians: An Exegetical Commentary* (Grand Rapids: Baker Academic, 2002), 342–44.

Categories and Examples[4]

PRONOUNS

TYPE	SAMPLE FORMS	NT EXAMPLE
PERSONAL	ἐγώ ("I"); μου ("my"); σύ (sg, "you"); ὑμῶν (pl, "your"); αὐτοῦ ("his").	**ἡμεῖς** δὲ οὐκ ἐσμὲν ὑποστολῆς εἰς ἀπώλειαν ("But **we** are not like those who turn away from God to their own destruction" Heb 10:39 NLT).
DEMONSTRATIVE	Near: οὗτος (masc, "this"); αὗται (fem, "these").	**ταῦτα** δὲ αὐτοῦ ἐνθυμηθέντος ("But after he had considered **these things**" Matt 1:20).
	Far: ἐκεῖνο (neut, "that"); ἐκεῖνοι (masc, "those").	ἐν δὲ ταῖς ἡμέραις **ἐκείναις** παραγίνεται Ἰωάννης ὁ βαπτιστής ("In **those** days John the Baptist came" Matt 3:1)
RELATIVE	οἵ (masc pl, "who"); ἧς (fem sg, "of whom"); ὅ (neut sg, "which").	ἀνδρὶ μωρῷ, **ὅστις** ᾠκοδόμησεν αὐτοῦ τὴν οἰκίαν ἐπὶ τὴν ἄμμον ("a foolish man **who** built his house on the sand" Matt 7:26).
INTERROGATIVE	τίς (masc/fem sg, "who?"); τίνος (masc/fem sg, "of whom?"); τί ("what/why?").	**τί** κωλύει με βαπτισθῆναι; ("**What** is to prevent me from being baptized?" Acts 8:36 NRSV).
INDEFINITE	τις (masc sg, "anyone, someone"); τινες (masc pl, "certain ones").	ἐάν **τις** εἴπῃ . . . ("If **anyone** says . . ." 1 John 4:20).
REFLEXIVE	ἐμαυτόν ("myself"); ἑαυτούς (masc, "yourselves"); ἑαυτοῖς (masc, "to themselves").	**ἑαυτοὺς** πειράζετε εἰ ἐστὲ ἐν τῇ πίστει ("Examine **yourselves** to see whether you are in the faith" 2 Cor 13:5 NIV).
RECIPROCAL	ἀλλήλων ("one another").	ἀνεχόμενοι **ἀλλήλων** ("bearing with **one another**" Col 3:13).

Adverbs

Definition and Description

Adverbs usually modify verbs, but they can also modify adjectives, other adverbs, or substantives. Adverbs are not declinable, but some endings tend to be common. Adverbs of manner often end in -ως (καλῶς, ταχέως), whereas adverbs of place often end in -θεν (ἄνωθεν, μακρόθεν). Adverbs of manner will usually be translated in English as *-ly* words; adverbs of place will often be translated using *from*. Adverbs of time often end in -οτε (τότε, πότε), and numerical adverbs of degree may end in -ις (πολλάκις, ἑπτάκις). But adverbs are not limited to these endings; the two most common are -ως and -ον.

One of the most common words in the NT is καί, which is usually translated as a conjunction. But καί also functions as an adverb. Καί is a conjunction when it connects two grammatically equal elements; otherwise, it functions as an adverb and would mean something like "also" or "even."

How you classify an adverb will impact how you understand a text. For example, John 3:16 begins with οὕτως. The ESV begins this verse as "For God *so* loved the world," treating οὕτως as an adverb of degree. The Message is more explicit, rendering it, "This is *how much* God loved the world." The CSB, by contrast, takes οὕτως as an adverb of manner: "For God loved the world *in this way*."[5] As this example demonstrates, classification is not always straightforward.

---

[4] Andreas J. Köstenberger, Benjamin L. Merkle, and Robert L. Plummer, *Going Deeper with New Testament Greek: An Intermediate Study of the Grammar and Syntax of the New Testament*, rev. ed. (Nashville: B&H Academic, 2020), 426.

[5] The CSB is correct here in taking this as an adverb of manner.

Categories and Examples[6]

ADVERBS MODIFYING A VERB	
INDICATIVE	ὁ θάνατος οὐκ ἔσται **ἔτι** ("Death will be no **more**" Rev 21:4 NRSV).
INFINITIVE	Ἰωσὴφ . . . ἐβουλήθη **λάθρᾳ** ἀπολῦσαι αὐτήν ("Joseph . . . decided to divorce her **secretly**" Matt 1:19).
PARTICIPLE	ὁ σπείρων **φειδομένως φειδομένως** καὶ θερίσει ("The person who sows **sparingly** will also reap **sparingly**" 2 Cor 9:6).
IMPERATIVE	ἐπίστηθι **εὐκαίρως ἀκαίρως** ("be ready **in season** and **out of season**" 2 Tim 4:2 ESV).
SUBJUNCTIVE	ἵνα . . . **σωφρόνως** καὶ **δικαίως** καὶ **εὐσεβῶς** ζήσωμεν ἐν τῷ νῦν αἰῶνι ("to live in a **sensible**, **righteous**, and **godly** way in the present age" Titus 2:12).
ADVERBS MODIFYING AN ADJECTIVE OR ADVERB	
ADJECTIVE	[ἦσαν] χαλεποὶ **λίαν**, ὥστε μὴ ἰσχύειν τινὰ παρελθεῖν διὰ τῆς ὁδοῦ ἐκείνης ("They were **so** violent that no one could pass that way" Matt 8:28).
ADVERB	καὶ πρωῒ ἔννυχα **λίαν** ἀναστὰς ἐξῆλθεν καὶ ἀπῆλθεν εἰς ἔρημον τόπον ("**Very** early in the morning, while it was still dark, he got up, went out, and made his way to a deserted place" Mark 1:35).
USES OF THE ADVERB	
TIME (WHEN?)	**ἔπειτα** ἦλθον εἰς τὰ κλίματα τῆς Συρίας καὶ τῆς Κιλικίας ("**Afterward**, I went to the regions of Syria and Cilicia" Gal 1:21).
DEGREE (HOW MUCH?)	ἐγὼ ἦλθον ἵνα ζωὴν ἔχωσιν καὶ **περισσὸν** ἔχωσιν ("I came that they may have life, and have it **abundantly**" John 10:10 NASB).
MANNER (IN WHAT WAY?)	**ὁμοίως** ὁ ἐλεύθερος κληθεὶς δοῦλός ἐστιν Χριστου ("**Likewise** he who is called as a free man is Christ's slave" 1 Cor 7:22).
PLACE (WHERE?)	σὺ κάθου **ὧδε** καλῶς ("Sit **here** in a good place" Jas 2:3).
ADVERBS USED AS NOUNS OR ADJECTIVES	
NOUN	ἵνα γένηται καὶ **τὸ ἐκτὸς** αὐτοῦ καθαρόν ("so **the outside** of it may also become clean" Matt 23:26).
ADJECTIVE	πρὸς τὴν ἔνδειξιν τῆς δικαιοσύνης αὐτοῦ ἐν τῷ **νῦν** καιρῷ ("to demonstrate his righteousness at the **present** time" Rom 3:26 NIV).

[6] Köstenberger, Merkle, and Plummer, *Going Deeper with New Testament Greek*, 428–29.

GUIDED PRACTICE: MARK 8:22–26 (NA[28])

22 Καὶ ἔρχονται εἰς Βηθσαϊδάν. Καὶ φέρουσιν αὐτῷ τυφλὸν καὶ παρακαλοῦσιν αὐτὸν ἵνα
αὐτοῦ ἅψηται. 23 καὶ ἐπιλαβόμενος τῆς χειρὸς τοῦ τυφλοῦ ἐξήνεγκεν αὐτὸν ἔξω τῆς κώμης
καὶ πτύσας εἰς τὰ ὄμματα αὐτοῦ, ἐπιθεὶς τὰς χεῖρας αὐτῷ ἐπηρώτα αὐτόν· εἴ τι βλέπεις;

24 καὶ ἀναβλέψας ἔλεγεν· βλέπω τοὺς ἀνθρώπους ὅτι ὡς δένδρα ὁρῶ περιπατοῦντας.
25 εἶτα πάλιν ἐπέθηκεν τὰς χεῖρας ἐπὶ τοὺς ὀφθαλμοὺς αὐτοῦ, καὶ διέβλεψεν καὶ ἀπεκατέστη
καὶ ἐνέβλεπεν τηλαυγῶς ἅπαντα. 26 καὶ ἀπέστειλεν αὐτὸν εἰς οἶκον αὐτοῦ λέγων· μηδὲ εἰς
τὴν κώμην εἰσέλθῃς.

VOCABULARY AIDS (WORDS 26X TO 50X)

8:22, 23 **τυφλός** *blind* (50x)

8:22 **ἅπτω** *to touch, hold, grasp* (middle/passive); *to light, ignite*; *cook* (active) (39x)

8:23, 26 **κώμη** *village* (27x)

8:23, 25 **ἐπιτίθημι** (ἐπί+τίθημι) *to lay on, place, put, add* (39x)

8:25 **ἅπας** *all, every* (36x)

VOCABULARY AIDS (WORDS 25X OR LESS)

8:22 **Βηθσαϊδά** *Bethsaida* (7x)

8:23 **ἐπιλαμβάνομαι** (ἐπί+λαμβάνω, aorist stem: λαβ) *to take hold of*; *to seize* (19x)

8:23 **ἐκφέρω** (ἐκ+φέρω) *to carry out, lead away* (8x)

8:23 **πτύω** *to spit* (3x)

8:23 **ὄμμα** *eye* (2x)

8:24 **ἀναβλέπω** (ἀνά+βλέπω) *to receive sight*; *to look up* (25x)

8:24 **δένδρον** *tree* (25x)

8:25 **εἶτα** *then, next* (15x)

8:25 **διαβλέπω** (διά+βλέπω) *to see clearly* (3x)

8:25 **ἀποκαθίστημι** (ἀπό+κατά+ἵστημι) *to restore, be healed, return* (8x)

8:25 **ἐμβλέπω** (ἐν+βλέπω) *to look intently*; *to give serious thought* (12x)

8:25 **τηλαυγῶς** (τῆλε+αὐγή) *clearly* (1x)

EXERCISE

I. Provide your translation under the Greek text above.

II Exegetical notes and questions: read the bullet points and answer the questions below.

Verse-by-Verse Questions

8:22

- Oftentimes, substantival adjectives have articles. But in this case, τυφλόν is anarthrous and yet fills the slot of the direct object as a substantive. This use is common when a substantival adjective is introduced; subsequent occurrences will usually be articular.

a) Why is αὐτοῦ in the genitive case? How is it functioning in the sentence?

8:23

b) What is the special article rule that applies to τῆς χειρὸς τοῦ τυφλοῦ? (Hint: There are three special rules to remember related to the article: [1] Granville Sharp Rule, [2] Colwell's Rule, and [3] Apollonius's Canon. See Chapter Four of this workbook.)

c) How would you translate εἰ? What is its function in the sentence?

d) Why do you think Jesus "brought him [the blind man] out of the village" (ἐξήνεγκεν αὐτὸν ἔξω τῆς κώμης) before he healed him?

8:24

e) What noun does περιπατοῦντας modify? How do you know that?

f) The syntax of the man's statement seems unnatural (e.g., the two "seeing" verbs, βλέπω and ὁρῶ). Why might this be the case? What is a possible explanation for this unnatural syntax?

8:25

g) What tenses are used for the three words of seeing: διέβλεψεν, ἀπεκατέστη, and ἐνέβλεπεν? What do these tenses signify, especially in relation to their respective verbal aspects?

8:26

h) What mood is εἰσέλθῃς, and what is its force when coupled with μηδέ?

Short Summary and Contextual Impact

III. Summarize the main idea of the passage and then discuss how it fits into the surrounding narrative.

Parsing and Classification

IV. Circle the pronouns, underline the adverbs, and then parse them both below. For the pronouns, label their type and identify the antecedent. For the adverbs, classify them into one of the following four uses: time, degree, manner, or place. Provide a brief explanation for your decisions.

Pronouns

8:22

1)

2)

3)

8:23

1)

2)

3)

4)

5)

8:25

1)

8:26

1)

2)

Adverbs[7]

8:25

1)

2)

3)

8:26

1)

---

[7] Some might want to consider ἔξω (8:23) and ὡς (8:24) in addition to the instances of adverbs to be listed below. These two words, however, are excluded in the current section in view of their respective syntactical functions in the text (ἔξω as a preposition, and ὡς as a comparative participle).

ANSWER KEY

I. Translation and Explanations

8:22 They came to Bethsaida. They brought a blind man to him and begged him to touch him. **23** He
took the blind man by the hand and brought him out of the village. Spitting on his eyes and laying
his hands on him, he asked him, "Do you see anything?"
24 He looked up[8] and said, "I see people—they look like trees walking."
25 Again Jesus placed his hands on the man's eyes. The man looked intently, and his sight was re-
stored, and he saw everything clearly.[9] **26** Then he sent him home, saying, "Don't even go into the
village."[10]

II. Answers to Exegetical Questions

Verse-by-Verse Questions

a) Some verbs take their direct object in the genitive case. This is characteristic of verbs of emotion, sharing, sensation, ruling, or separation. In 8:22, ἅψηται is a verb of sensation for which αὐτοῦ is serving as the direct object. Therefore, αὐτοῦ is in the genitive case.

b) Apollonius's Canon. This special rule says that, when a head noun is followed by a genitive noun, both will either have or lack an article. In 8:23, τυφλοῦ is a substantival adjective, filling the slot of a noun, so the rule applies.

c) Εἰ is not translated in 8:23. It can act as a marker of either direct or indirect questions. For indirect discourse, εἰ may be translated as "whether." For direct discourse, such as here, it would not be translated but would indicate that a question occurs.

d) Mark does not tell us why Jesus led the blind man out of the village before he healed him; however, it was likely to avoid the added attention the miracle would cause. This understanding fits with the so-called Messianic Secret motif in Mark's Gospel and is confirmed by the fact that Jesus told the man not to go back into the village after he was healed (8:26).[11]

e) In 8:24, περιπατοῦντας modifies ἀνθρώπους (not δένδρα) despite the distance between the two words. We know this because δένδρα is neuter, but both ἀνθρώπους and περιπατοῦντας are masculine. So, he saw people walking around who looked like trees, rather than people who looked like walking trees.

---

[8] The verb ἀναβλέπω itself could mean, depending on the context, "to look up," "to regain sight," or "to receive sight."

[9] The three words used for his recovered sight are διέβλεψεν, ἀπεκατέστη, and ἐνέβλεπεν. The first means "to see clearly," the second "to be healed," and the third "to see with insight." Regarding ἐνέβλεπεν, E. S. Johnson says, "In Mark's gospel ἐμβλέπω is always used with an intensive meaning, maintaining the root significance of the preposition ἐν, describing a kind of seeing 'into' by which people can understand a person or situation at a glance." See E. S. Johnson, "Mark VIII:22–26: The Blind Man from Bethsaida," *New Testament Studies* 25, no. 3 (April 1979), 378. So, this could be rendered, "He saw clearly, he was healed, and he could now clearly see (understand) everything."

[10] We use the *Christian Standard Bible* (Nashville: Holman Bible Publishers, 2020), which adopts the optimal equivalence approach, as our default translation across this workbook. Any deviations in the following explanations are our own. This clarification applies to not only this chapter but also the rest of the current workbook.

[11] For an overview of the Messianic Secret motif, see David E. Garland, *A Theology of Mark's Gospel: Good News about Jesus the Messiah, the Son of God*, ed. Andreas J. Köstenberger, Biblical Theology of the New Testament (Grand Rapids: Zondervan, 2015), 368–87.

f) In 8:24, the syntax is likely unnatural due to Mark reporting the actual words of the blind man from that moment. Or, as Rodney Decker writes, "The ragged nature of the syntax may well be the sign of a very close translation of what the man actually said—in the emotion of the moment, his words may have been jumbled, blurted out in excited anticipation of what was transpiring."[12]

g) In 8:25, διέβλεψεν and ἀπεκατέστη are aorist whereas ἐνέβλεπεν is imperfect. The first two represent the act of healing which was portrayed as a whole and as a completed action. The imperfect, on the other hand, conveys that the formerly blind man received vision, a new reality that continued from that time on.

h) In 8:26, εἰσέλθῃς is an aorist subjunctive verb. Coupled with μηδέ, the aorist subjunctive verb has a prohibitive sense (prohibitive subjunctive), "Do not even go into . . ."

III. Short Summary and Contextual Impact

Summary: In Bethsaida, a blind man is brought to Jesus for healing. Jesus takes him outside the village, spits on his eyes, lays hands on him, and heals him in two stages. It isn't until Jesus lays his hands on the blind man a second time that he sees clearly.

Contextual Impact: This passage marks the beginning of the Way Discourse (8:22–10:52) in which Jesus leads his disciples toward Jerusalem and focuses more on his disciples, helping them understand his identity and mission. The two-stage healing illustrates the disciples slowly increasing in understanding of who Jesus is and why he has come. In the preceding passage, Jesus rebuked them for not yet understanding (8:17, 18, 21). In the following pericope (8:27–33), Peter confesses Jesus as the Christ but fails to embrace Jesus's mission to come and die and, as a result, is rebuked. Just as in the two-stage healing of the current episode, Peter starts to see who Jesus is, but he needs additional help to see him clearly. With the entire Way Discourse in view, as the only two sight-healing stories in Mark's narrative and as the very passages surrounding the threefold passion-resurrection prediction cycle (8:27–10:45), 8:22–26 and 10:46–52 together form an inclusio and hint that the disciples' spiritual sight must be healed. (See, e.g., R. T. France, *The Gospel of Mark: A Commentary on the Greek Text*, New International Greek Testament Commentary [Grand Rapids: Eerdmans, 2002], 320–21, for further discussion.)

IV. Parsing and Classification of the Key Grammatical Concepts for the Lesson: Pronouns and Adverbs

Pronouns

8:22

1) αὐτῷ: αὐτός; 3 masc sg dat; *he*, *she*, *it*; *self*, *same*; *they* (when pl)
    - Personal: antecedent = Jesus. The antecedent is in 6:30. This is a basic personal pronoun. No special cases apply.

2) αὐτόν: αὐτός; 3 masc sg acc; *he*, *she*, *it*; *self*, *same*; *they* (when pl)
    - Personal: antecedent = Jesus. The antecedent is in 6:30. This is a basic personal pronoun. No special cases apply. The most recent explicit reference to Jesus is in 6:30. All other references to Jesus since

[12] Rodney J. Decker, *Mark 1–8: A Handbook on the Greek Text*, ed. Martin M. Culy, Baylor Handbook on the Greek New Testament (Waco: Baylor University Press, 2014), 217–18.

then are as personal pronouns or as the implied subject of verbs. The next explicit reference to Jesus is in 8:27. The scarcity of explicit references to Jesus reveals that he is the main character in Mark's narrative.

3) αὐτοῦ: αὐτός; 3 masc sg gen; *he*, *she*, *it*; *self*, *same*; *they* (when pl)
   - *Personal*: antecedent = τυφλόν, the blind man. This is a basic personal pronoun. No special cases apply.

8:23

1) αὐτόν: αὐτός; 3 masc sg acc; *he*, *she*, *it*; *self*, *same*; *they* (when pl)
   - *Personal*: antecedent = τυφλοῦ, the blind man. This is a basic personal pronoun. No special cases apply.

2) αὐτοῦ: αὐτός; 3 masc sg gen; *he*, *she*, *it*; *self*, *same*; *they* (when pl)
   - *Personal*: antecedent = τυφλοῦ, the blind man. This is a basic personal pronoun. No special cases apply.

3) αὐτῷ: αὐτός; 3 masc sg dat; *he*, *she*, *it*; *self*, *same*; *they* (when pl)
   - *Personal*: antecedent = τυφλοῦ, the blind man. This is a basic personal pronoun. No special cases apply.

4) αὐτόν: αὐτός; 3 masc sg acc; *he*, *she*, *it*; *self*, *same*; *they* (when pl)
   - *Personal*: antecedent = τυφλοῦ, the blind man. This is a basic personal pronoun. No special cases apply.

5) τι: τις; neut sg acc; *something*, *anything*, *a certain one*
   - *Indefinite*: antecedent = N/A. This is an indefinite pronoun, and thus it does not have an antecedent.

8:25

1) αὐτόῦ: αὐτός; 3 masc sg gen; *he*, *she*, *it*; *self*, *same*; *they* (when pl)
   - *Personal*: antecedent = τυφλοῦ, the blind man. This is a basic personal pronoun. No special cases apply.

8:26

1) αὐτόν: αὐτός; 3 masc sg acc; *he*, *she*, *it*; *self*, *same*; *they* (when pl)
   - *Personal*: antecedent = τυφλοῦ, the blind man. This is a basic personal pronoun. No special cases apply.

2) αὐτοῦ: αὐτός; 3 masc sg gen; *he*, *she*, *it*; *self*, *same*; *they* (when pl)
   - *Personal*: antecedent = τυφλοῦ, the blind man. This is a basic personal pronoun. No special cases apply.

Adverbs

8:25

1) εἶτα: not declinable; *then*, *next*
   - *Time*: It describes the time the action occurred (thus, addressing "when?").

2) πάλιν: not declinable; *again*
   - *Degree*: It indicates that Jesus performed the action yet another time (thus, addressing "how much?").

3) τηλαυγῶς: not declinable; *clearly*
   - *Manner*: It describes in what manner the blind man was now able to see (thus, addressing "in what way?").

8:26

1) μηδέ: not declinable; *nor*, *and not*
   - Time: This word indicates that the man was not to enter the village, at least not immediately, thus addressing the temporal dimension.[13]

Now, rewrite your translation of the entire passage in the GUIDED PRACTICE section, reflecting the above exegetical procedure.

[13] In Mark 8:26, μηδέ and εἰσέλθῃς (aorist subjunctive) together express an idea of prohibition (prohibitory subjunctive, "Don't even go into . . .") and is direct discourse, which is introduced by the participle, λέγων.

REFERENCES

Danker, Frederick William, et al. *A Greek-English Lexicon of the New Testament and other Early Christian Literature*. 3rd ed. Chicago: University of Chicago Press, 2000.

Decker, Rodney J. *Mark 1–8: A Handbook on the Greek Text*. Ed. Martin M. Culy. Baylor Handbook on the Greek New Testament. Waco: Baylor University Press, 2014.

France, R. T. *The Gospel of Mark*. The New International Greek Testament Commentary. Grand Rapids: Eerdmans, 2002.

Garland, David E. *A Theology of Mark's Gospel: Good News about Jesus the Messiah, the Son of God*. Ed. Andreas J. Köstenberger. Biblical Theology of the New Testament. Grand Rapids: Zondervan, 2015.

Hoehner, Harold W. *Ephesians: An Exegetical Commentary*. Grand Rapids: Baker Academic, 2002.

Johnson, E. S. "Mark VIII. 22–26: The Blind Man from Bethsaida." *New Testament Studies* 25, no. 3 (April 1979): 370–83.

Köstenberger, Andreas J., Benjamin L. Merkle, and Robert L. Plummer. *Going Deeper with New Testament Greek: An Intermediate Study of the Grammar and Syntax of the New Testament*. Rev. ed. Nashville: B&H Academic, 2020.

Mathewson, David L. and Elodie Ballantine Emig. *Intermediate Greek Grammar: Syntax for Students of the New Testament*. Grand Rapids: Baker Academic, 2016.

Merkle, Benjamin L. *Exegetical Gems from Biblical Greek*. Grand Rapids: Baker Academic, 2019.

Mounce, William D. *Basics of Biblical Greek Grammar*. Ed. Verlyn D. Verbrugge and Christopher A. Beetham. 4th ed. Grand Rapids: Zondervan, 2019.

Runge, Steven E. *Discourse Grammar of the Greek New Testament: A Practical Introduction for Teaching and Exegesis*. Peabody, MA: Hendrickson, 2010.

Wallace, Daniel B. *Greek Grammar Beyond the Basics: An Exegetical Syntax of the New Testament*. Grand Rapids: Zondervan, 1996.

CHAPTER THREE

//////////////////

MARK 8:27–9:1

WITH ATTENTION TO GENITIVES AND INFINITIVES

GRAMMAR REVIEW:

Genitives

Definition and Description

The genitive is an exegetically significant case in the Greek noun system because it can be interpreted in many ways. Genitives are considered to be the case of *description*, *quality*, or *separation*. They usually act adjectivally, modifying nouns, whereas datives usually have an adverbial force, modifying verbs (although you will see many exceptions to this statement). Genitives have a wide-ranging syntactical use, but they will often be translated using *of* or *from*. Genitives typically follow the noun they qualify, but the order may be reversed for emphasis.

How we interpret the genitive can impact the course of history! One example of how the interpretation of a genitive is theologically significant comes from Rom 1:17a: δικαιοσύνη γὰρ **θεοῦ** ἐν αὐτῷ ἀποκαλύπτεται ("For in it the righteousness **of God** is revealed"). Martin Luther traced his life-changing understanding of salvation by faith alone to his understanding of this verse. He came to believe that it spoke of a status *given by* God instead of an attribute of God *to which* we must attain. These differences are alternative ways of understanding the meaning of the genitive θεοῦ in this verse. It could be an attributive genitive, a possessive genitive, a genitive of source, an objective genitive, or a subjective genitive. Each reading presents a different understanding of this verse and emphasizes our need to rightly understand how the genitive is used.[1]

Categories and Examples[2]

ADJECTIVAL USES OF THE GENITIVE		
DESCRIPTION	Further limits or describes the head noun, but other common genitival categories do not capture the specific nuance.	βάπτισμα **μετανοίας** ("a baptism **of repentance**" Mark 1:4).

[1] See any of the Greek-based Romans commentaries, e.g., Thomas R. Schreiner, *Romans*, 2nd ed., Baker Exegetical Commentary on the New Testament (Grand Rapids: Baker, 2018).

[2] Andreas J. Köstenberger, Benjamin L. Merkle, and Robert L. Plummer, *Going Deeper with New Testament Greek: An Intermediate Study of the Grammar and Syntax of the New Testament*, rev. ed. (Nashville: B&H Academic, 2020), 108–9.

ADJECTIVAL USES OF THE GENITIVE (CONTINUED)		
ATTRIBUTIVE	Denotes an attribute or innate quality of the head term, conveying an emphatic adjectival idea.	τῷ ῥήματι τῆς **δυνάμεως** αὐτοῦ ("by his **powerful** word" Heb 1:3).
POSSESSION	Identifies ownership regarding the noun it modifies, often using a possessive pronoun.	καὶ εἰσελθόντες εἰς τὸν οἶκον **Φιλίππου** ("we entered the house **of Philip**" Acts 21:8).
RELATIONSHIP	Denotes a family relationship such as a person's parent or spouse. The word indicating the relationship is often omitted and must be inferred.	Ἰάκωβον τὸν **τοῦ Ζεβεδαίου** ("James the son **of Zebedee**" Matt 4:21).
SOURCE	Indicates the origin of the head noun ("from").	τὴν **τοῦ θεοῦ** δικαιοσύνην ("the righteousness **of God**" Rom 10:3).
MATERIAL OR CONTENT	Indicates the material of which the head term is made or specifies the content of an object or abstract noun.	Material: γόμον **χρυσοῦ** ("cargo **of gold**" Rev 18:12). Content: ποτήριον **ὕδατος** ("a cup **of water**" Mark 9:41).
PARTITIVE	Whether by itself or in conjunction with the preposition ἀπό or ἐκ, the articular noun in the genitive denotes the whole of which the head noun is a part.	ἓν **τῶν πλοίων** ("one **of the boats**" Luke 5:3).
VERBAL USES OF THE GENITIVE		
SUBJECTIVE	Functions semantically as the subject of the verbal idea implied in the head noun, producing the action.	τίς ἡμᾶς χωρίσει ἀπὸ τῆς ἀγάπης **τοῦ Χριστοῦ**; ("Who can separate us from the love **of Christ**?" Rom 8:35).
OBJECTIVE	Functions semantically as the direct object of the verbal idea implicit in the head noun, receiving the action.	ἔχετε πίστιν **θεοῦ** ("Have faith **in God**" Mark 11:22).
ADVERBIAL USES OF THE GENITIVE		
TIME OR PLACE	Indicates the location in time or space in which an action occurs. The focus is on kind or quality.	Time: ὁ ἐλθὼν πρὸς αὐτὸν **νυκτὸς** τὸ πρῶτον ("who had previously come to him **at night**" John 19:39). Place: μετὰ δὲ τὴν μετοικεσίαν **Βαβυλῶνος** ("After the exile **to Babylon**" Matt 1:12 NIV).
SEPARATION	Indicates motion away from or distance, whether literally or figuratively ("from").	ἀποστήσονταί τινες **τῆς πίστεως** ("some will depart **from the faith**" 1 Tim 4:1).
MEANS OR AGENCY	Conveys the impersonal means or personal agent by which a given action is carried out ("by").	Means: ὁ γὰρ θεὸς ἀπείραστός ἐστιν **κακῶν** ("since God is not tempted **by evil**" Jas 1:13). Agency: δεῦτε, οἱ εὐλογημένοι **τοῦ πατρός** μου ("Come, you who are blessed **by** my **Father**" Matt 25:34).

ADJECTIVAL USES OF THE GENITIVE (CONTINUED)		
COMPARISON	Used to denote comparison in conjunction with a comparative adjective ("than").	μείζων ἐστὶν ὁ θεὸς **τῆς καρδίας** ἡμῶν ("God is greater **than** our **heart**" 1 John 3:20).
PRICE	Indicates the price that is paid or the value that attaches to a given item.	ἠγοράσθητε . . . **τιμῆς** ("you have been bought **with a price**" 1 Cor 6:20 NASB).
OTHER USES OF THE GENITIVE		
APPOSITION	The genitive of apposition provides an alternate designation (simple) of a genitive head noun or provides an explanatory (epexegetical) restatement of a head noun in any case.	Simple: διὰ Ἰερεμίου **τοῦ προφήτου** ("through Jeremiah **the prophet**" Matt 2:17).
		Epexegetical: τὴν δωρεὰν **τοῦ ἁγίου πνεύματος** ("the gift **of the Holy Spirit**" Acts 2:38).
DIRECT OBJECT	Verbs of sensation, emotion, or volition, sharing, ruling, or separation take their direct object in the genitive case (instead of the accusative case).	μή **τινος** ὑστερήσατε; ("you did not lack **anything**, did you?" Luke 22:35 NASB).

Infinitives[3]

Definition and Description

As its name might suggest, infinitives (like participles) are non-finite verbs, meaning that they do not decline (change endings for person and number). Infinitives in English have *to* in front of them, for example, *to read.* Translations of Greek infinitives also often include *to*, but there are many other ways they can be translated.

Whereas participles are verbal adjectives, infinitives are verbal nouns. Like verbs, they have tense-forms (but only present, aorist or perfect), aspect (perfective, imperfective, and stative), and voice (active, middle, and passive). Infinitives can also take a direct object and an adverbial modifier. They can have a subject, but it will almost always be in the accusative case instead of the nominative case. Like nouns, they can be articular (in which case the article is always singular and neuter), they can serve as the object of a preposition (in which case they will always be articular), and they can be modified by an adjective.

There are 2,291 infinitives in the NT; 1,744 are anarthrous, and of the 547 articular infinitives, two-thirds are part of a prepositional phrase. As you work through the different categories of infinitives, you will see many verbal cues that an infinitive likely follows. They are also identified by their endings of -αι or -ειν (except in the case of contract verbs).

Categories and Examples[4]

ADVERBIAL INFINITIVES		
COMPLEMENTARY	"Completes" the verbal idea of another verb.	καὶ ἡμεῖς <u>ὀφείλομεν</u> ἀλλήλους **ἀγαπᾶν** ("<u>we</u> also <u>ought</u> **to love** one another" 1 John 4:11 NASB).
PURPOSE	Communicates the goal or intent of an action or state expressed by the controlling verb.	Μὴ νομίσητε ὅτι ἦλθον **καταλῦσαι** τὸν νόμον ("Don't think that I came **to abolish** the Law" Matt 5:17).

[3] Mark's Gospel contains 200 infinitives, which is the fourth most of any NT book.
[4] Köstenberger, Merkle, and Plummer, *Going Deeper with New Testament Greek*, 379–80.

ADVERBIAL INFINITIVES (CONTINUED)		
RESULT	Communicates the actual or conceived result of an action or state expressed by the controlling verb.	ἔπλησαν ἀμφότερα τὰ πλοῖα ὥστε **βυθίζεσθαι** αὐτά ("they . . . filled both the boats, so that they **began to sink**" Luke 5:7 ESV)
TEMPORAL[5]		
Previous Time	The action of the infinitive occurs before the action of the controlling verb (μετὰ τό + infinitive).	Μετὰ δὲ τὸ **παραδοθῆναι** τὸν Ἰωάννην ἦλθεν ὁ Ἰησοῦς εἰς τὴν Γαλιλαίαν ("After John **was arrested**, Jesus went to Galilee" Mark 1:14).
Contemporaneous Time	The action of the infinitive occurs simultaneously with the action of the controlling verb (ἐν τῷ + infinitive).	ἐν τῷ **σπείρειν** αὐτὸν ἃ μὲν ἔπεσεν παρὰ τὴν ὁδόν ("As he **sowed**, some seed fell along the path" Matt 13:4).
Subsequent Time	The action of the infinitive occurs after the action of the controlling verb (πρὸ τοῦ or πρίν [ἤ] + infinitive).	πρὸ τοῦ σε Φίλιππον **φωνῆσαι** . . . εἶδόν σε ("Before Philip **called** you, . . . I saw you" John 1:48).
CAUSE	Communicates the reason or ground for the action of the controlling verb, answering "Why?" (διὰ τό + infinitive).	οὐκ ἔχετε διὰ τὸ μὴ **αἰτεῖσθαι** ὑμᾶς ("You do not have because you **do** not **ask**" Jas 4:2).
MEANS	Conveys the way the action of the controlling verb is performed, answering "How?" (ἐν τῷ+ infinitive).	ὁ θεὸς . . . ἀπέστειλεν αὐτὸν εὐλογοῦντα ὑμᾶς ἐν τῷ **ἀποστρέφειν** ἕκαστον ἀπὸ τῶν πονηριῶν ὑμῶν ("God . . . sent him . . . to you to bless you by **turning** each of you from your evil ways" Acts 3:26).
SUBSTANTIVAL INFINITIVES		
SUBJECT	Functions as the subject (or predicate nominative) of a finite verb.	**τὸ ζῆν** Χριστὸς καὶ **τὸ ἀποθανεῖν** κέρδος ("**to live** is Christ, and **to die** is gain" Phil 1:21 ESV).
DIRECT OBJECT	Functions as the direct object of a finite verb.	ὁ πατὴρ . . . τῷ υἱῷ ἔδωκεν ζωὴν **ἔχειν** ἐν ἑαυτῷ ("the Father . . . has granted to the Son **to have** life in himself" John 5:26).
INDIRECT DISCOURSE	Used with verbs of speaking or perception to communicate indirect discourse.	καὶ ἀπεκρίθησαν μὴ **εἰδέναι** πόθεν ("So they answered that **they did** not **know** where it came from" Luke 20:7 ESV).
EXPLANATORY	Further defines, clarifies, or qualifies a noun or adjective.	ἔδωκεν αὐτοῖς ἐξουσίαν τέκνα θεοῦ **γενέσθαι** ("he gave them the right **to be** children of God" John 1:12).
INDEPENDENT INFINITIVES		
IMPERATIVAL	Functions as an imperative (or hortatory subjunctive).	**χαίρειν** μετὰ χαιρόντων ("**Rejoice** with those who rejoice" Rom 12:15).
ABSOLUTE	Functions independently of the rest of the sentence, having no syntactical relation to other words or phrases.	Ἰάκωβος . . . ταῖς δώδεκα φυλαῖς ταῖς ἐν τῇ διασπορᾷ **χαίρειν** ("James . . . To the twelve tribes in the dispersed abroad. **Greetings**" Jas 1:1).

[5] To be clear, "Previous Time," "Contemporaneous Time," and "Subsequent Time" are subcategories under "Temporal."

GUIDED PRACTICE: MARK 8:27–9:1 (NA[28])

8:27 Καὶ ἐξῆλθεν ὁ Ἰησοῦς καὶ οἱ μαθηταὶ αὐτοῦ εἰς τὰς κώμας Καισαρείας τῆς Φιλίππου· καὶ
ἐν τῇ ὁδῷ ἐπηρώτα τοὺς μαθητὰς αὐτοῦ λέγων αὐτοῖς· τίνα με λέγουσιν οἱ ἄνθρωποι εἶναι;
28 οἱ δὲ εἶπαν αὐτῷ λέγοντες [ὅτι] Ἰωάννην τὸν βαπτιστήν, καὶ ἄλλοι Ἠλίαν, ἄλλοι δὲ ὅτι
εἷς τῶν προφητῶν. 29 καὶ αὐτὸς ἐπηρώτα αὐτούς· ὑμεῖς δὲ τίνα με λέγετε εἶναι; ἀποκριθεὶς ὁ
Πέτρος λέγει αὐτῷ· σὺ εἶ ὁ χριστός. 30 καὶ ἐπετίμησεν αὐτοῖς ἵνα μηδενὶ λέγωσιν περὶ αὐτοῦ.

31 Καὶ ἤρξατο διδάσκειν αὐτοὺς ὅτι δεῖ τὸν υἱὸν τοῦ ἀνθρώπου πολλὰ παθεῖν καὶ
ἀποδοκιμασθῆναι ὑπὸ τῶν πρεσβυτέρων καὶ τῶν ἀρχιερέων καὶ τῶν γραμματέων καὶ
ἀποκτανθῆναι καὶ μετὰ τρεῖς ἡμέρας ἀναστῆναι· 32 καὶ παρρησίᾳ τὸν λόγον ἐλάλει. καὶ
προσλαβόμενος ὁ Πέτρος αὐτὸν ἤρξατο ἐπιτιμᾶν αὐτῷ. 33 ὁ δὲ ἐπιστραφεὶς καὶ ἰδὼν τοὺς
μαθητὰς αὐτοῦ ἐπετίμησεν Πέτρῳ καὶ λέγει· ὕπαγε ὀπίσω μου, σατανᾶ, ὅτι οὐ φρονεῖς τὰ τοῦ
θεοῦ ἀλλὰ τὰ τῶν ἀνθρώπων.

[34] Καὶ προσκαλεσάμενος τὸν ὄχλον σὺν τοῖς μαθηταῖς αὐτοῦ εἶπεν αὐτοῖς· εἴ τις θέλει ὀπίσω
μου ἀκολουθεῖν, ἀπαρνησάσθω ἑαυτὸν καὶ ἀράτω τὸν σταυρὸν αὐτοῦ καὶ ἀκολουθείτω μοι.
[35] ὃς γὰρ ἐὰν θέλῃ τὴν ψυχὴν αὐτοῦ σῶσαι ἀπολέσει αὐτήν· ὃς δ᾽ ἂν ἀπολέσει τὴν ψυχὴν
αὐτοῦ ἕνεκεν ἐμοῦ καὶ τοῦ εὐαγγελίου σώσει αὐτήν. [36] τί γὰρ ὠφελεῖ ἄνθρωπον κερδῆσαι
τὸν κόσμον ὅλον καὶ ζημιωθῆναι τὴν ψυχὴν αὐτοῦ; [37] τί γὰρ δοῖ ἄνθρωπος ἀντάλλαγμα
τῆς ψυχῆς αὐτοῦ; [38] ὃς γὰρ ἐὰν ἐπαισχυνθῇ με καὶ τοὺς ἐμοὺς λόγους ἐν τῇ γενεᾷ ταύτῃ τῇ
μοιχαλίδι καὶ ἁμαρτωλῷ, καὶ ὁ υἱὸς τοῦ ἀνθρώπου ἐπαισχυνθήσεται αὐτόν, ὅταν ἔλθῃ ἐν τῇ
δόξῃ τοῦ πατρὸς αὐτοῦ μετὰ τῶν ἀγγέλων τῶν ἁγίων.

[9:1] Καὶ ἔλεγεν αὐτοῖς· ἀμὴν λέγω ὑμῖν ὅτι εἰσίν τινες ὧδε τῶν ἑστηκότων οἵτινες οὐ μὴ
γεύσωνται θανάτου ἕως ἂν ἴδωσιν τὴν βασιλείαν τοῦ θεοῦ ἐληλυθυῖαν ἐν δυνάμει.

VOCABULARY AIDS (WORDS 26X TO 50X)

8:27 **κώμη** *village* (27x)
8:27 **Φίλιππος** (φίλος+ἵππος) *Philip* (36x)
8:28 **Ἠλίας** *Elijah* (29x)
8:30, 32, 33 **ἐπιτιμάω** (ἐπί+τιμάω) *to rebuke, to warn* (29x)
8:31 **πάσχω** *to experience; suffer, endure* (42x)
8:32 **παρρησία** (παρά+ῥῆμα) *boldness, frankness, openness* (31x)
8:33 **ἐπιστρέφω** (ἐπί+στρέφω) *to turn back, return, turn* (36x)
8:33, 34 **ὀπίσω** (+gen) *after* (prep); *back* (adv) (35x)
8:33 **σατανᾶς** *Satan* (Heb. *adversary*) (36x)
8:33 **φρονέω** *to be wise, to think* (26x)
8:34 **προσκαλέω** (πρός+καλέω) *to call, summon* (29x)
8:34 **σταυρός** *cross* (27x)
8:38 **γενεά** *generation* (43x)
8:38 **ἁμαρτωλός** *sinner, sinful* (47x)

VOCABULARY AIDS (WORDS 25X OR LESS)

8:27 **Καισάρεια** *Caesarea* (17x)
8:28 **βαπτιστής** (βαπτίζω) *washer, baptizer, Baptist* (12x)
8:31 **ἀποδοκιμάζω** (ἀπό+δοκιμάζω) *to reject* (9x)
8:32 **προσλαμβάνω** (πρός+λαμβάνω, aorist stem: λαβ) *to take aside* (12x)
8:34 **ἀπαρνέομαι** (ἀπό+ἀρνέομαι) *to deny, renounce* (11x)
8:35 **ἕνεκα** (+gen) *because of, for the sake of* (24x)
8:36 **ὠφελέω** *to gain; to benefit* (15x)
8:36 **κερδαίνω** *to gain* (17x)
8:36 **ζημιόω** *to punish, to lose* (6x)
8:37 **ἀντάλλαγμα** (ἀντί+ἄλλος) *something as an exchange* (2x)
8:38 **ἐπαισχύνομαι** (ἐπί+αἰσχύνομαι) *to be ashamed* (11x)
8:38 **μοιχαλίς** *adulteress* (7x)
9:1 **γεύομαι** *to taste, experience* (15x)

EXERCISE

I. Provide your translation under the Greek text above.

II. Exegetical notes and questions: read the bullet points and answer the questions below.

Verse-by-Verse Questions

8:27

a) Is ἐξῆλθεν singular or plural? What is the significance of its number?

8:29

b) The fronted pronoun ὑμεῖς is grammatically unnecessary in the sentence. Why might it have been included?

- Χριστός has not shown up in the Gospel since 1:1. This passage marks the beginning of a deeper revelation of Jesus's identity as the Messiah.

8:30

c) Why is αὐτοῖς in the dative instead of the accusative?

8:31

- Τῶν πρεσβυτέρων καὶ τῶν ἀρχιερέων καὶ τῶν γραμματέων: these represented the three main groups of leaders among the Jews. All were going to reject Jesus.
- Μετὰ τρεῖς ἡμέρας ἀναστῆναι: "after three days to rise." This time designation for Jesus's resurrection is unique to Mark. In both Matthew and Luke, one finds τῇ τρίτῃ ἡμέρᾳ ἐγερθῆναι: "on the third day be raised." The differences are reconciled by the fact that the Jews counted any portion of a day as one day. *After three days* was the same as *the day after tomorrow*, so the two renderings are equivalent.

8:32

d) Why is παρρησίᾳ in the dative? What is its function in the sentence?

8:33

e) This verse begins with ὁ δέ. Rodney Decker points out that this was a common literary device to indicate a switch in speakers or participants in a narrative.[6] It should be translated as *but he* or *and he*, although "*he*" may be slotted later in the translation. In this sentence, ὁ is a nominative subject to which verb?

8:34

f) What are the three imperatives in this verse, and what are their tenses?

8:35

g) This verse, along with vv. 36 and 37, uses ψυχή, which can refer to being physically alive or being alive in a spiritual, eternal sense (often translated as soul). How would you translate it in these verses? Would you use the same translation for each instance? Why?

8:37

h) This verse begins with τί γὰρ δοῖ ἄνθρωπος ἀντάλλαγμα. The prior verse starts out similarly: τί γὰρ ὠφελεῖ ἄνθρωπον κερδῆσαι. What is the tense, voice, and mood of δοῖ and of ὠφελεῖ?

---

[6] Rodney J. Decker, *Mark 1–8: A Handbook on the Greek Text*, ed. Martin M. Culy, Baylor Handbook on the Greek New Testament (Waco: Baylor University Press, 2014), 42.

9:1

- The phrase ἀμὴν λέγω ὑμῖν is uttered 13 times in Mark by Jesus. It introduces something to which Jesus wanted his audience to pay particular attention.

i) What does the statement in Mark 9:1 mean and how is it connected to the following episode?

Additional Questions

j) How does the preceding passage (8:22–26) contribute to our understanding of the current episode, especially Peter's response to Jesus's first passion prediction?

k)

Short Summary and Contextual Impact

III. Summarize the main idea of the passage and then discuss how it fits into the surrounding narrative.

Parsing and Classification

IV. Circle the genitive substantives (including nouns, pronouns, participles, and adjectives) and underline all the infinitives in the text, and parse them below. Then classify each entry according to the categories given in the grammar review above. Provide a brief explanation for your decisions. If a word is an object of a preposition, label it as "object of the preposition." Each of the prepositional phrases must also be further classified according to their functions in the text. To get an idea about how to further classify prepositional phrases here and the rest of this workbook, please consult, in advance, the pertinent examples on pp. 40–42 and 136–37 below. The numbers below each verse signify how many genitives or infinitives appear in the pertinent verse.

Genitives

8:27

1)

2)

3)

4)

8:28

1)

8:30

1)

8:31

1)

2)

3)

4)

8:33

1)

2)

3)

4)

8:34

1)

2)

3)

8:35

1)

2)

3)

4)

8:36

1)

8:37

1)

2)

8:38[7]

1)

2)

3)

4)

9:1

1)

2)

3)

---

[7] Since this section is focused on genitive **substantives**, the attributive adjective ἁγίων (holy) in 8:38 is not included here.

Infinitives

8:27

1)

8:29

1)

8:31

1)

2)

3)

4)

5)

8:32

1)

8:34

1)

8:35

1)

8:36

1)

2)

ANSWER KEY

I. Translation and explanations

8:27 Jesus went out with his disciples to the villages of Caesarea Philippi. And on the road he asked
his disciples, "Who do people say that I am?"[8]
28 They answered him, "John the Baptist; others, Elijah; still others, one of the prophets."
29 "But you," he asked them, "who do you say that I am?"
Peter answered him, "You are the Messiah." 30 And he strictly warned them to tell no one about
him.
31 Then he began to teach them that it was necessary for the Son of Man to suffer many things and
be rejected by the elders, chief priests, and scribes, be killed, and rise after three days. 32 He spoke
openly about this. Peter took him aside and began to rebuke him. 33 But turning around and looking at his disciples, he rebuked Peter and said, "Get behind me, Satan! You are not thinking about
God's concerns but human concerns."
34 Calling the crowd along with his disciples, he said to them, "If anyone wants to follow after
me, let him deny himself, take up his cross, and follow me. 35 For whoever wants to save his life
will lose it, but whoever loses his life because of me and the gospel will save it. 36 For what does
it benefit someone to gain the whole world and yet lose his life? 37 What can anyone give in exchange for his life? 38 For whoever is ashamed of me and my words in this adulterous and sinful
generation, the Son of Man will also be ashamed of him when he comes in the glory of his Father
with the holy angels."
9:1 Then he said to them, "Truly I tell you, there are some standing here who will not taste death
until they see the kingdom of God come in power."

II. Answers to exegetical questions

Verse-by-Verse Questions

a) In 8:27, ἐξῆλθεν is singular, even though Jesus and his disciples are involved. Dan Wallace explains that when a compound subject has a verb in the singular, it is because the author wants to highlight one of the subjects.[9] In this case, Jesus is the focus, and his disciples are ancillary.

b) In v. 29, ὑμεῖς is doubly emphatic in that it is both unnecessary and has been placed at the front of the question: "But who do *you* say that I am?"

c) In v. 30, αὐτοῖς is in the dative because the verb, ἐπιτιμάω, takes its direct object in the dative. This is characteristic of certain types of verbs, including those that have to do with areas of discipleship—worshiping, obeying, trusting, serving, and so on.

---

[8] The last part of this verse has difficult syntax and is hard to translate: τίνα με λέγουσιν οἱ ἄνθρωποι εἶναι. Wallace addresses this instance, in which two accusatives are associated with an equative infinitive verb. Daniel B. Wallace, *Greek Grammar Beyond the Basics: An Exegetical Syntax of the New Testament* (Grand Rapids: Zondervan, 1996), 195n71. He notes the interrogative pronoun τίνα is the predicate term, and με serves as the subject of the equative infinitive verb, εἶναι. Thus, one could translate this as, "People say of me that I am who?" The CSB rendering reads better in English and maintains this meaning: "Who do people say that I am?"

[9] Wallace, 401.

d) In v. 32, παρρησίᾳ is a dative of manner, describing the way Jesus was now communicating with his disciples. This is in contrast to his previous teaching, which often left them wondering what he was talking about. Now, Jesus was speaking plainly. Still, since what he said did not align with their preconceived notions of what the Messiah was supposed to do, they did not understand him.

e) In v. 33, ὁ is a nominative subject to ἐπετίμησεν and λέγει.

f) In v. 34, the three imperatives are ἀπαρνησάσθω, ἀράτω, and ἀκολουθείτω. The first two are aorist, and the third is in the present tense. One explanation is that the first two commands are seen as prerequisites that must be accomplished before the third, *following*, can begin.

g) In v. 35, both meanings of ψυχή are probably in view. Martyrdom was a real possibility for Jesus's followers, so loss of physical life was certainly in view. But Jesus is also addressing eternal consequences in this discourse. R. T. France suggests maintaining the ambiguity and wordplay in these verses by translating ψυχή as *life* throughout.[10] The CSB uses "life" in v. 35 to keep the martyrdom notion in mind but switches to "soul" in vv. 36 and 37, where eternal consequences are in view.

h) In v. 37, δοῖ is aorist, active, subjunctive, whereas in v. 36, ὠφελεῖ is present, active, indicative. The implied answer to both questions is no.

As an interesting side note, notice the spelling of δοῖ. The "textbook" spelling for δίδωμι in the aorist 3rd person subjunctive would be δῷ. Decker points out that Mark sometimes uses a "vernacular" spelling of words; he does the same in 4:29, where he spells the aorist subjunctive 3rd singular of παραδίδωμι as παραδοῖ instead of παραδῷ.[11]

i) The statement in 9:1 conveys the idea that some of the people standing in the crowd would not die before seeing that the kingdom of God has come in power. They will not necessarily see events leading to its arrival; rather, at some point, they will come to understand that it has arrived. This statement seems to be tied to the transfiguration, which comes next, at least as its partial fulfillment. The time stamp of "after six days" in v. 2 connects the saying in v. 1 with what follows.

Additional Questions

j) Peter's understanding of Jesus's messiahship, which represents the understanding of the disciples, is comparable to the blind man's condition in the preceding passage after the first phase of his healing process: He was able to see things but not clearly (8:24). Peter has confessed Jesus as the Messiah (8:29), yet without a clear understanding as to what that confession entails, as indicated by his subsequent interaction with Jesus (8:32–33).

III. Short Summary and Contextual Impact

Summary: Jesus asks his disciples whom others say and, more importantly, whom they say he is. Peter confesses Jesus as the Messiah, after which Jesus foretells his death and resurrection. Following a heated interaction with Peter after the announcement of Jesus's upcoming death, Jesus

---

[10] R. T. France, *The Gospel of Mark: A Commentary on the Greek Text*, The New International Greek Testament Commentary (Grand Rapids, MI: Eerdmans, 2002), 340–41.

[11] Decker, *Mark 1–8*, 107–8.

teaches his disciples and the gathered crowd about the cost of following him as a disciple. A disciple must deny himself and take up his cross.

Contextual Impact: In the Way Discourse (8:22–10:52), Jesus prepares his followers for the difficulties that will lie ahead, both for him and for his followers. Jesus's disciples, along with the Jews in general, had a fundamental misunderstanding about what the Messiah's role was going to be. Jesus may have referred to himself as the Son of Man due to its lack of connotations of a conquering king, which had come to be associated with the title Messiah. In this passage, Jesus starts to reveal himself more fully to his disciples, but he does not yet want them to reveal to others that he is the Messiah. That would continue to feed the existing misunderstanding about his purpose and mission. Instead, he prepares the disciples for his coming death and resurrection as he gives his first of three passion predictions (8:31); the next two come in 9:31 and 10:33–34. Notably, in each of these three instances, there is the pattern of a prediction, followed by the disciples' misunderstanding, followed by teaching on discipleship. Jesus depicts discipleship as costly and humbling, but truly worthy. In his journey with his disciples, Jesus keeps teaching them about these truths. He is working to upend expectations of a conquering messianic king, according to which those around him would anticipate positions of honor and glory.

IV. Parsing and Classification of the Key Grammatical Concepts for the Lesson: Genitives and Infinitives

Genitives

8:27

1) αὐτοῦ: αὐτός; 3 masc sg gen; *he/she/it*, *self*, *same*, *they*
   - *Possession*: The disciples "belong" to Jesus.

2) Καισαρείας: Καισάρεια; fem sg gen; *Caesarea*
   - *Description*: Caesarea describes which villages. Alternatively, this can be seen as a partitive genitive.

3) Φιλίππου: Φίλιππος; masc sg gen; *Philip*
   - *Description*: Same as for Caesarea.

4) αὐτοῦ: αὐτός; 3 masc sg gen; *he/she/it*, *self*, *same*, *they*
   - *Possession*: The disciples "belong" to Jesus.

8:28

1) προφητῶν: προφήτης; masc plur gen; *prophet*
   - *Partitive*: The prophets are the whole of which "one" (εἷς) is a part.

8:30

1) αὐτοῦ: αὐτός; 3 masc sg gen; *he/she/it*, *self*, *same*, *they*
   - *Object of the Preposition*: αὐτοῦ is the object of the preposition περί, so it can just be labeled accordingly. The prepositional phrase would be classified as one of reference.

8:31

1) ἀνθρώπου: ἄνθρωπος; masc sg gen; *man*, *human*
   - *Relationship*: Not the typical genitive of relationship, since ἄνθρωπος does not refer to a specific person here, but it still indicates that Jesus has a relationship with mankind. Ultimately, however, ὁ υἱὸς τοῦ ἀνθρώπου should be taken idiomatically and as a likely reference to Dan 7:13 ("one like a son of man").

2) πρεσβυτέρων: πρεσβύτερος; masc plur gen; *older*, *elder*
   - *Object of the Preposition*: This is a substantival adjective and is an object of the preposition ὑπό. The prepositional phrase indicates agency of ἀποδοκιμασθῆναι ("to be rejected").

3) ἀρχιερέων: ἀρχιερεύς; masc plur gen; *high priest*
   - *Object of the Preposition*: This is an object of the preposition ὑπό. The prepositional phrase indicates agency of ἀποδοκιμασθῆναι ("to be rejected").

4) γραμματέων: γραμματεύς; masc plur gen; *scribe*
   - *Object of the Preposition*: This is an object of the preposition ὑπό. The prepositional phrase indicates agency of ἀποδοκιμασθῆναι ("to be rejected").

8:33

1) αὐτοῦ: αὐτός; 3 masc sg gen; *he*/*she*/*it*, *self*, *same*, *they*
   - *Possession*: The disciples "belong" to Jesus.

2) μου: ἐγώ; 1 sg gen; *I*, *we*
   - *Object of the Preposition*: This is an object of the improper preposition ὀπίσω. Many improper prepositions take their object in the genitive.

3) θεοῦ: θεός; masc sg gen; *God*
   - *Attributive*: Attributive is the best fit. The translation could be rendered "Godly things."

4) ἀνθρώπων: ἄνθρωπος; masc plur gen; *man*, *human*
   - *Attributive*: Attributive is the best fit. The translation could be rendered "human things."

8:34

1) αὐτοῦ: αὐτός; 3 masc sg gen; *he*/*she*/*it*, *self*, *same*, *they*
   - *Possession*: The disciples "belong" to Jesus.

2) μου: ἐγώ; 1 sg gen; *I*, *we*
   - *Object of the Preposition*: This is an object of the improper preposition ὀπίσω. Many improper prepositions take their object in the genitive.

3) αὐτοῦ: αὐτός; 3 masc sg gen; *he*/*she*/*it*, *self*, *same*, *they*
   - *Possession*: The disciple of Jesus must bear his or her personal cross and follow him.

8:35

1) αὐτοῦ: αὐτός; 3 masc sg gen; *he*/*she*/*it*, *self*, *same*, *they*
   - *Possession*: Refers to the person's own life.

2) αὐτοῦ: αὐτός; 3 masc sg gen; *he*/*she*/*it*, *self*, *same*, *they*
   - *Possession*: Refers to the person's own life.

3) ἐμοῦ: ἐγώ; 1 sg gen; *I*, *we*
   - Object of the Preposition: This is part of a compound object of the improper preposition ἕνεκεν. Many improper prepositions take their object in the genitive.

4) εὐαγγελίου: εὐαγγέλιον; neut sg gen; *good news*, *gospel*
   - Object of the Preposition: This is part of a compound object of the improper preposition ἕνεκεν. Many improper prepositions take their object in the genitive. The phrase ἕνεκεν ἐμοῦ καὶ τοῦ εὐαγγελίου is an example of hendiadys, as one's commitment to Jesus and to the gospel is one and the same.

8:36

1) αὐτοῦ: αὐτός; 3 masc sg gen; *he/she/it*, *self*, *same*, *they*
   - Possession: Refers to the person's life.

8:37

1) ψυχῆς: ψυχή; fem sg gen; *soul*, *life*
   - Objective: It is the object of the verbal idea behind the noun ἀντάλλαγμα, "to exchange."

2) αὐτοῦ: αὐτός; 3 masc sg gen; *he/she/it*, *self*, *same*, *they*
   - Possession: Refers to the person's life.

8:38

1) ἀνθρώπου: ἄνθρωπος; masc sg gen; *man*, *human*
   - Relationship: Not the typical genitive of relationship, since ἄνθρωπος does not refer to a specific person here, but it still indicates that Jesus has a relationship with mankind. Ultimately, however, ὁ υἱὸς τοῦ ἀνθρώπου should be taken idiomatically and as a likely reference to Dan 7:13 ("one like a son of man").

2) πατρός: πατήρ; masc sg gen; *father*
   - Possession: Refers to the glory that Jesus's Father possesses.

3) αὐτοῦ: αὐτός; 3 masc sg gen; *he/she/it*, *self*, *same*, *they*
   - Relationship: Refers to Jesus's Father.

4) ἀγγέλων: ἄγγελος; masc plur gen; *messenger*, *angel*
   - Object of the Preposition: Object of the preposition μετά; the prepositional phrase would be classified as "association."

9:1

1) ἑστηκότων: (substantive participle) ἵστημι; perf act part masc plur gen; *to stand*, *place*, *put*
   - Partitive: The genitive is the whole ("those standing here") of the part ("some").

2) θανάτου: θάνατος; masc sg gen; *death*
   - Direct Object: Direct object of γεύσωνται ("taste"). Verbs of sensation take a genitive direct object.

3) θεοῦ: θεός; masc sg gen; *God*
   - Possession: Refers to the kingdom that God possesses.

   or
   - Subjective: In the sense that God reigns.

Infinitives

8:27

1) εἶναι: εἰμί; pres act inf; *to be*, *to exist*
   - Indirect Discourse: Indirect discourse, following λέγουσιν.

8:29

1) εἶναι: εἰμί; pres act inf; *to be*, *to exist*
   - Indirect Discourse: Indirect discourse, following λέγετε.

8:31

1) διδάσκειν: διδάσκω; pres act inf; *to teach*
   - Complementary: Completes the verb ἤρξατο.

2) παθεῖν: πάσχω; aor act inf; *to experience*, *to suffer*, *to endure*
   - Subject: Serves as one of four infinitive subjects of δεῖ. Some might classify it as a complementary infinitive that completes the verbal idea introduced by δεῖ ("it is necessary"). Then, the impersonal pronoun "it" would be regarded as the subject. However, even in this case, there is no difference in the sense because what "it" refers to is specified by the infinitive. This explanation also applies to numbers 3–5 below.

3) ἀποδοκιμασθῆναι: ἀποδοκιμάζω; aor pass inf; *to reject*
   - Subject: Serves as one of four infinitive subjects of δεῖ.

4) ἀποκτανθῆναι: ἀποκτείνω; aor pass inf; *to kill*
   - Subject: Serves as one of four infinitive subjects of δεῖ.

5) ἀναστῆναι: ἀνίστημι; aor act inf; *to raise up*, *to arise*
   - Subject: Serves as one of four infinitive subjects of δεῖ.

8:32

1) ἐπιτιμᾶν: ἐπιτιμάω; pres act inf; *to rebuke*
   - Complementary: Completes the verb ἤρξατο.

8:34

1) ἀκολουθεῖν: ἀκολουθέω; pres act inf; *to follow*
   - Complementary: Completes the verb θέλει.

8:35

1) σῶσαι: σῴζω; aor act inf; *to save*, *to maintain*, *to preserve*
   - Complementary: Completes the verb θέλει.

8:36

1) κερδῆσαι: κερδαίνω; aor act inf; *to gain*
   - Subject: Subject of ὠφελεῖ.

2) ζημιωθῆναι: ζημιόω; aor pass inf; *to punish*, *to lose*
   - *Subject*: Subject of ὠφελεῖ.

Now, rewrite your translation of the entire passage in the GUIDED PRACTICE section, reflecting the above syntactical procedure.

REFERENCES

Danker, Frederick William, et al. *A Greek-English Lexicon of the New Testament and other Early Christian Literature*. 3rd ed. Chicago: The University of Chicago Press, 2000.

Decker, Rodney J. *Mark 1–8: A Handbook on the Greek Text*. Ed. Martin M. Culy. Baylor Handbook on the Greek New Testament. Waco: Baylor University Press, 2014.

France, R. T. *The Gospel of Mark*. The New International Greek Testament Commentary. Grand Rapids: Eerdmans, 2002.

Köstenberger, Andreas J., Benjamin L. Merkle, and Robert L. Plummer. *Going Deeper with New Testament Greek: An Intermediate Study of the Grammar and Syntax of the New Testament*. Rev. ed. Nashville: B&H Academic, 2020.

Mathewson, David L. and Elodie Ballantine Emig. *Intermediate Greek Grammar: Syntax for Students of the New Testament*. Grand Rapids: Baker Academic, 2016.

Merkle, Benjamin L. *Exegetical Gems from Biblical Greek*. Grand Rapids: Baker Academic, 2019.

Moo, Douglas. *The Epistle to the Romans*. The New International Commentary on the New Testament. Grand Rapids: Eerdmans, 1996.

Strauss, Mark L. *Mark*. Zondervan Exegetical Commentary on the New Testament. Grand Rapids: Zondervan Academic, 2014.

Wallace, Daniel B. *Greek Grammar Beyond the Basics: An Exegetical Syntax of the New Testament*. Grand Rapids: Zondervan, 1996.

Williams, Joel. *Mark*. Exegetical Guide to the Greek New Testament. Nashville: B&H Academic, 2020.

CHAPTER FOUR

////////////////

MARK 9:2–13

WITH ATTENTION TO PERFECT INDICATIVES, PLUPERFECTS, AND ARTICLES

GRAMMAR REVIEW:

Perfect Indicatives

Definition and Description

Perfects are the least common of the five major verb tenses, comprising only 5 percent of the indicative verbs found in the New Testament. If you add in pluperfects, it is 6 percent. Because of its relative rarity, one should take note when the author decided to use a perfect tense form and discern why he might have made that selection.

The primary force of the perfect tense is its stative aspect. It is sometimes defined as indicating a completed past action resulting in a present state. The perfect tense can be viewed as a combination of the aorist tense/perfective aspect (for the action) and the present tense/imperfective aspect (for the result). The interpreter's job is to determine which side is being emphasized in a particular text.

Beginning grammars may suggest translating a perfect with the helping verb *has* or *have*, but in many cases, the sense will be best conveyed by translating it into English with the present tense or as a simple past tense. Translation will depend on which category is the best fit for the word in a particular context. Consider John 19:30: ὅτε οὖν ἔλαβεν τὸ ὄξος [ὁ] Ἰησοῦς εἶπεν· **τετέλεσται**, καὶ κλίνας τὴν κεφαλὴν παρέδωκεν τὸ πνεῦμα. All major Bible translations convey the perfect-tense verb, τετέλεσται, with the present tense, as "It is finished."

Categories and Examples[1]

PERFECT INDICATIVE		
INTENSIVE	Emphasizes the present state of the verb brought about by a past action.	**ἀφέωνταί** σοι αἱ ἁμαρτίαι σου ("your sins **are forgiven** you" Luke 5:20 ESV).
CONSUMMATIVE	Emphasizes the completed action that brought about the resulting state.	τὸν καλὸν ἀγῶνα **ἠγώνισμαι** ("**I have fought** the good fight" 2 Tim 4:7).

[1] Andreas J. Köstenberger, Benjamin L. Merkle, and Robert L. Plummer, *Going Deeper with New Testament Greek: An Intermediate Study of the Grammar and Syntax of the New Testament*, rev. ed. (Nashville: B&H Academic, 2020), 309.

PERFECT INDICATIVE (CONTINUED)		
DRAMATIC	Vividly portrays a past event or state of affairs.	ἀπελθὼν **πέπρακεν** πάντα ὅσα εἶχεν ("he went and **sold** everything he had" Matt 13:46).
PRESENT STATE	Used with certain verbs that lost their perfect significance and conveys a present tense-form meaning.	τὰς ἐντολὰς **οἶδας** ("**You know** the commandments" Luke 18:20).
GNOMIC	Communicates a customary or general truth.	ὁ δὲ μὴ πιστεύων ἤδη **κέκριται** ("but anyone who does not believe is already **condemned**" John 3:18).
ITERATIVE	The action of the verb occurred at intervals.	ὃ **ἑωράκαμεν** τοῖς ὀφθαλμοῖς ἡμῶν ("what **we have seen** with our eyes" 1 John 1:1).

Pluperfects

Definition and Description

According to Maximilian Zerwick, the pluperfect is "a *past* state of affairs constituted by an action still further in the past."[2] Or as Köstenberger, Merkle, and Plummer write, "When a narrator is telling a story, that story is already a past event. But when the narrator needs to describe something that took place prior to this narrative, then the pluperfect is often used."[3]

Concerning aspect, the pluperfect, like the perfect, generally conveys a stative aspect. But whereas the perfect refers to a past action resulting in a present state, the pluperfect is used of a past action which resulted in a past state. It can be viewed as a combination of the aorist tense/perfective aspect (for the action) and the imperfect tense/imperfective aspect (for the result).

Only 86 pluperfects appear in the NT constituting 1 percent of the indicative verbs. The pluperfect usually has an augment, reduplication, κ tense formative (1st pluperfect only), an ει connecting vowel, and secondary ending.

Categories and Examples[4]

PLUPERFECT INDICATIVE		
INTENSIVE	Emphasizes the (past) results brought about by a past action.	εἰς ὃν **πεπιστεύκεισαν** ("in whom **they had believed**" Acts 14:23).
CONSUMMATIVE	Emphasizes the completion of a past action.	οἱ . . . μαθηταὶ αὐτοῦ **ἀπεληλύθεισαν** εἰς τὴν πόλιν ("His disciples **had gone** into town" John 4:8).
PAST STATE	Used with certain verbs that convey a past state with no antecedent action.	ὅτι **ᾔδεισαν** αὐτόν ("because **they knew** him" Mark 1:34).

Articles

Definition and Description

The article is the most common word used in the NT, appearing twice as frequently as the nearest competitor, καί. Both its presence and its absence are signficant for interpretation. Greek does not have an indefinite article (the

---

[2] Maximilian Zerwick, *Biblical Greek: Illustrated by Examples*, English ed., adapted from the fourth Latin ed., vol. 114 of *Scripta Pontificii Instituti Biblici* (Rome: Scripta Pontificii Instituti Biblici, 1963), 98.

[3] Köstenberger, Merkle, and Plummer, *Going Deeper with New Testament Greek*, 305.

[4] Köstenberger, Merkle, and Plummer, 309.

English *a* or *an*), only a definite article (*the*). But not every appearance of the article should be translated as *the* or even translated at all.

There are three basic functions of the Greek article. First, the article is used to *conceptualize*, i.e., to turn words or phrases into substantives. Wallace writes, "The article is able to turn just about any part of speech into a noun and, therefore, a concept."[5] For example, "hungry" conveys a quality. But if you were to add an article and make it "the hungry," the addition of the article turns it into an entity. Second, the article is used to *identify*, i.e., to point out one thing from another. Third, the article is used to *mark something as definite* (*the* book versus *a* book). This is not to say that the lack of an article means something is indefinite; it only means that if an article is present, the word/phrase modified by it is definite.

Articles must precede their head noun (or substantive) and agree with it in case, number, and gender. One very helpful trait of the article is that it helps clarify the structure of a sentence, pointing out the subject, object, etc. This can be especially useful with an indeclinable noun—without the article, it is less obvious what role the noun is playing in the sentence. But, as a word of caution, the use of the article is not fully understood. According to Mathewson and Emig, "The presence and absence of the Greek article are not easily codified."[6] They also point out that sometimes the article's use is dependent on the author's stylistic preferences.[7]

Still, Wallace believes that the article is "one of the greatest gifts bequeathed by the Greeks to Western civilization,"[8] and that it is "one of the most fascinating areas of study in NT Greek grammar. It is also one of the most neglected and abused."[9] Therefore, if we want to be careful readers of the biblical text, we must give focused attention to the article.

Categories and Examples[10]

USES OF THE ARTICLE		
WITH SUBSTANTIVES	The article particularizes a substantive or uses it generically.	Identification: ποῦ ἐστιν **ὁ** τεχθεὶς βασιλεὺς τῶν Ἰουδαίων ("Where is **he** who has been born King of the Jews?" Matt 2:2).
		Par Excellence: **ὁ** προφήτης εἶ σύ; ("Are you **the** Prophet?" John 1:21).
		Monadic (One-of-a-Kind): οὕτως γὰρ ἠγάπησεν ὁ θεὸς τὸν κόσμον, ὥστε **τὸν** υἱὸν **τὸν** μονογενῆ ἔδωκεν ("For God so loved the world, that he gave his only Son" John 3:16 ESV).
		With Abstract Nouns: **ἡ** σωτηρία ἐκ τῶν Ἰουδαίων ἐστίν ("salvation is from the Jews" John 4:22).
		Previous Reference (Anaphoric): πόθεν οὖν ἔχεις **τὸ** ὕδωρ τὸ ζῶν; ("Where do You get **that** living water?" John 4:11 ESV).
		Generic: Προσέχετε ἀπὸ **τῶν** ψευδοπροφητῶν ("Be on your guard against false prophets" Matt 7:15).

[5] Daniel B. Wallace, *Greek Grammar Beyond the Basics: An Exegetical Syntax of the New Testament* (Grand Rapids: Zondervan, 1996), 209.

[6] David L. Mathewson and Elodie Ballantine Emig, *Intermediate Greek Grammar: Syntax for Students of the New Testament* (Grand Rapids: Baker Academic, 2016), 73.

[7] Mathewson and Emig, 73.

[8] Wallace, *Greek Grammar Beyond the Basics*, 207.

[9] Wallace, 207.

[10] Köstenberger, Merkle, and Plummer, *Going Deeper with New Testament Greek*, 178–79.

USES OF THE ARTICLE (CONTINUED)		
AS A PRONOUN	The article functions as a personal, relative, possessive, demonstrative, or alternate pronoun.	As Personal Pronoun: **οἱ** δὲ εἶπαν αὐτῷ ("**they** told him" Matt 2:5).
		As Relative Pronoun: δοξάσωσιν τὸν πατέρα ὑμῶν **τὸν** ἐν τοῖς οὐρανοῖς ("give glory to your Father **who** is in heaven" Matt 5:16 ESV).
		As Possessive Pronoun: ὁ δὲ διεῖλεν αὐτοῖς **τὸν** βίον ("And he divided **his** property between them" Luke 15:12 ESV).
		As Demonstrative Pronoun: **οἱ** . . . ἐν τῷ πλοίῳ προσεκύνησαν αὐτῷ ("**those** in the boat worshiped him" Matt 14:33).
		As Alternate Pronoun: αὐτὸς ἔδωκεν **τοὺς** μὲν ἀποστόλους ("He gave **some** as apostles" Eph 4:11 NASB).
ABSENCE OF ARTICLE	The absence of the article may convey that a given substantive is non-particular (indefinite or qualitative) or definite. If definite, this may be in conjunction with a proper name, a prepositional object, ordinal numbers, in predicate nominatives, as the complement in an object, complement construction, with monadic (one-of-a-kind) nouns, with abstract or generic nouns, with a pronominal adjective, or with technical expressions.	Indefinite: Καὶ εἶπεν τοῖς μαθηταῖς αὐτοῦ ἵνα πλοιάριον προσκαρτερῇ αὐτῷ ("Then he told his disciples to have a small boat ready for him" Mark 3:9).
		Qualitative: πλήρης χάριτος καὶ ἀληθείας ("full of grace and truth" John 1:14).
		Definite: Prepositional Object: Χαίρετε ἐν κυρίῳ ("Rejoice in the Lord" Phil 4:4). Predicate Nominative: θεοῦ εἰμι υἱός ("I am the Son of God." Matt 27:43 ESV).
		Proper Name: Παῦλος καὶ Σιλᾶς προσευχόμενοι ("Paul and Silas were praying" Acts 16:25).
SPECIAL RULES	Granville Sharp Rule: When a single article governs two singular, personal, non-proper substantives of the same case that are joined by καί, they frequently refer to the same person.	**τοῦ** μεγάλου θεοῦ καὶ σωτῆρος ἡμῶν Ἰησοῦ Χριστοῦ ("our great God and Savior, Jesus Christ" Titus 2:13).
	Colwell's Rule: A definite predicate nominative does not usually take the article when preceding the copula (linking verb).	θεὸς ἦν ὁ λόγος ("the Word was God" John 1:1).
	Apollonius's Canon: When two nouns are in a genitive construction, both the head noun and the noun in the genitive case either have or lack the article.	**ὁ** λόγος **τοῦ** θεοῦ = "**the** Word of God" (John 10:35) or λόγου . . . θεοῦ (1 Pet 1:23).

GUIDED PRACTICE: MARK 9:2–13 (NA[28])

9:2 Καὶ μετὰ ἡμέρας ἓξ παραλαμβάνει ὁ Ἰησοῦς τὸν Πέτρον καὶ τὸν Ἰάκωβον καὶ τὸν
Ἰωάννην καὶ ἀναφέρει αὐτοὺς εἰς ὄρος ὑψηλὸν κατ᾽ ἰδίαν μόνους. καὶ μετεμορφώθη
ἔμπροσθεν αὐτῶν, 3 καὶ τὰ ἱμάτια αὐτοῦ ἐγένετο στίλβοντα λευκὰ λίαν, οἷα γναφεὺς
ἐπὶ τῆς γῆς οὐ δύναται οὕτως λευκᾶναι. 4 καὶ ὤφθη αὐτοῖς Ἠλίας σὺν Μωϋσεῖ καὶ ἦσαν
συλλαλοῦντες τῷ Ἰησοῦ. 5 καὶ ἀποκριθεὶς ὁ Πέτρος λέγει τῷ Ἰησοῦ· ῥαββί, καλόν ἐστιν
ἡμᾶς ὧδε εἶναι, καὶ ποιήσωμεν τρεῖς σκηνάς, σοὶ μίαν καὶ Μωϋσεῖ μίαν καὶ Ἠλίᾳ μίαν.
6 οὐ γὰρ ᾔδει τί ἀποκριθῇ, ἔκφοβοι γὰρ ἐγένοντο. 7 καὶ ἐγένετο νεφέλη ἐπισκιάζουσα αὐτοῖς,
καὶ ἐγένετο φωνὴ ἐκ τῆς νεφέλης· οὗτός ἐστιν ὁ υἱός μου ὁ ἀγαπητός, ἀκούετε αὐτοῦ. 8 καὶ
ἐξάπινα περιβλεψάμενοι οὐκέτι οὐδένα εἶδον ἀλλὰ τὸν Ἰησοῦν μόνον μεθ᾽ ἑαυτῶν.

[9] Καὶ καταβαινόντων αὐτῶν ἐκ τοῦ ὄρους διεστείλατο αὐτοῖς ἵνα μηδενὶ ἃ εἶδον
διηγήσωνται, εἰ μὴ ὅταν ὁ υἱὸς τοῦ ἀνθρώπου ἐκ νεκρῶν ἀναστῇ. [10] καὶ τὸν λόγον ἐκράτησαν
πρὸς ἑαυτοὺς συζητοῦντες τί ἐστιν τὸ ἐκ νεκρῶν ἀναστῆναι.

[11] Καὶ ἐπηρώτων αὐτὸν λέγοντες· ὅτι λέγουσιν οἱ γραμματεῖς ὅτι Ἠλίαν δεῖ ἐλθεῖν πρῶτον;
[12] ὁ δὲ ἔφη αὐτοῖς· Ἠλίας μὲν ἐλθὼν πρῶτον ἀποκαθιστάνει πάντα· καὶ πῶς γέγραπται ἐπὶ
τὸν υἱὸν τοῦ ἀνθρώπου ἵνα πολλὰ πάθῃ καὶ ἐξουδενηθῇ; [13] ἀλλὰ λέγω ὑμῖν ὅτι καὶ Ἠλίας
ἐλήλυθεν, καὶ ἐποίησαν αὐτῷ ὅσα ἤθελον, καθὼς γέγραπται ἐπ᾽ αὐτόν.

VOCABULARY AIDS (WORDS 26X TO 50X)

9:2	**παραλαμβάνω** (παρά+λαμβάνω, aorist stem: λαβ) *to take along* (49x)
9:2	**Ἰάκωβος** *James* (43x)
9:2	**ἔμπροσθεν** (ἐν+πρός+θεν) (+gen) *before*, *in front of* (48x)
9:4, 5, 11, 12, 13	**Ἠλίας** *Elijah* (29x)
9:8	**οὐκέτι** (οὐ+ἔτι) *no longer* (47x)
9:10	**κρατέω** *to grasp*, *be strong*, *take possession*, *to keep*, *to hold onto* (47x)
9:12	**πάσχω** *to experience*; *suffer*, *endure* (42x)

VOCABULARY AIDS (WORDS 25X OR LESS)

9:2	**ἕξ** *six* (13x)
9:2	**ἀναφέρω** (ἀνά+φέρω) *to bring up, raise up, bear, pay, add to, offer up* (10x)
9:2	**ὑψηλός** *high, proud* (11x)
9:2	**μεταμορφόω** (μετά+μορφή) *to change form* (4x)
9:3	**στίλβω** *to shine* (1x)
9:3	**λευκός** *white* (25x)
9:3	**λίαν** *exceedingly* (12x)
9:3	**οἷος** *such as, as*; (adv) *for instance* (14x)
9:3	**γναφεύς** *cloth refiner* (1x)
9:3	**λευκαίνω** *to whiten* (2x)
9:4	**συλλαλέω** (σύν+λαλέω) *to speak with* (6X)
9:5	**ῥαββί** *Rabbi* (Heb. *my teacher*) (15x)
9:5	**σκηνή** *tent*; *tabernacle*; *stage* (20x)
9:6	**ἔκφοβος** (ἐκ+φόβος) *terrified* (2x)
9:7	**νεφέλη** *cloud* (25x)
9:7	**ἐπισκιάζω** (ἐπί+σκιά) *to overshadow* (5x)
9:8	**ἐξάπινα** (ἐκ+ἄφνω) *suddenly* (1x)
9:8	**περιβλέπω** (περί+βλέπω) *to look around* (7x)
9:9	**διαστέλλω** (διά+στέλλω) *to strictly order, command* (8x)
9:9	**διηγέομαι** (διά+ἄγω) *to describe in detail*; *tell, explain* (8x)
9:10	**συζητέω** (σύν+ζητέω) *to argue, question* (10x)
9:12	**ἀποκαθίστημι** (ἀπό+κατά+ἵστημι) *to restore, return* (8x)
9:12	**ἐξουδενέω** (ἐκ+οὐδέ+εἷς) *to treat with contempt*; *scorn, despise* (1x)

EXERCISE

I. Provide your translation under the Greek text above.

II. Exegetical notes and questions: read the bullet points and answer the questions below.

Verse-by-Verse Questions

9:2

a) Παραλαμβάνει and ἀναφέρει are both in what tense? Why? How would you translate these verbs?

b) Μετὰ ἡμέρας ἓξ ("after six days") is the most specific time marker narrated between events in Mark's Gospel.[11] Why do you think Mark is so specific here?

9:3

- The verb στίλβω is employed only here in the NT, but in the LXX, it is used to describe the "radiance of stars or the luster of metals."[12]

9:4

c) What type of construction is used in ἦσαν συλλαλοῦντες?

9:5

d) How should ἀποκριθείς be translated? What is its use?

---

[11] Also note the significant temporal marker contained in the passion predictions (μετὰ τρεῖς ἡμέρας; 8:31; 9:31; 10:34) which is not located between episodes and should, thus, be distinguished from the time indicator in 9:2.

[12] *BDAG*, 945.

e) What construction is καλόν ἐστιν ἡμᾶς ὧδε εἶναι, and how does καλόν function in it?

9:6

f) Verse 6 starts out with οὐ γὰρ ᾔδει. English translations will render it as "For he did not know . . ." Why is γάρ the second word in the given Greek clause instead of the first? Moreover, for which portion of the text, in particular, does this γάρ clause provide the rationale?

9:7

g) In the clause, καὶ ἐγένετο νεφέλη **ἐπισκιάζουσα** αὐτοῖς, what type of participle would you consider ἐπισκιάζουσα to be, and how would you translate this clause?

h) In the clause, οὗτός ἐστιν ὁ υἱός μου ὁ ἀγαπητός, how do you know which nominative is the subject and which nominative is the predicate?

9:9

i) How would you classify the participle καταβαινόντων? What role does it play in the sentence?

j) How would you classify and translate this ἵνα clause: ἵνα μηδενὶ ἃ εἶδον διηγήσωνται?

9:10

k) In the phrase, τί ἐστιν τὸ ἐκ νεκρῶν ἀναστῆναι, what role does τό play? With which word is it associated?

9:11

l) Explain the two uses of ὅτι.

9:13

m) Note both instances of καί. What is this construction called, and what is its typical translation?

Additional Questions

n) In 9:11, the disciples ask Jesus why the scribes say Elijah must come first. Jesus addresses their question but also asks them one of his own about the Son of Man's prophesied suffering. The logic of the narrative flow is not straightforward. How would you explain the flow of thought and the logic of the questions and answers in 9:11–13?

Short Summary and Contextual Impact

III. Summarize the main idea of the passage and then discuss how it fits into the surrounding narrative.

Parsing and Classification

IV. Circle the perfect and pluperfect indicatives in the text, underline the articles, and parse them all below. Then classify each one according to the categories given in the grammar review above. Provide a brief explanation for your decisions.

Perfect Indicatives

9:12

1)

9:13

1)

2)

Pluperfect Indicatives

9:6

1)

Articles (using specific categories, e.g., "identification")

9:2

1)

2)

3)

4)

9:3

1)

2)

9:4

1)

9:5

1)

2)

9:7

1)

2)

3)

9:8

1)

9:9

1)

2)

3)

9:10

1)

2)

9:11

1)

9:12

1)

2)

3)

ANSWER KEY

I. Translation and explanations

9:2 After six days Jesus took Peter, James, and John and led them up a high mountain by themselves
to be alone. He was transfigured in front of them, 3 and his clothes became dazzling—extremely
white as no launderer on earth could whiten them. 4 Elijah appeared to them with Moses, and they
were talking with Jesus. 5 Peter said to Jesus, "Rabbi, it's good for us to be here. Let's set up three
shelters: one for you, one for Moses, and one for Elijah"—6 because he did not know what to say,
since they were terrified.
7 A cloud appeared, overshadowing them, and a voice came from the cloud: "This is my beloved
Son; listen to him!"
8 Suddenly, looking around, they no longer saw anyone with them except Jesus.
9 As they were coming down the mountain, he ordered them to tell no one what they had seen until
the Son of Man had risen from the dead. 10 They kept this word to themselves, questioning what
"rising from the dead" meant.
11 Then they asked him, "Why do the scribes say that Elijah must come first?"
12 "Elijah does come first and restores all things," he replied. "Why then is it written that the Son of
Man must suffer many things and be treated with contempt? 13 But I tell you that Elijah has come,
and they did whatever they pleased to him, just as it is written about him."

II. Answers to exegetical questions

Verse-by-Verse Questions

a) In 9:2, παραλαμβάνει and ἀναφέρει are both in the present tense, which is known as the historical present. Historical presents often mark a new paragraph, a new location and/or a new character. Translate them as past tense in English: [*Jesus*] *took*; [*he*] *led them up*.

b) In 9:2, the specificity of elapsed time between pericopes serves to tie them together, leading the reader to understand one in light of the other. In Mark 9:1, Jesus had just said that some standing there would not die before seeing that the kingdom of God had come. The story of the transfiguration would seem to be at least a partial fulfillment of this prophecy.

c) In 9:4, συλλαλοῦντες is a periphrastic participle in an *imperfect* construction (imperfect of εἰμί + present ptc), meaning "were talking with." Instead of pairing the "to be" verb with a participle, the same meaning could have been rendered via a single finite verb in the imperfect tense—συνελάλουν.

d) In 9:5, ἀποκριθείς is paired with λέγει as a redundant participle of speaking and would not be translated separately. This pairing is idiomatic and is frequent when someone is replying to a question or, as in this case, when a person is responding to a situation.

e) Regarding καλόν ἐστιν ἡμᾶς ὧδε εἶναι in 9:5, ἡμᾶς ὧδε εἶναι is an infinitive clause, acting as the subject of ἐστιν; καλόν is a predicate adjective. Woodenly, this means, "For us to be here is good."

f) The γάρ in 9:6 is a post-positive conjunction in that it can never appear first in a sentence. (The word δέ is another common post-positive conjunction.) The first γάρ clause in 9:6 (οὐ γὰρ ᾔδει τί ἀποκριθῇ) provides the rationale for v. 5 as a whole rather than just the direct discourse in v. 5. In other words, Mark clarifies through this γάρ clause why Peter responded in the way described in v. 5. The second γάρ clause in v. 6 (ἔκφοβοι γὰρ ἐγένοντο), on the other hand, offers the rationale for the first γάρ clause in the same verse.

g) In 9:7, one finds καὶ ἐγένετο νεφέλη **ἐπισκιάζουσα** αὐτοῖς. Williams sees ἐπισκιάζουσα as a participle of *result*.[13] If so, the clause should be translated as something like: "and a cloud came and overshadowed them" (cf. CSB). However, another rendering is also possible. If, as Decker suggests, ἐπισκιάζουσα is the lone Markan example of a perfective periphrastic participle, the aorist verb ἐγένετο should not be translated independently.[14] Instead, it needs to be taken collectively with the participle ἐπισκιάζουσα for the single idea of "and the cloud overshadowed them" (cf. ESV).[15] Williams's and Decker's renderings are more natural than taking ἐπισκιάζουσα as an attributive participle modifying νεφέλη ("a cloud that overshowed them came"). The latter reading is possible grammatically, but it does not make good sense because it requires a preceding instance where the cloud overshadowed these disciples.

h) In 9:7, the clause οὗτός ἐστιν ὁ υἱός μου ὁ ἀγαπητός has nominatives both before and after ἐστιν. To determine which is the subject in situations like this, the following should be considered in the given order: (1) the subject will be the pronoun, (2) the subject will be articular, and (3) the subject will appear first in order.[16] Thus, οὗτός is the subject, and the clause should be translated, "This is my beloved Son."

i) In 9:9, καταβαινόντων is a genitive absolute (temporal), given that it is in the genitive case, anarthrous, at the front of the sentence, and its subject is different from that of the rest of the sentence. It provides background information, setting the stage for what comes next.

j) The ἵνα in 9:9 should be seen as introducing the direct object of the verb διεστείλατο and more specifically an indirect discourse (μηδενὶ ἃ εἶδον **διηγήσωνται**), providing the content of what Jesus commanded (thus, imperatival in force). Therefore, διεστείλατο αὐτοῖς ἵνα μηδενὶ ἃ εἶδον **διηγήσωνται** could be rendered "he ordered them that they should tell no one what they had seen" (our own translation). Alternatively, it can be translated with an indirect discourse infinitive: "he ordered them to tell no one what they had seen" (CSB).

k) In 9:10, the τό in the phrase τί ἐστιν τὸ ἐκ νεκρῶν ἀναστῆναι is associated with the infinitive ἀναστῆναι. It marks the infinitive as the subject of ἐστιν. It is also anaphoric, referencing Jesus's rising from the dead, just mentioned at the end of v. 9. If τό is not functioning anaphorically, it would leave open the possibility that the disciples were discussing what rising from the dead would look like for *them*.

l) In 9:11, the first use of ὅτι initiates direct discourse with the question, "why?" According to Decker, the use of ὅτι, equivalent to ὅ τι,[17] as "why" is unique to Mark in the NT. It is used this way, however, in the LXX.[18] The second use introduces indirect discourse, translated as "that."

---

[13] Joel F. Williams, *Mark*, ed. Andreas J. Köstenberger and Robert W. Yarbrough, Exegetical Guide to the Greek New Testament (Nashville: B&H Academic, 2020), 151.

[14] Rodney J. Decker, *Mark 1–8: A Handbook on the Greek Text*, ed. Martin M. Culy, Baylor Handbook on the Greek New Testament (Waco: Baylor University Press, 2014), xxxi.

[15] Wallace notes that the basic concept behind a periphrastic participle is a "*round-about* way of saying what could be expressed by a single verb," in which a verb of being is paired with a participle. See Wallace, *Greek Grammar Beyond the Basics*, 647.

[16] For a detailed analysis proving this order, see Lane C. McGaughy, *Toward a Descriptive Analysis of EINAI as a Linking Verb in New Testament Greek* (SBLDS 6; Missoula, MT: Society of Biblical Literature, 1972). To see further discussion on McGaughy's work, consult Eugene Van Ness Goetchius, "Review of *Toward a Descriptive Analysis of EINAI as a Linking Verb in New Testament Greek,* by Lane C. McGaughy," *Journal of Biblical Literature,* 95 (1976), 147–49; D. A. Carson, "Syntactical and Text-Critical Observations on John 20:30–31: One More Round on the Purpose of the Fourth Gospel," *Journal of Biblical Literature* 124, no. 4 (2005), 693–714.

[17] The space between ὅ and τι here is intended.

[18] Decker, *Mark 1–8*, 57.

m) The two occurrences of καί in 9:13 are known as *paired* or *correlative conjunctions*. This correlative construction should be translated as *both . . . and*. Some other paired conjunctions are μήτε . . . μήτε (*neither . . . nor*), οὔτε . . . οὔτε (*neither . . . nor*), τε . . . τε (*as . . . so*), ἤ . . . ἤ (*either . . . or*), and μέν . . . δέ (*on the one hand . . . on the other hand*).

Additional Questions

n) In 9:11–13, the logic of the dialogue may appear to be confusing. In essence, one should note that what has been written of the Messiah and his suffering (9:12–13, with αὐτόν [9:13] referring to Jesus; cf. 14:21) determines not only his course but also the fate of his Elijah-like forerunner, that is, John the Baptizer (6:14–29). The disciples are wondering how Elijah's coming fits into the picture since they know that the Messiah is fulfilling prophecy. In other words, how are they to understand the fact that Elijah was supposed to come on the scene first? Jesus is responding to the disciples by first questioning their assumption about what the coming of the Messiah is going to look like. Jesus asks them, if Elijah is first coming to restore all things, how does it make sense that the Son of Man—the Messiah—is going to suffer? Their understanding of what it means to "restore all things" must need revision given that Elijah has already come, and he has been mistreated and has suffered. Here, Jesus teaches that the glorious ministry of restoration may appear to be, instead, dishonorable to the eyes of man/the world (cf. 8:33; 1 Cor 1:18–31).[19]

III. Short Summary and Contextual Impact

Summary: Jesus leads Peter, James, and John up a mountain, where he is transfigured before them and where he converses with Elijah and Moses. Peter offers to pitch a tent for Jesus, Moses, and Elijah each, after which God speaks to the disciples from a cloud and identifies Jesus as his Son, commanding that they must listen to him. Then Elijah and Moses suddenly disappear. When Jesus and his disciples are returning from the mountain, Jesus guides these disciples into a crucial conversation on his resurrection and his passion, the latter of which is explained in association with the suffering of John the Baptist, that is, the Elijah-like forerunner of the Messiah.

Contextual Impact: In the Way Discourse of Mark (8:22–10:52), Jesus focuses on his disciples, clarifying his true identity and mission for them. In the preceding passage, Jesus and his disciples discussed who he is, and Peter confessed him as the Messiah. But then, when Jesus began to share his upcoming rejection and death, Peter admonished him, thus revealing that he did not yet grasp what Jesus had come to do. In response, Jesus gave a lesson on what discipleship entails. Then he remarks that some of those standing there would not die until they see the coming of God's kingdom (9:1).

The time stamp "after six days" (9:2) ties 9:1 to what comes next: the scene of transfiguration (9:2–8). Jesus reveals his glory to the three inner-group disciples at the mount of transfiguration. His glory is seen when he changes physically, converses with Elijah and Moses, and is affirmed by God the Father, who speaks from a cloud, telling the disciples that Jesus is his Son and that they must listen to him. This divine voice from the cloud is in response to their earlier, negative reaction toward Jesus's passion prediction. Moses and Elijah loomed large in Second Temple Judaism, but in this scene, Jesus is exalted far above those heroes of Israel.

What happens at the transfiguration is part of the preparation for what awaits Jesus and the disciples in Jerusalem. The disciples are offered a glimpse of Jesus's true identity, a glimpse powerful enough to help them overcome doubt when their visions of an earthly kingdom fails to materialize.

---

[19] Cf. Mark L. Strauss, *Mark*, Zondervan Exegetical Commentary on the New Testament (Grand Rapids: Zondervan, 2014), 388–89.

IV. Parsing and Classification of the Key Grammatical Concepts for the Lesson: Perfect Indicatives, Pluperfects, and Articles

Perfect Indicatives

9:12

1) γέγραπται: γράφω; 3 sg perf pass ind; *to write*, *engrave*, *inscribe*, *record*
   - *Intensive*: The emphasis is the current state of *being written*, not the past action.[20]

9:13

1) ἐλήλυθεν: ἔρχομαι; 3 sg perf act ind; *to come*, *go*
   - *Consummative*: Focus is on the fact that Elijah has come. It could also be seen as dramatic. In either case, the emphasis is on the act of Elijah's coming.

2) γέγραπται: γράφω; 3 sg perf pass ind; *to write*, *engrave*, *inscribe*, *record*
   - *Intensive*: The emphasis is the current state of *being written*, not the past action.

Pluperfect Indicatives

9:6

1) ᾔδει: οἶδα; 3 sg pluperf act ind; *to know*
   - *Past State*: This category is common for οἶδα.

Articles (using specific categories, e.g., "identification")

9:2

1) ὁ: ὁ; masc sg nom; *the*, *who*, *which*
   - *Identification*: Used before the proper noun Ἰησοῦς.

2) τόν (1st): ὁ; masc sg acc; *the*, *who*, *which*
   - *Identification*: Used before the proper noun Πέτρον.

3) τόν (2nd): ὁ; masc sg acc; *the*, *who*, *which*
   - *Identification*: Used before the proper noun Ἰάκωβον.

4) τόν (3rd): ὁ; masc sg acc; *the*, *who*, *which*
   - *Identification*: Used before the proper noun Ἰωάννην.

9:3

1) τά: ὁ; neut plur nom; *the*, *who*, *which*
   - *Identification*: Identifies the cloak which Jesus was wearing.

---

[20] The verb γέγραπται in 9:12 and 9:13 is a divine passive in that the implied agent is God.

2) τῆς: ὁ; fem sg gen; *the*, *who*, *which*
   - *Identification*: Identifies the ground or earth.

9:4

1) τῷ: ὁ; masc sg dat; *the*, *who*, *which*
   - *Identification*: Used before the proper noun Ἰησοῦ.

9:5

1) ὁ: ὁ; masc sg nom; *the*, *who*, *which*
   - *Identification*: Used before the proper noun Πέτρος.

2) τῷ: ὁ; masc sg dat; *the*, *who*, *which*
   - *Identification*: Used before the proper noun Ἰησοῦ.

9:7

1) τῆς: ὁ; fem sg gen; *the*, *who*, *which*
   - *Previous Reference*: References the cloud mentioned earlier in the sentence.

2) ὁ (1st): ὁ; masc sg nom; *the*, *who*, *which*
   - *Monadic*: Jesus is being identified as God's (unique) Son, modified by *beloved*.

3) ὁ (2nd): ὁ; masc sg nom; *the*, *who*, *which*
   - *Identification*: This use of the article is an example of the *second attributive position*; in this case, we apply the default category of *identification*.

9:8

1) τόν: ὁ; masc sg acc; *the*, *who*, *which*
   - *Identification*: Used before the proper noun Ἰησοῦν.

9:9

1) τοῦ (1st): ὁ; neut sg gen; *the*, *who*, *which*
   - *Previous Reference*: References the mountain mentioned in 9:2.

2) ὁ: ὁ; masc sg nom; *the*, *who*, *which*
   - *Monadic*: Jesus is God's unique Son.

3) τοῦ (2nd): ὁ; masc sg gen; *the*, *who*, *which*
   - *Apollonius's Canon*: The genitive noun, according to Apollonius's Canon, must be articular since the head noun has an article.

9:10

1) τόν: ὁ; masc sg acc; *the*, *who*, *which*
   - *Identification*: It identifies the word or statement that Jesus had uttered.

2) τό: ὁ; neut sg nom; *the*, *who*, *which*
   - *Previous Reference*: Modifies the infinitive ἀναστῆναι, marking it as the subject of ἐστιν. It is anaphoric because it looks back to Jesus's statement about his rising from the dead in v. 9.

9:11

1) οἱ: ὁ; masc plur nom; *the*, *who*, *which*
   - *Identification*: Identifies the scribes.

9:12

1) ὁ: ὁ; masc sg nom; *the*, *who*, *which*
   - *Personal Pronoun*: According to the pattern, ὁ is paired with δέ, and it is translated as the personal pronoun "he."

2) τόν: ὁ; masc sg acc; *the*, *who*, *which*
   - *Monadic*: Jesus is God's unique Son.

3) τοῦ: ὁ; masc sg gen; *the*, *who*, *which*
   - *Apollonius's Canon*: The genitive noun, according to Apollonius's Canon, must be articular since the head noun has an article.

Now, rewrite your translation of the entire passage in the GUIDED PRACTICE section, reflecting the above exegetical procedure.

REFERENCES

Danker, Frederick William, et al. *A Greek-English Lexicon of the New Testament and other Early Christian Literature*. 3rd ed. Chicago: The University of Chicago Press, 2000.

Decker, Rodney J. *Mark 1–8: A Handbook on the Greek Text*. Ed. Martin M. Culy. Baylor Handbook on the Greek New Testament. Waco: Baylor University Press, 2014.

———. *Mark 9–16: A Handbook on the Greek Text*. Ed. Martin M. Culy. Baylor Handbook on the Greek New Testament. Waco: Baylor University Press, 2014.

Evans, Craig A. *Mark 8:27–16:20*. Word Biblical Commentary, vol 34b. Grand Rapids: Zondervan, 1988.

France, R. T. *The Gospel of Mark*. The New International Greek Testament Commentary. Grand Rapids: Eerdmans, 2002.

Köstenberger, Andreas J., Benjamin L. Merkle, and Robert L. Plummer. *Going Deeper with New Testament Greek: An Intermediate Study of the Grammar and Syntax of the New Testament*. Rev ed. Nashville: B&H Academic, 2020.

Mathewson, David L. and Elodie Ballantine Emig. *Intermediate Greek Grammar: Syntax for Students of the New Testament*. Grand Rapids: Baker Academic, 2016.

Merkle, Benjamin L. *Exegetical Gems from Biblical Greek*. Grand Rapids: Baker Academic, 2019.

Strauss, Mark L. *Mark*. Zondervan Exegetical Commentary on the New Testament. Grand Rapids: Zondervan Academic, 2014.

Wallace, Daniel B. *Greek Grammar Beyond the Basics: An Exegetical Syntax of the New Testament*. Grand Rapids: Zondervan, 1996.

Williams, Joel. *Mark*. Ed. Andreas J. Köstenberger and Robert W. Yarbrough. Exegetical Guide to the Greek New Testament. Nashville: B&H, 2020.

Zerwick, Maximilian. *Biblical Greek Illustrated by Examples*. English ed., adapted from the fourth Latin ed. Vol. 114 of *Scripta Pontificii Instituti Biblici*. Rome: Pontificio Istituto Biblico, 1963.

CHAPTER FIVE

/////////////////

MARK 9:14–29

WITH ATTENTION TO PARTICIPLES AND VOCATIVES

GRAMMAR REVIEW:

Participles[1]

Definition and Description

Participles are a very common and an extremely versatile part of speech in the Greek NT. As participles appear 6,658 times, learning how to interpret them is crucial to understanding most texts. A participle is a declinable verbal adjective. Like verbs, they have tense/aspect, voice, can take an object, and, like adjectives, they have gender, number, and case. This complexity is often what makes participles so difficult for students to master. As Wallace says, "The participle is difficult to master because it is so versatile. But this very versatility makes it capable of a rich variety of nuances, as well as a rich variety of abuses."[2]

Most participles—69 percent—are in the nominative case, while 14 percent are accusative, 11 percent are genitive, 5 percent are dative, and 1 percent are vocative. As to tense, 55 percent are present, 34 percent are aorist, 10 percent are perfect, and about 1 percent are future.

There is debate over how time relates to participles. The more traditional view argues that participles do encode time but that it is a relative time that is derived from the *controlling* verb rather than the speaker.[3] In other words, rather than indicating something as past, present, or future with respect to the speaker/author, the participle indicates something as being before, contemporaneous with, or subsequent to the verb. A second view argues that time is entirely absent from participles and that word order is determinative for understanding the function of participles.[4] A third, nuanced view argues that aspect is primary, time is absent, and context is the only way to determine the function of a participle.[5] While adjudicating between these views is beyond the scope of this workbook, as you consider participles in the pericope below, we encourage you to focus on aspect and context to help discern how the participle is being used.

---

[1] Mark's Gospel contains 562 participles, which is the fourth most of any book in the NT.

[2] Daniel B. Wallace, *Greek Grammar Beyond the Basics: An Exegetical Syntax of the New Testament* (Grand Rapids: Zondervan, 1996), 613.

[3] Wallace, 614–15.

[4] Stanley E. Porter, *Idioms of the Greek New Testament*, 2nd. ed. reprinted, Biblical Languages: Greek 2 (Sheffield, UK: Sheffield Academic, 1999), 188.

[5] Andreas J. Köstenberger, Benjamin L. Merkle, and Robert L. Plummer, *Going Deeper with New Testament Greek: An Intermediate Study of the Grammar and Syntax of the New Testament*, rev. ed. (Nashville: B&H Academic, 2020), 324–25.

To classify a participle, first determine if it is adjectival or adverbial. If an article precedes the participle, it must be adjectival. If there is no article, it may be either adjectival or adverbial. How one classifies a participle can have a significant impact on the meaning of a text. Consider the following example.

In the CSB, 1 Peter 5:6–7 reads, "Humble yourselves, therefore, under the mighty hand of God, so that he may exalt you at the proper time, **casting** all your cares on him, because he cares about you." The NIV renders this as, "Humble yourselves, therefore, under God's mighty hand, that he may lift you up in due time. **Cast** all your anxiety on him because he cares for you." The Greek word translated both as *casting* and as *cast*, is ἐπιρίψαντες. In the first example, the translators understand ἐπιρίψαντες to be an adverbial participle of *means*, explaining *how* one humbles oneself. In the second example, it is considered to be an imperatival participle, i.e., an additional command and, therefore, separate from *humble yourselves*. The first understanding is likely correct and rendering it as a participle of means shows us the way we are to humble ourselves. As Wallace notes, "Taking the participle as means enriches our understanding of both verbs: Humbling oneself is not a negative act of self-denial per se, but a positive one of active dependence on God for help."[6] From this example, one gets a glimpse of just how important the study of participles is for understanding the Greek NT.

Categories and Examples[7]

ADJECTIVAL PARTICIPLES		
ATTRIBUTIVE	Modifies an expressed noun (agreeing with it in gender, case, and number) and usually has a definite article.	ὁ δὲ ἐχθρὸς ὁ **σπείρας** αὐτά ("and the enemy **who sowed** them" Matt 13:39).
SUBSTANTIVAL	Usually has a definite article but becomes a virtual noun (substantive).	ὁ **νικῶν** κληρονομήσει ταῦτα ("The one **who conquers** will inherit these things" Rev 21:7).
VERBAL PARTICIPLES (ADVERBIAL)		
TEMPORAL	The aorist participle communicates perfective aspect, depicting an action as simply occurring or having occurred.	***Perfective aspect:*** καθαρισμὸν τῶν ἁμαρτιῶν **ποιησάμενος** ἐκάθισεν ("**After making purification** for sins, he sat down" Heb 1:3).
	The present participle communicates imperfective aspect, portraying an action as ongoing.	***Imperfective aspect:*** **παράγων** εἶδεν ἄνθρωπον ("As he **was passing by**, he saw a man" John 9:1).
MEANS	Answers the question "How?" the main verb was accomplished (add "by" or "by means of").	ἀπόλουσαι τὰς ἁμαρτίας σου **ἐπικαλεσάμενος** τὸ ὄνομα αὐτοῦ ("Have your sins washed away by **calling on** the name of the Lord" Acts 22:16 NLT).
MANNER	Answers "how" the main verb was performed and is often translated as an adverb.	ἐπορεύοντο **χαίροντες** ("they went out . . . **rejoicing**" Acts 5:41).
CAUSE	Answers the question "Why?" providing the cause, reason, or grounds by which an action is accomplished (add "because," "since," or "for").	ἡμεῖς δὲ ἡμέρας **ὄντες** νήφωμεν ("But **since we are** of *the* day, let's be sober" 1 Thess 5:8 NASB).

[6] Wallace, *Greek Grammar Beyond the Basics*, 630.

[7] Köstenberger, Merkle, and Plummer, *Going Deeper with New Testament Greek*, 347–48.

VERBAL PARTICIPLES (ADVERBIAL) (CONTINUED)		
CONDITION	The participial phrase functions as the protasis ("if" clause) of a conditional statement (add "if").	οὐδὲν ἀπόβλητον μετὰ εὐχαριστίας **λαμβανόμενον** ("nothing is to be rejected **if it is received** with thanksgiving" 1 Tim 4:4).
CONCESSION	The action of the main verb takes place in spite of the circumstances related to the participle (add "although," "even though," or "though").	τυφλὸς **ὢν** ἄρτι βλέπω ("**though I was** blind, now I see" John 9:25 ESV).
PURPOSE	Indicates the purpose of the main verb's action (add "in order to," "so that," or "that").	ὃς ἐληλύθει **προσκυνήσων** εἰς Ἰερουσαλήμ ("He had come **to worship** in Jerusalem" Acts 8:27).
RESULT	Indicates the actual result (and not merely the intended result) of the main verb's action (add "so that," "with the result that," or "that").	ἵνα ἦτε τέλειοι καὶ ὁλόκληροι ἐν μηδενὶ **λειπόμενοι** ("so that you may be mature and complete, [**and as a result**] **lacking** nothing" Jas 1:4).
VERBAL PARTICIPLES (OTHERS)		
ATTENDANT CIRCUMSTANCE	Coordinates to the main verb, thus taking on the mood of this verb (whether indicative, imperative, or subjunctive).	**ἐγερθεὶς** παράλαβε τὸ παιδίον ("**Get up**! Take the child" Matt 2:13).
GENITIVE ABSOLUTE	A special use of the adverbial participle found in the genitive case that provides background information.	**Καθημένου** δὲ αὐτοῦ . . . προσῆλθον αὐτῷ οἱ μαθηταὶ ("**While** he **was sitting** . . . the disciples approached him" Matt 24:3).
IMPERATIVAL	The participle functions independently as an imperative.	αἱ γυναῖκες, **ὑποτασσόμεναι** τοῖς ἰδίοις ἀνδράσιν ("wives, **submit yourselves** to your own husbands" 1 Pet 3:1).
PLEONASTIC	A redundant expression usually using ἀποκριθείς or λέγων, often untranslated, as in the example.	**Ἀποκριθεὶς** δὲ ὁ Πέτρος εἶπεν αὐτῷ ("But Peter said to him" Matt 15:15 ESV).
COMPLEMENTARY	Completes the idea of another (main) verb, usually verbs of completion.	Ὡς δὲ ἐπαύσατο **λαλῶν** ("When he had finished **speaking**" Luke 5:4).
INDIRECT DISCOURSE	A statement of what someone said. The participle will be in the accusative case and will be anarthrous.	πᾶν πνεῦμα ὃ ὁμολογεῖ Ἰησοῦν Χριστὸν ἐν σαρκὶ **ἐληλυθότα** ἐκ τοῦ θεοῦ ἐστιν ("Every spirit that confesses that Jesus Christ **has come** in the flesh is from God" 1 John 4:2).
PERIPHRASTIC PARTICIPLES		
PRESENT	Present of εἰμί + present ptc	οἱ ἄνδρες . . . **εἰσὶν** . . . **διδάσκοντες** τὸν λαόν ("The men . . . **are** . . . **teaching** the people" Acts 5:25).
IMPERFECT	Imperfect of εἰμί [ἤμην] + present ptc	**ἦν** . . . **διδάσκων** αὐτοὺς ("**he was teaching** them" Matt 7:29).

PERIPHRASTIC PARTICIPLES (CONTINUED)		
FUTURE	Future of εἰμί [ἔσομαι] + present ptc	καὶ **ἔσεσθε μισούμενοι** ὑπὸ πάντων διὰ τὸ ὄνομά μου ("**You will be hated** by everyone because of my name" Matt 10:22).
PERFECT	Present of εἰμί + perfect ptc	Τῇ γὰρ χάριτί **ἐστε σεσῳσμένοι** διὰ πίστεως ("For by grace **you are saved** through faith" Eph 2:8 ESV).
PLUPERFECT	Imperfect of εἰμί [ἤμην] + perfect ptc	ἐπίστευσαν ὅσοι **ἦσαν τεταγμένοι** εἰς ζωὴν αἰώνιον ("all who **had been appointed** to eternal life believed" Acts 13:48).
FUTURE PERFECT	Future of εἰμί [ἔσομαι] + perfect ptc	ὃ ἐὰν λύσῃς ἐπὶ τῆς γῆς **ἔσται λελυμένον** ἐν τοῖς οὐρανοῖς ("whatever you loose on earth **shall have been loosed** in heaven" Matt 16:19 NASB).

Vocatives

Definition and Description

The vocative is the case of direct address. According to Wallace, there are 317 vocatives in the NT: 292 of them are nouns, 24 are adjectives, and 1 is a participle.[8] This count can be a bit misleading, though, because the nominative case can also be used for direct address, and vocatives and nominatives have the same form in the plural as well as the singular first declension.[9] One way to distinguish between the vocative and the nominative is to remember that vocatives do not take an article. So, if the word in question has an article, it cannot be a vocative.[10] However, since the nominative and vocative serve the same function in these scenarios where their forms are identical, it is not of great importance to distinguish between them.

Vocatives can usually be identified by their use in the sentence. Concerning syntax, the vocative typically appears at the beginning of a sentence and functions independently from the rest of the sentence. Although some vocatives can be considered more emphatic than others and some can function appositionally, we will just classify all vocatives as a form of direct address, which is their basic function.

Categories and Examples[11]

USES OF THE VOCATIVE		
DIRECT ADDRESS	The use of the vocative to designate the person or thing being addressed.	**Λάζαρε**, δεῦρο ἔξω ("**Lazarus**, come out!" John 11:43).

[8] Wallace, *Greek Grammar Beyond the Basics*, 35. Here, Wallace counts only the vocatives and not the nominatives functioning as vocatives. That is why his count is substantially lower than what Bible software programs such as Accordance produce. According to Accordance, there are 775 vocatives: 611 of them are nouns, 115 of them are adjectives, and 49 are participles.

[9] For example, see John 17:25, Mark 9:19, and Luke 8:54.

[10] When the vocative is emphatic, it will sometimes appear with the particle ὦ in front of it. This particle should not be confused with the definite article.

[11] Köstenberger, Merkle, and Plummer, *Going Deeper with New Testament Greek*, 72.

GUIDED PRACTICE: MARK 9:14–29 (NA[28])

9:14 Καὶ ἐλθόντες πρὸς τοὺς μαθητὰς εἶδον ὄχλον πολὺν περὶ αὐτοὺς καὶ γραμματεῖς
συζητοῦντας πρὸς αὐτούς. 15 καὶ εὐθὺς πᾶς ὁ ὄχλος ἰδόντες αὐτὸν ἐξεθαμβήθησαν καὶ
προστρέχοντες ἠσπάζοντο αὐτόν. 16 καὶ ἐπηρώτησεν αὐτούς· τί συζητεῖτε πρὸς αὐτούς; 17 Καὶ
ἀπεκρίθη αὐτῷ εἷς ἐκ τοῦ ὄχλου· διδάσκαλε, ἤνεγκα τὸν υἱόν μου πρὸς σέ, ἔχοντα πνεῦμα
ἄλαλον· 18 καὶ ὅπου ἐὰν αὐτὸν καταλάβῃ ῥήσσει αὐτόν, καὶ ἀφρίζει καὶ τρίζει τοὺς ὀδόντας
καὶ ξηραίνεται· καὶ εἶπα τοῖς μαθηταῖς σου ἵνα αὐτὸ ἐκβάλωσιν, καὶ οὐκ ἴσχυσαν. 19 ὁ δὲ
ἀποκριθεὶς αὐτοῖς λέγει· ὦ γενεὰ ἄπιστος, ἕως πότε πρὸς ὑμᾶς ἔσομαι; ἕως πότε ἀνέξομαι
ὑμῶν; φέρετε αὐτὸν πρός με. 20 καὶ ἤνεγκαν αὐτὸν πρὸς αὐτόν. καὶ ἰδὼν αὐτὸν τὸ πνεῦμα
εὐθὺς συνεσπάραξεν αὐτόν, καὶ πεσὼν ἐπὶ τῆς γῆς ἐκυλίετο ἀφρίζων. 21 καὶ ἐπηρώτησεν
τὸν πατέρα αὐτοῦ· πόσος χρόνος ἐστὶν ὡς τοῦτο γέγονεν αὐτῷ; ὁ δὲ εἶπεν· ἐκ παιδιόθεν·
22 καὶ πολλάκις καὶ εἰς πῦρ αὐτὸν ἔβαλεν καὶ εἰς ὕδατα ἵνα ἀπολέσῃ αὐτόν· ἀλλ᾽ εἴ τι δύνῃ,

βοήθησον ἡμῖν σπλαγχνισθεὶς ἐφ’ ἡμᾶς. 23 ὁ δὲ Ἰησοῦς εἶπεν αὐτῷ· τὸ εἰ δύνῃ, πάντα δυνατὰ
τῷ πιστεύοντι. 24 εὐθὺς κράξας ὁ πατὴρ τοῦ παιδίου ἔλεγεν· πιστεύω· βοήθει μου τῇ ἀπιστίᾳ.
25 ἰδὼν δὲ ὁ Ἰησοῦς ὅτι ἐπισυντρέχει ὄχλος, ἐπετίμησεν τῷ πνεύματι τῷ ἀκαθάρτῳ λέγων
αὐτῷ· τὸ ἄλαλον καὶ κωφὸν πνεῦμα, ἐγὼ ἐπιτάσσω σοι, ἔξελθε ἐξ αὐτοῦ καὶ μηκέτι εἰσέλθῃς
εἰς αὐτόν. 26 καὶ κράξας καὶ πολλὰ σπαράξας ἐξῆλθεν· καὶ ἐγένετο ὡσεὶ νεκρός, ὥστε τοὺς
πολλοὺς λέγειν ὅτι ἀπέθανεν. 27 ὁ δὲ Ἰησοῦς κρατήσας τῆς χειρὸς αὐτοῦ ἤγειρεν αὐτόν, καὶ
ἀνέστη.

28 Καὶ εἰσελθόντος αὐτοῦ εἰς οἶκον οἱ μαθηταὶ αὐτοῦ κατ’ ἰδίαν ἐπηρώτων αὐτόν· ὅτι
ἡμεῖς οὐκ ἠδυνήθημεν ἐκβαλεῖν αὐτό; 29 καὶ εἶπεν αὐτοῖς· τοῦτο τὸ γένος ἐν οὐδενὶ δύναται
ἐξελθεῖν εἰ μὴ ἐν προσευχῇ.

VOCABULARY AIDS (WORDS 26X TO 50X)

9:18 **ἰσχύω** *to be able, be strong* (28x)
9:19 **γενεά** *generation* (43x)
9:21 **πόσος** *how much? how many?* (27x)
9:25 **ἐπιτιμάω** (ἐπί+τιμάω) *to rebuke, to warn* (29x)
9:25 **ἀκάθαρτος** *unclean* (32x)
9:27 **κρατέω** *to grasp, be strong, take possession* (47x)

VOCABULARY AIDS (WORDS 25X OR LESS)

9:14, 16 **συζητέω** (σύν+ζητέω) *to argue, question* (10x)
9:15 **ἐκθαμβέω** (ἐκ+θαμβέω) *to be alarmed, amazed, awe-struck* (4x)
9:15 **προστρέχω** (πρός+τρέχω) *to run out; to run to* (3x)
9:17, 25 **ἄλαλος** *speechless, mute* (3x)
9:18 **καταλαμβάνω** (κατά+λαμβάνω, aorist stem: λαβ) *to take, overtake, reach* (15x)
9:18 **ῥήσσω** *to cause to fall down, to throw down* (6x)
9:18, 20 **ἀφρίζω** *to foam* (2x)
9:18 **τρίζω** *to scream, to gnash or grind teeth* (1x)
9:18 **ξηραίνω** *to dry up, be paralyzed, become rigid* (15x)
9:19 **πότε** *when?* (19x)
9:19 **ἀνέχω** (ἀνά+ἔχω) *to lift; esteem; hinder, stop; bear with, be patient* (15x)
9:20 **συσπαράσσω** (σύν+σπαράσσω) *to throw into convulsions* (2x)
9:20 **κυλίω** *to roll, wallow, throw down* (1x)
9:21 **παιδιόθεν** (παῖς+θεν) *from childhood* (1x)
9:22 **πολλάκις** *often* (18x)
9:22, 24 **βοηθέω** *to help* (8x)
9:22 **σπλαγχνίζομαι** *to have compassion* (12x)
9:24 **ἀπιστία** *unbelief* (11x)
9:25 **ἐπισυντρέχω** (ἐπί+σύν+τρέχω) *to gather rapidly* (1x)
9:25 **κωφός** *speechless, deaf* (14x)
9:25 **ἐπιτάσσω** (ἐπί+τάσσω) *to command, order* (10x)
9:25 **μηκέτι** (μή+ἔτι) *no longer, no more* (22x)
9:26 **σπαράσσω** *to tear apart; to throw into convulsions* (3x)
9:26 **ὡσεί** (ὡς+εἰ) *like, as, about* (21x)
9:29 **γένος** *family, race, kind; offspring* (20x)
9:29 **προσευχή** (πρός+εὐχή) *prayer* (36x)

EXERCISE

I. Provide your translation under the Greek text above.

II. Exegetical notes and questions: read the bullet points and answer the questions below.

Verse-by-Verse Questions

9:14

- The participle συζητοῦντας could mean simply "discussing" or "arguing." Hostility is often implied when it is followed by πρός, as in this example.

9:15

a) Mark is known for his abundant use of εὐθύς. It is often translated as "immediately," but it can simply mean "then." How did you translate it in this sentence? Why did you translate it that way?

b) Ὄχλος is singular, and yet the verbs and modifying participles are plural. How do you explain this?

9:17

c) How would you parse ἤνεγκα?

9:18

d) Ὅπου ἐάν can mean "whenever" or "wherever." How did you translate it in this instance? Why did you translate it that way?

9:19

e) What is the function of ὁ δέ and why does Mark use δέ (instead of καί) at this point?

9:22

f) In the clause, εἴ τι δύνῃ, δύνῃ is from δύναμαι ("to be able"), which typically takes a complementary infinitive. Where is the infinitive? How did you translate this conditional clause?

g) What type of conditional statement is εἴ τι δύνῃ (1st, 2nd, 3rd, or 4th class)?

9:23

h) Jesus begins his response to the father with τὸ εἰ δύνῃ. What is the function of τό? How did you translate this clause?

i) Where is the verb in the statement πάντα δυνατὰ τῷ πιστεύοντι?

9:25

j) The adjective κωφός can mean either mute or deaf. How did you translate it in this context? Why did you translate it that way?

9:29

k) How would you parse and classify ἐξελθεῖν?

Short Summary and Contextual Impact

III. Summarize the main idea of the passage and then discuss how it fits into the surrounding narrative.

Parsing and Classification

IV. Circle the participles and underline the vocatives in the text and parse them below. Then classify each one according to the categories given in the grammar review above. Provide a brief explanation for your decisions.

Participles

9:14

1)

2)

9:15

1)

2)

9:17

1)

9:19

1)

9:20

1)

2)

3)

9:22

1)

9:23

1)

9:24

1)

9:25

1)

2)

9:26

1)

2)

9:27

1)

9:28

1)

Vocatives

9:17

1)

9:19

1)

2)

Extra Questions on 9:25 (nominatives used in place of vocatives)

1)

2)

3)

ANSWER KEY

I. Translation and explanations

9:14 When they came to the disciples, they saw a large crowd around them and scribes disputing
with them. 15 When the whole crowd saw him, they were amazed and ran to greet him. 16 He
asked them, "What are you arguing with them about?" 17 Someone from the crowd answered him,
"Teacher, I brought my son to you. He has a spirit that makes him unable to speak. 18 Whenever
it seizes him, it throws him down, and he foams at the mouth, grinds his teeth, and becomes rigid.
I asked your disciples to drive it out, but they couldn't." 19 He replied to them, "You unbelieving
generation, how long will I be with you? How long must I put up with you? Bring him to me."
20 So they brought the boy to him. When the spirit saw him, it immediately threw the boy into convulsions. He fell to the ground and rolled around, foaming at the mouth. 21 "How long has this been
happening to him?" Jesus asked his father. "From childhood," he said. 22 "And many times it has
thrown him into fire or water to destroy him. But if you can do anything, have compassion on us
and help us." 23 Jesus said to him, "'If you can'? Everything is possible for the one who believes."
24 Immediately the father of the boy cried out, "I do believe; help my unbelief!" 25 When Jesus saw
that a crowd was quickly gathering, he rebuked the unclean spirit, saying to it, "You mute and deaf
spirit, I command you: Come out of him and never enter him again." 26 Then it came out, shrieking
and throwing him into terrible convulsions. The boy became like a corpse, so that many said, "He's
dead." 27 But Jesus, taking him by the hand, raised him, and he stood up.
28 After he had gone into the house, his disciples asked him privately, "Why couldn't we drive it
out?" 29 And he told them, "This kind can come out by nothing but prayer."

II. Answers to exegetical questions

Verse-by-Verse Questions

a) In 9:15, εὐθύς should probably be translated "immediately." This rendering fits better with the context of the scene, especially the crowd's decisive action to run to Jesus and the sense of immediacy implied in such an action.

b) In 9:15, ὄχλος is a collective singular noun. Collective singular nouns usually take singular verbs, but on occasion, they will take plural verbs.[12] In this instance, the collective singular noun takes two plural verbs, with each of them accompanied by a plural adverbial participle.

c) In 9:17, ἤνεγκα is from φέρω and is 1st sg aor act ind. It is not intuitive to associate the two with each other based on their forms, as φέρω has three different roots. The present tense uses φερ, the future act/mid employs οἰ, and all other forms take ἐνεκ.[13]

d) In 9:18, ὅπου ἐάν could be translated as either "wherever" or "whenever." Bible translations differ. Although either rendering makes sense, "wherever" is more likely from the fact that, in v. 22, the father complains about the dangerous places in which the demon convulses his son.[14]

---

[12] Wallace, *Greek Grammar Beyond the Basics*, 400–401.

[13] William D. Mounce, *The Morphology of Biblical Greek*, ed. Verlyn D. Verbrugge (Grand Rapids: Zondervan, 1994), 265.

[14] Joel Williams, *Mark*, ed. Andreas J. Köstenberger and Robert W. Yarbrough, Exegetical Guide to the Greek New Testament (Nashville: B&H Academic, 2020), 155.

e) In 9:19, ὁ δέ should be translated "(and) he." Using δέ instead of καί is a common way to show a change in speakers (or to mark a shift or development in the narrative). It is also very common to pair δέ with the article when the latter is functioning as a personal pronoun. See Mark 8:31 for an example of using καί when the speaker did not change.

f) In 9:22, εἴ τι δύνῃ has an implied infinitive, ποιεῖν, so this phrase could be translated "if you are able to do anything."

g) In 9:22, εἴ τι δύνῃ is a 1st class conditional clause, whose premise is assumed to be true for the sake of argument. Here, given the father's weak state of faith (v. 24), he might have had more of a hope than an expectation.

h) In 9:23, Jesus begins his response to the father with τὸ εἰ δύνῃ. This is a partial restatement of the father's previous statement. The article τό serves to nominalize the clause, making it a nominative substantive.[15] Wallace calls this usage a nominative of exclamation. He states that it is "a primitive use of the language where emotion overrides syntax."[16] The article does not get translated. The clause could be rendered, "If you are able!"

i) In 9:23, πάντα δυνατὰ τῷ πιστεύοντι has an implied verb, ἐστίν. An implied ἐστίν is common in exclamations.[17]

j) In 9:25, κωφόν is best translated as "deaf," since ἄλαλον is paired with it. The adjective ἄλαλος unambiguously means "speechless" or "mute."

k) In 9:29, ἐξελθεῖν is an aorist active infinitive from ἐξέρχομαι. It is a complementary infinitive, coupled with δύναται. The word δύναμαι is the most common helper verb, which usually takes an infinitive to complete its thought.[18]

III. Short Summary and Contextual Impact

Summary: When Jesus and the three disciples return from the mountain where Jesus's transfiguration took place, they encounter a crowd arguing with the other disciples about why those disciples were unable to heal a demon-possessed boy. Jesus says to the boy's father that, with faith, anything is possible. Though the initial instances of the exorcism make the boy appear to be dead, the demon is cast out, and the boy is healed. Subsequently, Jesus tells his disciples, who failed in their exorcism attempts, that this work does require prayer.

Contextual Impact: This pericope demonstrates both Jesus's unique authority and the need for his disciples to rely on God, that is, to pray. In the Way Discourse (8:22–10:52), Jesus is focused on teaching and preparing his disciples for what he knows lies ahead of them when they reach Jerusalem. This exorcism by Jesus, coming after the disciples' failure, provides another teaching moment. The disciples would likely have felt insulted when the boy's father reported their failure in exorcism. They would also have been baffled by their lack of ability, considering their previous successes (Mark 6). When they ask Jesus privately why they were unable to exorcise the demon,

---

[15] Rodney J. Decker, *Mark 9–16: A Handbook on the Greek Text*, ed. Martin M. Culy, of *Baylor Handbook on the Greek New Testament* (Waco: Baylor University Press, 2014), 19.
[16] Wallace, *Greek Grammar Beyond the Basics*, 59–60.
[17] Decker, *Mark 9–16*, 20.
[18] Wallace, *Greek Grammar Beyond the Basics*, 598.

Jesus instructs them that "this kind" can only come out with prayer. The meaning of "this kind" is not entirely clear, but the focus of Jesus's statement is that prayer is mandatory. The disciples had probably fallen into the trap of thinking that their previous successes in exorcism had come from a power they had come to possess within themselves. This incident of failure reminds them that they are only vessels, mere servants, in the kingdom of God. Their role is to be one of service, and they must consistently depend on God to be successful in that role. The following passage reveals that the disciples indeed need this lesson.

Moreover, that the boy had been declared by the crowd to be dead before Jesus raised him seems to imply the power of resurrection in the Lord Jesus (cf. 5:35–43), especially given that the current passage is located between the first and the second passion-resurrection predictions (8:31; 9:31). Jesus has indeed conquered the power of death through his own death and his resurrection!

IV. Parsing and Classification of the Key Grammatical Concepts for the Lesson: Participles and Vocatives

Participles

9:14

1) ἐλθόντες: ἔρχομαι; aor act part masc plur nom; *to come*, *go*
   - <u>*Temporal*</u> (*perfective*): antecedent time. The aorist tense communicates a perfective aspect. This is describing what they saw after they came to the disciples.

2) συζητοῦντας: συζητέω (σύν+ζητέω); pres act part masc plur acc; *to argue*, *question*
   - <u>*Attributive*</u>: It modifies γραμματεῖς, describing what the scribes are doing.

9:15

1) ἰδόντες: ὁράω; aor act part masc plur nom; *to see*, *view*, *perceive*
   - <u>*Temporal*</u> (*perfective*): antecedent time. The aorist tense communicates a perfective aspect. This is describing the crowd's reaction after they saw Jesus.

2) προστρέχοντες: προστρέχω (πρός+τρέχω); pres act part masc plur nom; *to run out*; *to run to*
   - <u>*Temporal*</u> (*imperfective*): contemporaneous time. The present tense communicates an imperfective aspect. The picture is of the crowd shouting their greetings as they were running up to Jesus.

9:17

1) ἔχοντα: ἔχω; pres act part masc sg acc; *to have*
   - <u>*Cause*</u>: The man is giving the reason for bringing his son. The participle could, however, also be seen as attributive, modifying υἱόν.

9:19

1) ἀποκριθείς: ἀποκρίνομαι (ἀπό+κρίνω); aor pass part masc sg nom; *to answer*, *reply*
   - <u>*Pleonastic*</u>: Paired with λέγει, this is a redundant participle of speech.

9:20

1) ἰδὼν: ὁράω; aor act part masc sg nom; *to see*, *view*, *perceive*
   - <u>*Temporal*</u> (*perfective*): antecedent time. The aorist tense communicates a perfective aspect. This is describing the demon's reaction after it saw Jesus. Note that the participle is masculine; the gender should

match that of its subject, πνεῦμα, which is neuter. Decker suggests this is because the demon assumes the inhabited boy's gender.[19]

2) πεσών: πίπτω; aor act part masc sg nom; *to fall*
   - Temporal (*perfective*): antecedent time. The aorist tense communicates a perfective aspect. It is describing what the boy did before rolling around.

3) ἀφρίζων: ἀφρίζω; pres act part masc sg nom; *to foam*
   - Temporal (*imperfective*): contemporaneous time. The present tense communicates an imperfective aspect. The picture is of the boy rolling around and foaming at the mouth. It could also be construed as a participle of manner, describing how the boy was rolling about.

9:22

1) σπλαγχνισθείς: σπλαγχνίζομαι; aor pass part masc sg nom; *to have compassion*
   - Means: Describes the means by which Jesus might help in the man's view.

9:23

1) πιστεύοντι: πιστεύω; pres act part masc sg dat; *to believe*, *trust*
   - Substantival: Translated as "one who believes." It functions as a dative of advantage.

9:24

1) κράξας: κράζω; aor act part masc sg nom; *to call out*; *clamor*; *to croak*
   - Pleonastic: Paired with ἔλεγεν, it is a redundant participle of speech.

9:25

1) ἰδών: ὁράω; aor act part masc sg nom; *to see*, *view*, *perceive*
   - Temporal (*perfective*): antecedent time. The aorist tense communicates a perfective aspect. It is describing what Jesus did before rebuking the demon. Alternatively, it could be taken as a participle of cause, describing why Jesus then rebuked the demon.

2) λέγων: λέγω; pres act part masc sg nom; *to say*, *speak*, *tell*
   - Pleonastic: Paired with ἐπετίμησεν, it is a redundant participle of speech. Alternatively, it could be taken as a participle of means, explaining how Jesus rebuked the demon.

9:26

1) κράξας: κράζω; aor act part masc sg nom; *to call out*; *clamor*; *to croak*
   - Temporal (*perfective*): antecedent time. The aorist tense communicates a perfective aspect. This is describing what the demon did before coming out of the boy.

2) σπαράξας: σπαράσσω; aor act part masc sg nom; *to tear apart*; *to throw into convulsions*
   - Temporal (*perfective*): antecedent time. The aorist tense communicates a perfective aspect. This is describing what the demon did before coming out of the boy.

[19] Decker, *Mark 9–16*, 17, referencing Ezra Palmer Gould, *A Critical and Exegetical Commentary on the Gospel according to St. Mark*, International Critical Commentary (New York: C. Scribner's Sons, 1922), 168–69.

9:27

1) κρατήσας: κρατέω; aor act part masc sg nom; *to grasp*, *be strong*, *take possession*
   - *Means*: Describes the way Jesus raised the boy up. It could also be taken as temporal, antecedent time.

9:28

1) εἰσελθόντος: εἰσέρχομαι (εἰς+ἔρχομαι); aor act part masc sg gen; *to enter*
   - *Genitive Absolute*: It provides background information and a change of scene. It meets all the requirements of a genitive absolute: its subject (Jesus) is different from that of the main clause (the disciples), it is in the genitive, it comes at the beginning of the sentence, it is anarthrous, it is adverbial in function, and it is temporal in sense.

Vocatives

9:17

1) διδάσκαλε: διδάσκαλος; noun; masc sg voc; *teacher*
   - *Direct Address*: This is the only category.

9:19

1) γενεά: γενεά; noun; fem sg voc; *generation*
   - *Direct Address*: This is the only category.

2) ἄπιστος: ἄπιστος; adjective; fem sg voc; *incredible, unbelievable, unbelieving*
   - *Direct Address*: This is the only category.

Extra Questions on 9:25 (nominatives used in place of vocatives)

1) ἄλαλον: ἄλαλος; adjective; neut sg nom; *speechless*
   - *Direct Address*

2) κωφόν: κωφός; adjective; neut sg nom; *speechless*, *deaf*
   - *Direct Address*

3) πνεῦμα: πνεῦμα; noun; neut sg nom; *wind*, *breath*, *spirit*
   - *Direct Address*.

Now, rewrite your translation of the entire passage in the GUIDED PRACTICE section, reflecting the above exegetical procedure.

REFERENCES

Danker, Frederick William, et al. *A Greek-English Lexicon of the New Testament and other Early Christian Literature*. 3rd ed. Chicago: The University of Chicago Press, 2000.

Decker, Rodney J. *Mark 1–8: A Handbook on the Greek Text*. Ed. Martin M. Culy. Baylor Handbook on the Greek New Testament. Waco: Baylor University Press, 2014.

———. *Mark 9–16: A Handbook on the Greek Text*. Ed. Martin M. Culy. Baylor Handbook on the Greek New Testament. Waco: Baylor University Press, 2014.

Evans, Craig A. *Mark 8:27–16:20*. Word Biblical Commentary, vol 34b. Grand Rapids: Zondervan, 1988.

France, R. T. *The Gospel of Mark*. The New International Greek Testament Commentary. Grand Rapids: Eerdmans, 2002.

Gould, Ezra Palmer. *A Critical and Exegetical Commentary on the Gospel according to St. Mark*. International Critical Commentary. New York: C. Scribner's Sons, 1922.

Köstenberger, Andreas J., Benjamin L. Merkle, and Robert L. Plummer. *Going Deeper with New Testament Greek: An Intermediate Study of the Grammar and Syntax of the New Testament*. Rev. ed. Nashville: B&H Academic, 2020.

Mathewson, David L. and Elodie Ballantine Emig. *Intermediate Greek Grammar: Syntax for Students of the New Testament*. Grand Rapids: Baker Academic, 2016.

Merkle, Benjamin L. *Exegetical Gems from Biblical Greek*. Grand Rapids: Baker Academic, 2019.

Mounce, William D. *The Morphology of Biblical Greek*. Ed. Verlyn D. Verbrugge. Grand Rapids: Zondervan, 1994.

Porter, Stanley E. *Idioms of the Greek New Testament*. 2nd ed. reprinted. Biblical Languages: Greek 2. Sheffield, UK: Sheffield Academic Press, 1999.

Strauss, Mark L. *Mark*. Zondervan Exegetical Commentary on the New Testament. Grand Rapids: Zondervan Academic, 2014.

Wallace, Daniel B. *Greek Grammar Beyond the Basics: An Exegetical Syntax of the New Testament*. Grand Rapids: Zondervan, 1996.

Williams, Joel. *Mark*. Ed. Andreas J. Köstenberger and Robert W. Yarbrough. Exegetical Guide to the Greek New Testament. Nashville: B&H Academic, 2020.

CHAPTER SIX

////////////////

MARK 9:30–37

WITH ATTENTION TO DATIVES AND ACCUSATIVES

GRAMMAR REVIEW:

Dative

Definition and Description

The core idea behind the dative is the concept of *indirect object*. It can be a simple indirect object (I threw the ball *to you*) or it can be more complicated. It can communicate location, time, means, agency, or manner. It can communicate advantage (or disadvantage), reference, or possession. The dative is, thus, a flexible grammatical category and primarily context will truly tell you how it is being used.

Sometimes, a New Testament author chooses to use a certain dative because it shares a stem or a concept with the head verb. Other times, the author might use the dative appositionally—to further describe another dative noun.

Wallace points out that in Koine Greek, the simple dative was being phased out and replaced by prepositional phrases.[1] So, as you read through the Greek New Testament, you should notice that often the same function is fulfilled by prepositional phrases that would have been fulfilled by a simple dative.

Categories and Examples[2]

PURE DATIVE		
INDIRECT OBJECT	Indicates the one for whom or in whose interest an act is performed.	δὸς δόξαν **τῷ θεῷ** ("Give glory **to God**" John 9:24).
PERSONAL INTEREST (ADVANTAGE OR DISADVANTAGE)	Denotes the person (or rarely, the thing) to whose benefit or detriment a verbal action occurs.	***Advantage***: ὡς νύμφην κεκοσμημένην **τῷ ἀνδρὶ** αὐτῆς ("like a bride adorned **for** her **husband**" Rev 21:2).
		Disadvantage: ἡ δὲ Ἡρῳδιὰς ἐνεῖχεν **αὐτῷ** ("So Herodias held a grudge **against him**" Mark 6:19).

[1] Daniel B. Wallace, *Greek Grammar Beyond the Basics: An Exegetical Syntax of the New Testament* (Grand Rapids: Zondervan, 1996), 138.
[2] Andreas J. Köstenberger, Benjamin L. Merkle, and Robert L. Plummer, *Going Deeper with New Testament Greek: An Intermediate Study of the Grammar and Syntax of the New Testament*, rev. ed. (Nashville: B&H Academic, 2020), 140–41.

PURE DATIVE (CONTINUED)		
REFERENCE OR RESPECT	Limits the extent to which something is presented as true, qualifying a statement that would otherwise not be true.	**τῇ ἁμαρτίᾳ** ἀπέθανεν ἐφάπαξ ("he died **to sin** once for all time" Rom 6:10).
POSSESSION	Unique construction in which the dative possesses the subject of an equative verb (such as εἰμι or γίνομαι).	**ὑμῖν** γάρ ἐστιν ἡ ἐπαγγελία ("For the promise is **for you**" Acts 2:39).
LOCATIVE DATIVE		
PLACE	Pinpoints the literal physical location of a noun in the dative case.	τοὺς περὶ αὐτὸν **κύκλῳ** καθημένους ("those sitting **in a circle** around him" Mark 3:34).
SPHERE	Identifies the figurative or metaphorical location (i.e., sphere or realm) of a noun in the dative case.	ἀναστενάξας **τῷ πνεύματι** αὐτοῦ ("Sighing deeply **in** his **spirit**" Mark 8:12).
TIME	Indicates the point in time (location in time) at which the action of a verb is accomplished.	Καὶ **τῇ ἡμέρᾳ τῇ τρίτῃ** γάμος ἐγένετο ("**On the third day** a wedding took place" John 2:1).
INSTRUMENTAL DATIVE		
MEANS	Denotes the impersonal means by which the action of a given verb is accomplished.	κατακόπτων ἑαυτὸν **λίθοις** ("cutting himself **with stones**" Mark 5:5).
MANNER	Denotes the manner in which the action of a given verb is accomplished.	**παρρησίᾳ** τὸν λόγον ἐλάλει ("He spoke **openly** about this" Mark 8:32).
AGENCY	Denotes the personal agency by which the action of a given verb is accomplished.	εἰ δὲ **πνεύματι** ἄγεσθε ("But if you are led **by the Spirit**" Gal 5:18).
ASSOCIATION	Denotes the person or thing with which a person is associated or by which a person is accompanied.	συνταφέντες **αὐτῷ** ἐν τῷ βαπτισμῷ ("having been buried **with him** in baptism" Col 2:12 ESV).
OTHER USES		
CAUSE	Indicates the basis or reason of the action of a given verb, whether external (occasion) or internal (motivation).	ἐγὼ δὲ **λιμῷ** ὧδε ἀπόλλυμαι ("here I am dying [**because**] **of hunger**!" Luke 15:17).
COGNATE DATIVE	Use of a dative noun that is a cognate (of the same stem) to the verb it modifies either formally or conceptually.	<u>ἐξέστησαν</u> . . . **ἐκστάσει** μεγάλῃ ("<u>they were</u> **utterly** <u>astounded</u>" Mark 5:42).
APPOSITION	Two related substantives refer to the same person or thing.	ἐν τῷ Βεελζεβοὺλ **ἄρχοντι** τῶν δαιμονίων ("by Beelzebul, **the ruler** of the demons" Matt 12:24).
DIRECT OBJECT	The dative occurs after certain verbs of trusting, obeying, serving, worshiping, thanksgiving, or following and functions as the direct object.	Εὐχαριστοῦμεν **τῷ θεῷ** . . . πάντοτε ("We always thank **God**" Col 1:3).

Accusative

Definition and Description

The basic role of the accusative is its function as a limitation on the extension of a verb. Wallace, in describing the limiting effect of the accusative, notes that it limits a verb as to its "extent, direction, or goal."[3] It is the *end* of an action. By far the most common use of an accusative is to communicate the *direct object* of a verb ("I kicked *the ball*"), but other *substantival* uses include the functional subject of an infinitive, apposition, double accusative, and cognate accusative. *Adverbial* uses include measure, manner, and respect.

The accusative and genitive are similar in that they both have a limiting function. However, the genitive is frequently related to nouns while the accusative is frequently related to verbs. Another nuance to keep in mind is that genitives limit as to quality, whereas accusatives limit as to quantity.[4]

The accusative and dative are similar since they are both predominantly related to verbs. Their functions differ, however, in that "the dative is concerned about that to which the action of the verb is related, located, or by which it is accomplished, while the accusative is concerned about the extent and the scope of the verb's action."[5]

Categories and Examples[6]

SUBSTANTIVAL USES OF THE ACCUSATIVE		
DIRECT OBJECT	Serves as the recipient of the action.	οὕτως γὰρ ἠγάπησεν ὁ θεὸς **τὸν κόσμον** ("For God so loved **the world**" John 3:16 ESV).
COGNATE ACCUSATIVE	Aligned with the verb regarding either the lexical root or the idea conveyed.	ἵνα <u>στρατεύῃ</u> ἐν αὐταῖς τὴν καλὴν **στρατείαν** ("that by them you <u>fight</u> the good **fight**" 1 Tim 1:18 NASB).
DOUBLE ACCUSATIVE	A verb requires more than one accusative object to complete the thought, taking either (1) a personal and impersonal object or (2) a direct and predicate object.	(1) <u>ὃν</u> αἰτήσει ὁ υἱὸς αὐτοῦ **ἄρτον** ("if his son asks <u>him</u> **for bread**" Matt 7:9 ESV). (2) ὁ δοὺς <u>ἑαυτὸν</u> **ἀντίλυτρον** ὑπὲρ πάντων ("who gave <u>himself</u> as **a ransom** for all" 1 Tim 2:6).
SUBJECT OF INFINITIVE	Functions as the subject of an infinitive, indicating the agent performing the action conveyed by the infinitive.	πρὸ τοῦ σε **Φίλιππον** φωνῆσαι . . . εἶδόν σε ("Before **Philip** called you . . . I saw you" John 1:48).
APPOSITION	Two accusatives are juxtaposed, both referring to the same person or thing, with the second accusative further specifying the first accusative.	καὶ ἐπὶ πῶλον **υἱὸν** ὑποζυγίου ("and on a colt, **the foal** of a donkey" Matt 21:5).
ADVERBIAL USES OF THE ACCUSATIVE		
MEASURE	Functions in essence like an adverb in that it specifies measure (time or space).	Καὶ προσελθὼν **μικρόν** ἔπεσεν ἐπὶ πρόσωπον αὐτοῦ ("And going **a little farther** he fell on his face" Matt 26:39 ESV).
MANNER	Functions in essence like an adverb in that it specifies manner.	δικαιούμενοι **δωρεὰν** τῇ αὐτοῦ χάριτι ("they are justified **freely** by his grace" Rom 3:24).
RESPECT	Restricts the reference of the verbal action, indicating in what regard an action is represented as true.	κατενύγησαν **τὴν καρδίαν** ("they were pierced **to the heart**" Acts 2:37).

[3] Wallace, *Greek Grammar Beyond the Basics*, 178.
[4] Wallace, 178.
[5] Wallace, 178.
[6] Köstenberger, Merkle, and Plummer, *Going Deeper with New Testament Greek*, 72–73.

GUIDED PRACTICE: MARK 9:30–37 (NA^{28})

9:30 Κἀκεῖθεν ἐξελθόντες παρεπορεύοντο διὰ τῆς Γαλιλαίας, καὶ οὐκ ἤθελεν ἵνα τις
γνοῖ· 31 ἐδίδασκεν γὰρ τοὺς μαθητὰς αὐτοῦ καὶ ἔλεγεν αὐτοῖς ὅτι ὁ υἱὸς τοῦ ἀνθρώπου
παραδίδοται εἰς χεῖρας ἀνθρώπων, καὶ ἀποκτενοῦσιν αὐτόν, καὶ ἀποκτανθεὶς μετὰ τρεῖς
ἡμέρας ἀναστήσεται. 32 οἱ δὲ ἠγνόουν τὸ ῥῆμα, καὶ ἐφοβοῦντο αὐτὸν ἐπερωτῆσαι.

33 Καὶ ἦλθον εἰς Καφαρναούμ. Καὶ ἐν τῇ οἰκίᾳ γενόμενος ἐπηρώτα αὐτούς· τί ἐν τῇ ὁδῷ
διελογίζεσθε; 34 οἱ δὲ ἐσιώπων· πρὸς ἀλλήλους γὰρ διελέχθησαν ἐν τῇ ὁδῷ τίς μείζων.
35 καὶ καθίσας ἐφώνησεν τοὺς δώδεκα καὶ λέγει αὐτοῖς· εἴ τις θέλει πρῶτος εἶναι, ἔσται
πάντων ἔσχατος καὶ πάντων διάκονος. 36 καὶ λαβὼν παιδίον ἔστησεν αὐτὸ ἐν μέσῳ αὐτῶν
καὶ ἐναγκαλισάμενος αὐτὸ εἶπεν αὐτοῖς· 37 ὃς ἂν ἓν τῶν τοιούτων παιδίων δέξηται ἐπὶ τῷ
ὀνόματί μου, ἐμὲ δέχεται· καὶ ὃς ἂν ἐμὲ δέχηται, οὐκ ἐμὲ δέχεται ἀλλὰ τὸν ἀποστείλαντά με.

VOCABULARY AIDS (WORDS 26X TO 50X)

9:32 **ἀγνοέω** *not to know, be ignorant* (22x)

9:35 **φωνέω** *call* (43x)

VOCABULARY AIDS (WORDS 25X OR LESS)

9:30 **κἀκεῖθεν** *and from there* (11x)

9:30 **παραπορεύομαι** *go by; pass by; go (through)* (5x)

9:33 **Καφαρναούμ** *Capernaum* (16x)

9:33 **διαλογίζομαι** *consider; ponder; reason; argue* (16x)

9:34 **σιωπάω** *be silent* (10x)

9:34 **διαλέγομαι** *converse, argue* (14x)

9:36 **ἐναγκαλίζομαι** *take into one's arms* (2x)

EXERCISE

I. Provide your translation under the Greek text above.

II. Exegetical notes and questions: read the bullet points and answer the questions below.

Verse-by-Verse Questions

9:30

a) Ἐξελθόντες is a nominative plural aorist active participle. How should it be classified syntactically?

b) Look at the phrase οὐκ ἤθελεν ἵνα τις γνοῖ. Why didn't Jesus want anybody to know? What is the significance of the answer to this question?

9:31

c) How should the 3rd singular imperfect active indicative ἐδίδασκεν be classified syntactically?

- Ὁ υἱὸς τοῦ ἀνθρώπου παραδίδοται εἰς χεῖρας ἀνθρώπων: the "Son of Man" in Daniel 7 is a remarkable figure who is highly exalted, receiving kingship and glory from the Ancient of Days (7:13–14). It would have been shocking for the disciples, if they were perceptive enough, to hear that the exalted "Son of Man" is supposed to be killed!

d) How should the present tense verb παραδίδοται be classified syntactically?

9:33

- The phrase ἐν τῇ ὁδῷ is repeated throughout Mark's gospel. This road to which this phrase refers ultimately leads to Golgotha, where Jesus will be crucified. Therefore, this phrase gives a sense of irony. While they were on the way to Golgotha where their Master would be crucified, *the disciples were arguing about who was the greatest among them*. This incident reveals the ever-present danger of selfish ambition; even the closest followers of Jesus are not immune.

9:35

e) How does the phrase εἴ τις θέλει πρῶτος εἶναι, ἔσται πάντων ἔσχατος καὶ πάντων διάκονος relate to Jesus's use of a child as a teaching metaphor?

9:36

f) The participle ἐναγκαλισάμενος comes from the rare verb ἐναγκαλίζομαι which is only used one other time in the NT (Mark 10:16). Both occurrences are in Mark and are in reference to children. Why do you think Mark used this verb here?

Additional Questions

g) How does Jesus's teaching about children and a childlike attitude contribute to Mark's teaching on discipleship?

h) How does the disciples' failure to understand Jesus's teaching about his sufferings (9:31–32) contribute to the overall presentation of Mark's narrative?

Short Summary and Contextual Impact

III. Summarize the main idea of the passage and then discuss how it fits into the surrounding narrative.

Parsing and Classification

IV. Circle the datives and underline the accusatives in the text, and parse them below (do not circle or underline the articles).[7] Then classify each entry according to the categories given in the grammar review above. Provide a brief explanation for your decisions. However, if a noun is the object of a preposition, classify it as an object of preposition.[8]

Datives

9:31

1)

9:33

1)

2)

9:34

1)

9:35

1)

---

[7] The limitation on the Greek article mainly has to do with the fact that there is another chapter (chap. 4 of this workbook) focusing on it. With that noted, it is still commendable to include the article together with the dative and accusative entries, when applicable, for further and more holistic practice.

[8] For an overview of the use of prepositions with case constructions, see Wallace, *Greek Grammar Beyond the Basics*, 360–62.

9:36

1)

2)

9:37

1)

Accusatives

9:31

1)

2)

3)

4)

5)

9:32

1)

2)

9:33

1)

2)

3)

9:34

1)

9:35

1)

9:36

1)

2)

3)

9:37 (excluding the accusative participle ἀποστείλαντά, the direct object of δέχεται)

1)

2)

3)

4)

5)

ANSWER KEY

I. Translation and explanations

30 Then they left that place and made their way through Galilee, but he did not want anyone to
know it. **31** For he was teaching his disciples and telling them, "The Son of Man is going to be betrayed into the hands of men. They will kill him, and after he is killed, he will rise three days later."
32 But they did not understand this statement, and they were afraid to ask him.
33 They came to Capernaum. When he was in the house, he asked them, "What were you arguing
about on the way?" **34** But they were silent, because on the way they had been arguing with one
another about who was the greatest. **35** Sitting down, he called the Twelve and said to them, "If anyone wants to be first, he must be last and servant of all." **36** He took a child, had him stand among
them, and taking him in his arms, he said to them, **37** "Whoever welcomes one little child such as
this in my name welcomes me. And whoever welcomes me does not welcome me, but him who
sent me."

II. Answers to exegetical questions

Verse-by-Verse Questions

a) In 9:30, the participle ἐξελθόντες should be classified as *attendant circumstance*. Thus, it should be translated as a finite verb ("left" or "went out/away") and connected to the main verb with the conjunction "and" (together rendered as "left . . . and passed through)."

b) The reason Jesus did not want anyone to know is specified by the γάρ clause in the next verse (9:31): "**For** he was teaching his disciples and telling them, 'The Son of Man is going to be betrayed into the hands of men. They will kill him, and after he is killed, he will rise three days later.'" The significance of Jesus's words is well-stated by France: "In 7:24 we are not told why he sought privacy. But here the new focus of the gospel is revealed by a more positive statement of purpose in the γάρ that follows. Jesus's mission is now to teach his disciples, and that takes priority over any public activity."[9]

c) In 9:31, ἐδίδασκεν should be syntactically classified as an inceptive imperfect.[10] Jesus took his disciples aside to begin instructing them about his passion.

d) In 9:31, παραδίδοται should be rendered as a futuristic present. This is true for two reasons: (1) At this point in the narrative, Jesus is not being handed over to the Jews and the Romans. That means the verb is either gnomic, historical, or futuristic. (2) Just a few words later, Mark uses the *future* verb ἀποκτενοῦσιν, clearly indicating that Jesus has been talking about future events (see also the future passive indicative form of παραδίδωμι used in the third passion prediction in 10:33).

e) In 9:35, Jesus uses the lowly status of a child as a teaching metaphor to demonstrate how the disciples should approach their own status. France says, "The child represents the lowest order in the social scale, the one

---

[9] R. T. France, *The Gospel of Mark: A Commentary on the Greek Text*, New International Greek Testament Commentary (Grand Rapids: Eerdmans, 2002), 371.

[10] For further study on the imperfect in Mark's Gospel, please see Rodney J. Decker, "The Function of the Imperfect Tense in Mark's Gospel," in *The Language of the New Testament: Context, History, and Development*, ed. Stanley E. Porter and Andrew W. Pitts (Leiden: Brill, 2013), 347–64.

who is under the authority and care of others and who has not yet achieved the right of self-determination. To 'become like a child' (Mt. 18:3) is to forgo status and to accept the lowest place, to be a 'little one' (Mt. 18:6, 10, 14; 10:42)."[11]

f) In Mark 9:36, the participle ἐναγκαλισάμενος was probably used to vividly display that Jesus embraces those with low status, or those who do not seek honor and glory for themselves. France notes that the use of this word makes the message Jesus is conveying "visual as well as verbal."[12]

Additional Questions

g) According to Garland, "Jesus emphasizes that they have the choice between grasping for power to dominate others and surrendering dominance over others to serve them. The first option will lead to their ultimate humiliation. The second option, humbling themselves for the sake of others, will lead to their ultimate exaltation (Matt 23:12; Luke 14:11; 18:14; Phil 2:8–9)."[13] This teaching in Mark about having a childlike attitude is primarily meant to contribute to the Gospel's overall message on rejecting worldly exaltation and embracing humiliation for the sake of following Jesus and serving others.

h) Mark's Gospel, especially the Way Discourse, emphasizes the disciples' inability to grasp Jesus's mission as one of suffering and death. They cannot fathom a Messiah who lays his life down vicariously. They desire a Messiah who pursues worldly exaltation because they want such exaltation for themselves. So, their inability to understand Jesus's teaching (and fear of asking about it!) exemplifies that the world cannot comprehend a Savior who accomplishes his salvific work through his own vicarious suffering. A Savior the world could easily comprehend would be one who conquers and acquires glory for himself.

III. Short Summary and Contextual Impact

Summary: Jesus the Messiah is on a mission to die "for many," but his disciples are only obsessed with their personal status. In response, Jesus teaches them that true exaltation is found in humbling oneself to serve others, including seemingly the most insignificant people.

Contextual impact: Mark 8:31–38 presents Jesus's teaching on how his disciples must follow him on the way to the cross; he teaches that following him is to "take up your cross," thus indicating that discipleship requires even the ultimate sacrifice. Mark 9:1–13 is the revelation of Jesus's glory on the mount of transfiguration. Mark 9:14–29 then narrates the disciples' failure to cast out a demon and, in contrast, Jesus's success; throughout the passage, it is taught that dependence on God is mandatory for discipleship. The current episode, 9:30–37, fits with the previous passages in that it provides additional teaching on what it means to be a disciple of Jesus. Discipleship is not only about giving up your life or about having faith in God/Jesus, but also about rejecting worldly ways of seeking status and embracing the lowliness of the Son of Man. The glorious Jesus seen at the transfiguration is uninterested in worldly status. To be his disciple is to accept humiliation, looking to the glorious Jesus for assurance that true discipleship is never in vain but will certainly be rewarded in the age to come.

---

[11] France, 374.
[12] France, 374.
[13] David E. Garland, *A Theology of Mark's Gospel: Good News about Jesus the Messiah, the Son of God*, ed. Andreas J. Köstenberger, Biblical Theology of the New Testament (Grand Rapids: Zondervan, 2015), 422.

IV. Parsing and Classification of the Key Grammatical Concepts for the Lesson: Datives and Accusatives

Datives

9:31

1) αὐτοῖς: αὐτός; 3 masc plur dat; *he*, *she*, *it*; *self*, *same*; *they* (when pl)
   - *Indirect Object*: It is a dative of indirect object because it is paired with a verb of speech; therefore, it is denoting the people *to whom* the speech is directed.

9:33

1) οἰκίᾳ: οἰκία; fem sg dat; *house*, *household*
   - *Object of a Preposition*: It is the object of the preposition ἐν.

2) ὁδῷ: ὁδός; fem sg dat; *way*, *road*, *highway*
   - *Object of a Preposition*: It is the object of the preposition ἐν.

9:34

1) ὁδῷ: ὁδός; fem sg dat; *way*, *road*, *highway*
   - *Object of a Preposition*: It is the object of the preposition ἐν.

9:35

1) αὐτοῖς: αὐτός; 3rd masc plur dat; *he*, *she*, *it*; *self*, *same*; *they* (when pl)
   - *Indirect Object*: It is a dative of indirect object because it is paired with a verb of speech; therefore, it denotes the people *to whom* the speech is directed.

9:36

1) μέσῳ: μέσος; neut sg dat; *middle*, *between*, *among*
   - *Object of a Preposition*: It is the object of the preposition ἐν.

2) αὐτοῖς: αὐτός; 3rd masc plur dat; *he*, *she*, *it*; *self*, *same*; *they* (when pl)
   - *Indirect Object*: It is a dative of indirect object because it is paired with a verb of speech; therefore, it denotes the people *to whom* the speech is directed.

9:37

1) ὀνόματί: ὄνομα; neut sg dat; *name*, *person*
   - *Object of a Preposition*: It is the object of the preposition ἐπί.

Accusatives

9:31

1) μαθητάς: μαθητής; masc plur acc; *disciple*, *pupil*
   - *Direct Object*: This is the direct object of the imperfect tense verb ἐδίδασκ4).

2) χεῖρας: χεῖρ; fem plur acc; *hand*
   - *Object of a Preposition:* It is the object of the preposition εἰς.

3) αὖτόν: αὐτός; masc sing acc; *he, she, it; self, same; they* (when pl)
   - *Direct Object:* This is an accusative of direct object. It is the object of the verb ἀποκτενοῦσιν.

4) τρεῖς: τρεῖς; fem plur acc; *three*
   - *Object of a Preposition*: It is the object of the preposition μετά5)

5) ἡμέρας: ἡμέρα; fem plur acc; *day*
   - *Object of a Preposition*: It is the object of the preposition μετά.

9:32

1) ῥῆμα: ῥῆμα; neut sg acc; *word*, *saying*, *statement*
   - *Respect*: It is an adverbial accusative of respect. This classification fits because it is narrowing the scope of the disciples' ignorance, i.e., it is not as though they were ignorant of all things, but rather that they were ignorant with respect to "this word."

2) αὐτόν: αὐτός; 3 masc sg acc; *he*, *she*, *it*; *self*, *same*; *they* (when pl)
   - *Direct Object*: This is an accusative of direct object. It is the object of the infinitive ἐπερωτῆσαι. Many verbs can take either a personal object or an impersonal object. The pronoun αὐτόν is the personal object of ἐπερωτῆσαι.

9:33

1) Καφαρναούμ: indeclinable; fem sg acc; *Capernaum*
   - *Object of a Preposition*: It is the object of the preposition εἰς.

2) αὐτούς: αὐτός; 3 masc plur acc; *he*, *she*, *it*; *self*, *same*; *they* (when pl)
   - *Direct Object*: This is an accusative of direct object. It is the object of the verb ἐπηρώτα.

3) τί: τίς; neut sing acc; *what, who, why*
   - *Direct Object:* This is an accusative of direct object. It is the object of the verb διελογίζεσθε.

9:34

1) ἀλλήλους: ἀλλήλων; masc plur acc; *each other*, *one another*
   - *Object of a Preposition*: It is the object of the preposition πρός.

9:35

1) δώδεκα: indeclinable; masc plur acc; *twelve*
   - *Direct Object*: This is an accusative of direct object. It is the object of the verb ἐφώνησεν. The article τούς (masc plur acc) helps us to identify the indeclinable number δώδεκα as masc plur acc.

9:36

1) παιδίον: παιδίον; neut sg acc; *child*, *infant*
   - *Direct Object*: This is an accusative of direct object. It is the object of the verb λαβών.

2) αὐτό: αὐτός; 3 neut sg acc; *he*, *she*, *it*; *self*, *same*; *they* (when pl)
   - *Direct Object*: This is an accusative of direct object. It is the object of the verb ἔστησεν.

3) αὐτό: αὐτός; 3 neut sg acc; *he*, *she*, *it*; *self*, *same*; *they* (when pl)
   - Direct Object: This is an accusative of direct object. It is the object of the participle ἐναγκαλισάμενος.

9:37 (excluding the accusative participle ἀποστείλαντά, the direct object of δέχεται)

1) ἕν: εἷς, μία, ἕν; neut sg acc; *one*
   - Direct Object: This is an accusative of direct object. It is the object of the verb δέξηται.

2) ἐμέ: ἐγώ; 1 sg acc; *I*, *me*, *my*
   - Direct Object: This is an accusative of direct object. It is the object of the verb δέχεται.

3) ἐμέ: ἐγώ; 1 sg acc; *I*, *me*, *my*
   - Direct Object: This is an accusative of direct object. It is the object of the verb δέχηται.

4) ἐμέ: ἐγώ; 1 sg acc; *I*, *me*, *my*
   - Direct Object: This is an accusative of direct object. It is the object of the verb δέχεται.

5) με: ἐγώ; 1 sg acc; *I*, *me*, *my*
   - Direct Object: This is an accusative of direct object. It is the object of the participle ἀποστείλαντά.

Now, rewrite your translation of the entire passage in the GUIDED PRACTICE section, reflecting the above exegetical procedure.

REFERENCES

Danker, Frederick William, et al. *A Greek-English Lexicon of the New Testament and other Early Christian Literature*. 3rd ed. Chicago: University of Chicago Press, 2000.

Decker, Rodney J. *Mark 1–8: A Handbook on the Greek Text*. Ed. Martin M. Culy. Baylor Handbook on the Greek New Testament. Waco: Baylor University Press, 2014.

———. *Mark 9–16: A Handbook on the Greek Text*. Ed. Martin M. Culy. Baylor Handbook on the Greek New Testament. Waco: Baylor University Press, 2014.

———. "The Function of the Imperfect Tense in Mark's Gospel," in *The Language of the New Testament: Context, History, and Development*, ed. Stanley E. Porter and Andrew W. Pitts. Leiden: Brill, 2013. Pages 347–64.

France, R. T. *The Gospel of Mark*. The New International Greek Testament Commentary. Grand Rapids: Eerdmans, 2002.

Garland, David E. *A Theology of Mark's Gospel: Good News about Jesus the Messiah, the Son of God*. Ed. Andreas J. Köstenberger. Biblical Theology of the New Testament. Grand Rapids: Zondervan, 2015.

Köstenberger, Andreas J., Benjamin L. Merkle, and Robert L. Plummer. *Going Deeper with New Testament Greek: An Intermediate Study of the Grammar and Syntax of the New Testament*. Rev. ed. Nashville: B&H Academic, 2020.

Wallace, Daniel B. *Greek Grammar Beyond the Basics: An Exegetical Syntax of the New Testament*. Grand Rapids: Zondervan, 1996.

Williams, Joel. *Mark*. Ed. Andreas J. Köstenberger and Robert W. Yarbrough. Exegetical Guide to the Greek New Testament. Nashville: B&H Academic, 2020.

CHAPTER SEVEN

////////////////

MARK 9:38–50

WITH ATTENTION TO PRESENT INDICATIVES AND SENTENCE STRUCTURE

GRAMMAR REVIEW:

Present Indicative

Definition and Description

The present indicative, as a tense-form, has an imperfective aspect. In other words, it portrays an action as incomplete. Wallace helpfully describes the aspect as *internal*—i.e., the event is being viewed from the inside, as it is happening, without regard to beginning or end.[1] It usually portrays an action as occurring *in the present*, but this is not always the case. In fact, Constantine R. Campbell argues that the present indicative describes actions in the present only about 70 percent of the time.[2] To discern the specific use of the present tense, one must consider other influences such as contextual, grammatical, and lexical factors.[3]

As a reminder, the indicative mood presents an action as *actual*, regardless of whether or not the action truly happened. In other words, it is simply a declarative statement: "I ran," "He will kneel," "We jump," and so on.

Categories and Examples[4]

PRESENT INDICATIVE		
PROGRESSIVE	An action that is in progress or ongoing.	κύριε, σῶσον, **ἀπολλύμεθα** ("Lord, save us! **We are perishing**!" Matt 8:25 NRSV).
DURATIVE	An action that began in the past and continues into the present.	ἀπ᾽ ἀρχῆς ὁ διάβολος **ἁμαρτάνει** ("the devil **has sinned** from the beginning" 1 John 3:8).

[1] Daniel B. Wallace, *Greek Grammar Beyond the Basics: An Exegetical Syntax of the New Testament* (Grand Rapids: Zondervan, 1996), 514.

[2] Constantine R. Campbell, *Advances in the Study of Greek: New Insights for Reading the New Testament* (Grand Rapids: Zondervan, 2015), 114.

[3] Andreas J. Köstenberger, Benjamin L. Merkle, and Robert L. Plummer, *Going Deeper with New Testament Greek: An Intermediate Study of the Grammar and Syntax of the New Testament*, rev. ed. (Nashville: B&H Academic, 2020), 257.

[4] Köstenberger, Merkle, and Plummer, 276.

PRESENT INDICATIVE (CONTINUED)		
ITERATIVE	An action that is performed repeatedly, regularly, or customarily.	πολλάκις . . . **πίπτει** εἰς τὸ πῦρ ("He often **falls** into the fire" Matt 17:15).
GNOMIC	A statement that is timeless (omni-temporal), universal, or generally true.	ἱλαρὸν . . . δότην **ἀγαπᾷ** ὁ θεός ("God **loves** a cheerful giver" 2 Cor 9:7).
INSTANTANEOUS	An action that is done instantaneously, usually by the very fact that it is spoken.	Καίσαρα **ἐπικαλοῦμαι** ("**I appeal** to Caesar!" Acts 25:11).
HISTORICAL	A past event that adds vividness to the event or gives literary prominence to some aspect of the story.	καὶ **ἔρχεται** πρὸς τοὺς μαθητάς ("Then **he came** to the disciples" Matt 26:40).
TENDENTIAL	An action was begun, attempted, or proposed, but not completed.	οἵτινες ἐν νόμῳ **δικαιοῦσθε** ("**You** who **are trying to be justified** by the law" Gal 5:4).
FUTURISTIC	An action that will occur in the future (often adds vividness or certainty).	μετὰ τρεῖς ἡμέρας **ἐγείρομαι** ("After three days **I will rise** again" Matt 27:63).
PERFECTIVE	Emphasizes the present state of a past action.	**ἀπέχουσιν** τὸν μισθὸν αὐτῶν ("**they have received** their reward" Matt 6:2 ESV).

Sentence Structure

Definition and Description

Köstenberger, Merkle, and Plummer describe a sentence as "a complete grammatical unit that includes or implies a subject and a predicate."[5] The subject is a person, place, or thing and is what the sentence is about. The predicate says something about the subject. Consider 1 John 1:5: θεὸς φῶς ἐστιν. θεός is the subject and φῶς is the predicate. As the subject, God is the focus, and we are being told something about him, namely, that he is light.

Unlike English, Greek can communicate a complete sentence in one simple word. John 11:35 says, ἐδάκρυσεν ὁ Ἰησοῦς. Jesus is the subject and the verb "wept" is the predicate. However, ἐδάκρυσεν alone could be a complete sentence, since the Greek verb includes a subject in its ending ("he," "she," "it") and contains a predicate.[6]

There are many components to a Greek sentence including words, phrases, and clauses. For a more thorough review of the components of a Greek sentence, please see Köstenberger, Merkle, and Plummer's *Going Deeper with New Testament Greek* on pages 442–49.

Categories and Examples[7]

COMPONENTS OF A GREEK SENTENCE		
COMPONENT	**DEFINITION**	**EXAMPLE**
WORD	A foundational sound unit (lex) with other functional sound units (morphemes) sometimes combined with it, so that a native speaker recognizes it as a grammatical entity referring to a person, place, thing, or action, or functioning in some other way in his language.	Φοίβην ("Phoebe" Rom 16:1).

[5] Köstenberger, Merkle, and Plummer, 443.
[6] Köstenberger, Merkle, and Plummer, 443. For an example of a one-verb sentence, refer to *τετέλεσται* ("It is finished") in John 19:30.
[7] Köstenberger, Merkle, and Plummer, 467–68.

PHRASE	Two or more words functioning together as a discrete grammatical unit, though lacking the sufficient components to be called a clause or sentence. Various kinds of phrases: Prepositional, Noun, Adverbial, Adjectival, Verbal.	τοῦ λοιποῦ, ἐνδυναμοῦσθε **ἐν κυρίῳ** καὶ **ἐν τῷ κράτει τῆς ἰσχύος αὐτοῦ** ("Finally, be strong **in the Lord** and **in the strength of his might**" Eph 6:10 NASB).
INDEPENDENT CLAUSE	A portion of a sentence that contains (or implies) a subject or predicate and is not subordinated to another portion of the sentence.	ἡνίκα δὲ ἐὰν ἐπιστρέψῃ πρὸς κύριον, **περιαιρεῖται τὸ κάλυμμα** ("But whenever anyone turns to the Lord, **the veil is taken away**" 2 Cor 3:16 NIV).
DEPENDENT CLAUSE	A portion of a sentence that contains (or implies) a subject or predicate and is subordinated to another portion of the sentence.	σὺ ὃ σπείρεις, οὐ ζῳοποιεῖται **ἐὰν μὴ ἀποθάνῃ** ("What you sow does not come to life **unless it dies**" 1 Cor 15:36)
TYPES OF GREEK SENTENCES (BY COMPONENTS)		
TYPE	**DEFINITION**	**EXAMPLE**
SIMPLE	A sentence that has one word or group of words functioning as the subject and one word or group of words functioning as the predicate.	ὁ πλοῦτος ὑμῶν σέσηπεν ("Your riches have rotted" Jas 5:2 ESV).
COMPOUND	A sentence composed of two or more independent clauses connected by one or more coordinating conjunctions.	καὶ εὐθὺς ἀπῆλθεν ἀπ᾽ αὐτοῦ ἡ λέπρα, καὶ ἐκαθαρίσθη ("Immediately the leprosy left him, and he was made clean" Mark 1:42).
COMPLEX	A sentence that includes both an independent clause and a subordinate (dependent) clause.	καὶ ἐγερθεὶς ἀπῆλθεν εἰς τὸν οἶκον αὐτοῦ ("And, after he arose, he departed to his house" Matt 9:7 author's translation).
COPULATIVE	A sentence that links two substantives with a copulative verb (i.e., εἰμί, γίνομαι, ὑπάρχω).	ὑμεῖς ἐστε τὸ φῶς τοῦ κόσμου ("You are the light of the world" Matt 5:14).
TYPES OF GREEK SENTENCES (BY FUNCTION)		
TYPE	**DEFINITION**	**EXAMPLE**
DECLARATIVE	Makes a statement of fact.	πάντες γὰρ οἱ προφῆται καὶ ὁ νόμος ἕως Ἰωάννου ἐπροφήτευσαν ("For all the prophets and the law prophesied until John came" Matt 11:13).
INTERROGATIVE	Asks a question.	ποῦ σου, θάνατε, τὸ νῖκος ("Where, death, is your victory?" 1 Cor 15:55).
IMPERATIVE	Gives a command or makes a request.	αἴτησόν με ὃ ἐὰν θέλῃς ("Ask me whatever you want" Mark 6:22).
EXCLAMATORY	Communicates an expression of strong feeling.	μὴ γένοιτο ("May it never be!" Rom 9:14 NASB).

GUIDED PRACTICE: MARK 9:38–50 (NA[28])

9:38 Ἔφη αὐτῷ ὁ Ἰωάννης· διδάσκαλε, εἴδομέν τινα ἐν τῷ ὀνόματί σου ἐκβάλλοντα δαιμόνια
καὶ ἐκωλύομεν αὐτόν, ὅτι οὐκ ἠκολούθει ἡμῖν. 39 ὁ δὲ Ἰησοῦς εἶπεν· μὴ κωλύετε αὐτόν. οὐδεὶς
γάρ ἐστιν ὃς ποιήσει δύναμιν ἐπὶ τῷ ὀνόματί μου καὶ δυνήσεται ταχὺ κακολογῆσαί με· 40 ὃς
γὰρ οὐκ ἔστιν καθ᾽ ἡμῶν, ὑπὲρ ἡμῶν ἐστιν.

41 Ὃς γὰρ ἂν ποτίσῃ ὑμᾶς ποτήριον ὕδατος ἐν ὀνόματι ὅτι Χριστοῦ ἐστε, ἀμὴν λέγω ὑμῖν
ὅτι οὐ μὴ ἀπολέσῃ τὸν μισθὸν αὐτοῦ.

42 Καὶ ὃς ἂν σκανδαλίσῃ ἕνα τῶν μικρῶν τούτων τῶν πιστευόντων [εἰς ἐμέ], καλόν ἐστιν
αὐτῷ μᾶλλον εἰ περίκειται μύλος ὀνικὸς περὶ τὸν τράχηλον αὐτοῦ καὶ βέβληται εἰς τὴν
θάλασσαν. 43 Καὶ ἐὰν σκανδαλίζῃ σε ἡ χείρ σου, ἀπόκοψον αὐτήν· καλόν ἐστίν σε κυλλὸν
εἰσελθεῖν εἰς τὴν ζωὴν ἢ τὰς δύο χεῖρας ἔχοντα ἀπελθεῖν εἰς τὴν γέενναν, εἰς τὸ πῦρ τὸ
ἄσβεστον. 45 Καὶ ἐὰν ὁ πούς σου σκανδαλίζῃ σε, ἀπόκοψον αὐτόν· καλόν ἐστίν σε εἰσελθεῖν εἰς

τὴν ζωὴν χωλὸν ἢ τοὺς δύο πόδας ἔχοντα βληθῆναι εἰς τὴν γέενναν. [47] Καὶ ἐὰν ὁ ὀφθαλμός
σου σκανδαλίζῃ σε, ἔκβαλε αὐτόν· καλόν σέ ἐστιν μονόφθαλμον εἰσελθεῖν εἰς τὴν βασιλείαν
τοῦ θεοῦ ἢ δύο ὀφθαλμοὺς ἔχοντα βληθῆναι εἰς τὴν γέενναν, [48] ὅπου ὁ σκώληξ αὐτῶν οὐ
τελευτᾷ καὶ τὸ πῦρ οὐ σβέννυται.

[49] Πᾶς γὰρ πυρὶ ἁλισθήσεται. [50] καλὸν τὸ ἅλας· ἐὰν δὲ τὸ ἅλας ἄναλον γένηται, ἐν τίνι αὐτὸ
ἀρτύσετε; ἔχετε ἐν ἑαυτοῖς ἅλα καὶ εἰρηνεύετε ἐν ἀλλήλοις.

VOCABULARY AIDS (WORDS 26X TO 50X)

9:38, 39 **κωλύω** *to hinder, prevent, forbid* (23x)
9:41 **ποτήριον** *cup* (34x)
9:42, 43, 45, 47 **σκανδαλίζω** *to cause to sin, cause to stumble* (29x)

VOCABULARY AIDS (WORDS 25X OR LESS)

9:39 **κακολογέω** *to speak evil of*; *revile*; *insult* (5x)
9:39 **ταχύς** *short time*; *soon*; *quickly* (13x)
9:41 **ποτίζω** *to give to drink*; *water* (15x)
9:42 **περίκειμαι** *to be around*; *be placed around* (9x)
9:42 **μύλος** *mill*; *millstone* (5x)
9:42 **ὀνικός** *of a donkey* (2x)
9:42 **τράχηλος** *neck* (10x)
9:43, 45 **ἀποκόπτω** *cut off*; *cut away* (7x)
9:43 **κυλλός** *crippled*; *deformed* (4x)
9:43, 45, 47 **γέεννα** *hell*; *Gehenna* (13x)
9:43 **ἄσβεστος** *unquenchable*, *inextinguishable* (5x)
9:45 **ἀποκόπτω** *to cut off*; *cut away* (7x)
9:45 **χωλός** *lame*, *crippled* (14x)
9:47 **μονόφθαλμος** *one-eyed* (2x)
9:48 **σκώληξ** *worm* (1x)
9:48 **τελευτάω** *to die* (11x)
9:48 **σβέννυμι** *quench*, *extinguish* (6x)
9:49 **ἁλίζω** *to salt* (verb, 3x)
9:50 **ἅλας** *salt* (noun, 8x)
9:50 **ἄναλος** *without salt* (1x)
9:50 **ἀρτύω** *to season*; *salt* (3x)
9:50 **εἰρηνεύω** *to be at peace*; *keep peace* (4x)

EXERCISE

I. Provide your translation under the Greek text above.

II. Exegetical notes and questions: read the bullet points and answer the questions below.

Verse-by-Verse Questions

9:38

a) What is the case of διδάσκαλε?

b) How is the masculine accusative singular present active participle ἐκβάλλοντα being used?

- France makes the point that ἀκολουθέω is almost always used in Mark with reference to Jesus, but here it is used with ἡμῖν. France describes the significance of this phenomenon: "What John is looking for is not so much personal allegiance and obedience to Jesus, but membership in the 'authorised' circle of his followers."[8]

9:39

c) How should the infinitive κακολογῆσαί be classified syntactically?

d) How does Mark 9:38–41 delineate what it means to follow Jesus?

9:41

e) How should the phrase ὃς γὰρ ἂν ποτίσῃ be translated? What role does ἂν play?

[8] R. T. France, *The Gospel of Mark: A Commentary on the Greek Text*, New International Greek Testament Commentary (Grand Rapids: Eerdmans, 2002), 377.

- οὐ μὴ ἀπολέσῃ—οὐ μή + aorist subjunctive is the strongest form of negation in Koine Greek. Jesus is communicating that the one who fulfills the condition described in the indefinite relative clause of the verse, will "*never* lose his reward."

9:42

f) How should the phrase καλόν ἐστιν αὐτῷ μᾶλλον be translated?

- μύλος ὀνικός—literally, "millstone of a donkey." This phrase means a "heavy millstone."

9:43, 45, 47

g) Verses 43, 45, and 47 all begin with conditional clauses. What class of condition are they?

- σκανδαλίζῳ—France makes the point that in the current context this verb implies more than simply "to cause to sin." It means to cause to stumble and refers more broadly to causing one's downfall.[9]
- Γέεννα (Hebrew originally) was a refuse dump outside of Jerusalem that burned continuously. Therefore, Jesus's use of it as an analogy to "the inextinguishable fire" of hell is both fitting and effective.

h) In the phrase τὸ πῦρ τὸ ἄσβεστον, how should the adjective ἄσβεστον be classified?

- The phrase ὁ σκώληξ αὐτῶν οὐ τελευτᾷ καὶ τὸ πῦρ οὐ σβέννυται is a reference to Isa 66:24. Jesus uses this phrase as a strong deterrence from sinning and causing others to fall away. The radical demands of vv. 43–47 are warranted since the alternative is the worst possible fate.

Additional Questions

i) How does 9:42–48 contribute to the Markan presentation of discipleship?

j) How does 9:49–50 fit with the preceding literary context?

---

[9] France, 380.

Short Summary and Contextual Impact

III. Summarize the main idea of the passage and then discuss how it fits into the surrounding narrative.

Parsing and Classification

IV. Circle the present indicatives in the text and parse them below. Then classify each one according to the categories given in the grammar review above. Provide a brief explanation for your decision.

Present Indicatives

9:39

1)

9:40

1)

2)

9:41

1)

2)

9:42

1)

2)

9:43

1)

9:45

1)

9:47

1)

9:48

1)

2)

Phrase/Clause Classification

Now, analyze the following phrases/clauses and classify each entry.

9:38

1) ἐν τῷ ὀνόματί

2) ἐκβάλλοντα δαιμόνια

9:39

1) ὁ δὲ Ἰησοῦς εἶπεν

9:42

1) καλόν ἐστιν αὐτῷ

2) περὶ τὸν τράχηλον

9:50

1) Καλὸν τὸ ἅλας

ANSWER KEY

I. Translation and explanations

38 John said to him, "Teacher, we saw someone driving out demons in your name, and we tried to
stop him because he wasn't following us."
39 "Don't stop him," said Jesus, "because there is no one who will perform a miracle in my name
who can soon afterward speak evil of me. **40** For whoever is not against us is for us. **41** And whoever
gives you a cup of water to drink in my name, because you belong to Christ—truly I tell you, he
will never lose his reward.
42 "But whoever causes one of these little ones who believes in me to fall away—it would[10] be
better for him if a heavy millstone were hung around his neck and he were thrown into the sea.
43 "And if your hand causes you to fall away, cut it off. It is better for you to enter life maimed
than to have two hands and go to hell, the unquenchable fire. **45** And if your foot causes you to fall
away, cut it off. It is better for you to enter life lame than to have two feet and be thrown into hell.
47 And if your eye causes you to fall away, gouge it out. It is better for you to enter the kingdom
of God with one eye than to have two eyes and be thrown into hell, **48** where their worm does not
die,[11] and the fire is not quenched.[12] **49** For everyone will be salted with fire. **50** Salt is good, but if
the salt should lose its flavor, how can you season it? Have salt among yourselves, and be at peace
with one another."

II. Answers to exegetical questions

Verse-by-verse questions

a) In 9:38, διδάσκαλε is a vocative, used for direct address.

b) In 9:38, ἐκβάλλοντα is functioning as an adjectival attributive participle modifying the direct object, τινα, or as a participle functioning as an object complement (which is complementary in relation to the direct object, τινα).

c) In 9:39, κακολογῆσαί should be classified as a complementary infinitive.

d) This text (9:38–9:41) helps the reader understand that being a disciple of Jesus is not about being part of an "in" group, but about being loyal and obedient to Jesus.

e) In 9:41, ἄν makes this an **indefinite** relative clause, which should be translated, "For who**ever** gives you a cup of water. . . ."

f) In 9:42, the phrase καλόν ἐστιν αὐτῷ μᾶλλον should be translated, "It would be better for him." This translation is accurate for two reasons: (1) when μᾶλλον appears with καλόν, καλόν functions as a comparative and (2) εἰ introduces a part that describes what σκανδαλίσῃ ἕνα τῶν μικρῶν τούτων τῶν πιστευόντων εἰς ἐμέ is **compared** to in the current context.

---

[10] The CSB rightly reflects the gnomic nature of these present indicatives.
[11] Or "will not die."
[12] Or "will not be quenched."

g) The conditional clauses in vv. 43, 45, and 47 are all 3rd class conditional clauses.[13] As a brief reminder, in 3rd class conditional clauses "the event in the protasis is presented somewhat more hypothetically by the speaker. It is more tentative than the 1st class conditional.[14]

h) In 9:43, the adjective ἄσβεστον should be classified as an adjective in the 2nd attributive position, which modifies the noun, πῦρ.

Additional Questions

i) These verses (9:42–48) fit especially with the Markan theme of self-denial and add to that theme by demonstrating that self-denial extends to refusing and resisting any sin that turns others away from their devotion to Jesus. It is important to note that self-denial is a necessary element of true discipleship according to Mark (e.g., 8:34; cf. 9:35).

j) These verses (9:49–50) describe several things: (1) the cost of following Jesus, (2) the horror of judgment, and (3) the necessity of preserving one another from sin (since salt's primary use in the first century was that of a preservative[15]). Thus, these verses depict the entailment of discipleship in line with the previous parts of the Way Discourse.

In addition, it can be noted that Mark connects the statements in vv. 49–50 with one another and with the preceding verses through a common-word link and a cognate connection. To begin with, the term "fire" (πῦρ) is a common word between v. 48 and v. 49. Next, the link through the "salt" cognates (ἁλίζω and ἅλας) is used between v. 49 and v. 50. Finally, the word "salt" (ἅλας) serves as a common thread across the sayings in v. 50. A similar method of combining statements through a common term is seen also in Mark 12:38–44.

III. Short Summary and Contextual Impact

Summary: This passage further delineates what it means to be a disciple. Discipleship is not about being among the "in" group but instead about publicly identifying with Jesus, taking radical steps to resist sin that drives others way from their devotion to Christ, and obeying the Messiah amid trials and persecutions.

Contextual impact: This passage describes many themes previously introduced in the Way Discourse, for instance, the cost of discipleship, which involves self-denial, as introduced in 8:34–37. The current passage further demonstrates the critical role that self-denial plays in discipleship, which is presented this time in connection to Jesus's warning against sin that leads others to stumble and fall away from their commitment to Jesus the Messiah.

---

[13] See Köstenberger, Merkle, and Plummer, *Going Deeper with New Testament Greek*, 448–49 for review of the different classes of conditional clauses.

[14] Köstenberger, Merkle, and Plummer, 448.

[15] France, *The Gospel of Mark,* 384. For an overview of all the different ways that salt was used in the first century, see W. D. Davies and Dale C. Allison, *A Critical and Exegetical Commentary on the Gospel According to Saint Matthew*, The International Critical Commentary on the Holy Scriptures of the Old and New Testaments (New York: T&T Clark, 2004), 472–73.

IV. Parsing & Classification of the Key Grammatical Concepts for the Lesson: Present Indicatives and Sentence Structure.

Present Indicative[16]

9:39

1) ἐστιν: εἰμί; 3 sg pres act ind; *to be, is*
   - Gnomic: Jesus is referring to what tends to be the case in general.

9:40

1) ἐστιν: εἰμί; 3 sg pres act ind; *to be, is*
   - Gnomic: It is almost proverbial in style and is intended to be a universal statement; something timeless.

2) ἐστιν: εἰμί; 3 sg pres act ind; *to be, is*
   - Gnomic: same as the immediately preceding entry

9:41)

1) ἐστε: εἰμί; 2 pl pres act ind; *to be, is*
   - Gnomic: Jesus is referring to what tends to be the case in general.

2) λέγω: λέγω; 1 sg pres act ind; *to say, to speak*
   - Instantaneous: It gives attention to the authoritative words that Jesus himself is speaking at the moment.

9:42

1) ἐστιν: εἰμί; 3 sg pres act ind; *to be, is*
   - Gnomic: This is part of a comparison between being drowned at the bottom of a lake and causing a "little one" that believes in Jesus to sin. It is a timeless truth that does not describe an actual action that takes place in time.

2) περίκειται: περίκειμαι; 3 sg pres mid ind; *to be around, to be placed around*
   - Gnomic: *See the explanation on ἐστιν (9:42) above.*

9:43

1) ἐστιν: εἰμί; 3 sg pres act ind; *to be, is*
   - Gnomic: *See the explanation on ἐστιν (9:42) above.*

9:45

1) ἐστιν: εἰμί; 3 sg pres act ind; *to be, is*
   - Gnomic: *See the explanation on ἐστιν (9:42) above.*

---

[16] Though there are no examples of the historical present in this pericope, it is a prominent feature of Mark's Gospel. For further review of the historical present, please see chapter 6, titled "Historical Present" in Steven E. Runge, *Discourse Grammar of the Greek New Testament: A Practical Introduction for Teaching and Exegesis* (Peabody, MA: Hendrickson, 2010).

9:47

1) ἐστιν: εἰμί; 3 sg pres act ind; *to be, is*
   - <u>*Gnomic*</u>: *See the explanation on ἐστιν (9:42) above.*

9:48

1) τελευτᾷ: τελευτάω; 3 sg pres act ind; *to come to an end, to die*
   - <u>*Futuristic*</u>: In New Testament theology, the second coming of Christ is when judgment happens, and therefore *Gehenna* is unpopulated until then. This verb is therefore futuristic.

2) σβέννυται: σβέννυμι; 3 sg pres pass ind; *to extinguish, to quench*
   - <u>*Futuristic*</u>: *See the explanation on τελευτᾷ (9:48) above.*

Phrase/Clause Classification

9:38

1) ἐν τῷ ὀνόματί: Prepositional Phrase

2) ἐκβάλλοντα δαιμόνια: Verbal Phrase

9:39

1) ὁ δὲ Ἰησοῦς εἶπεν: Independent Clause (This clause introduces the following direct discourse.)

9:42

1) καλόν ἐστιν αὐτῷ: Independent Clause (The subject is included in the verb, and the clause is to be translated, "it would be better for him" or "it is better for him.")

2) περὶ τὸν τράχηλον: Prepositional Phrase

9:50

1) καλὸν τὸ ἅλας: Independent Clause (If this phrase were τὸ ἅλας τὸ καλόν, it would be an adjectival phrase "the good salt"; however, as it stands, it is an independent clause "salt is good," with a subject, an implied verb, and a predicate adjective.)

Now, rewrite your translation of the entire passage in the GUIDED PRACTICE section, reflecting the above exegetical procedure.

REFERENCES

Danker, Frederick William, et al. *A Greek-English Lexicon of the New Testament and other Early Christian Literature*. 3rd ed. Chicago: University of Chicago Press, 2000.

Decker, Rodney J. *Mark 9–16: A Handbook on the Greek Text*. Ed. Martin M. Culy. Baylor Handbook on the Greek New Testament. Waco: Baylor University Press, 2014.

Campbell, Constantine R. *Advances in the Study of Greek: New Insights for Reading the New Testament*. Grand Rapids: Zondervan, 2015.

Davies, W. D., and Dale C. Allison. *A Critical and Exegetical Commentary on the Gospel According to Saint Matthew*. International Critical Commentary. New York: T&T Clark, 2004.

France, R. T. *The Gospel of Mark*. The New International Greek Testament Commentary. Grand Rapids: Eerdmans, 2002.

Köstenberger, Andreas J., Benjamin L. Merkle, and Robert L. Plummer. *Going Deeper with New Testament Greek: An Intermediate Study of the Grammar and Syntax of the New Testament*. Rev. ed. Nashville: B&H Academic, 2020.

Runge, Steven E. *Discourse Grammar of the Greek New Testament: A Practical Introduction for Teaching and Exegesis*. Peabody, MA: Hendrickson, 2010.

Wallace, Daniel B. *Greek Grammar Beyond the Basics: An Exegetical Syntax of the New Testament*. Grand Rapids: Zondervan, 1996.

Williams, Joel. *Mark*. Ed. Andreas J. Köstenberger and Robert W. Yarbrough. Exegetical Guide to the Greek New Testament. Nashville: B&H Academic, 2020.

CHAPTER EIGHT

////////////////

MARK 10:1–16

WITH ATTENTION TO FUTURE INDICATIVES AND PREPOSITIONS

GRAMMAR REVIEW:

Future Indicatives

Definition and Description

Although the Greek verbal system is highly aspectual, the future indicative is unique because it is often regarded as "aspectually neutral."[1] In other words, it is a tense-category alone, although Wallace believes that the future portrays an external aspect,[2] depicting an entire action from an outside perspective. Robertson notes that the future indicative may well have evolved out of the aorist somehow, given that it is largely punctiliar in nature.[3]

The future communicates action subsequent to some point in time. It also communicates the expectation of the author, which is why it is sometimes used in place of other moods like the subjunctive or the imperative. Almost all uses of the future tense in the New Testament are indicatives, appearing 1,609 times compared to only 12 future participles and 5 future infinitives.[4]

Categories and Examples[5]

FUTURE INDICATIVE		
PREDICTIVE	Predicts a future event.	αὐτὸς . . . **βαπτίσει** ὑμᾶς ἐν πνεύματι ἁγίῳ ("he **will baptize** you with the Holy Spirit" Mark 1:8).
IMPERATIVAL	Expresses a command.	ἅγιοι **ἔσεσθε**, ὅτι ἐγὼ ἅγιός ("**You shall be** holy, for I am holy" 1 Pet 1:16 ESV).

[1] Andreas J. Köstenberger, Benjamin L. Merkle, and Robert L. Plummer, *Going Deeper with New Testament Greek: An Intermediate Study of the Grammar and Syntax of the New Testament*, rev. ed. (Nashville: B&H Academic, 2020), 271.

[2] Daniel B. Wallace, *Greek Grammar Beyond the Basics: An Exegetical Syntax of the New Testament* (Grand Rapids: Zondervan, 1996), 566.

[3] A.T. Robertson, *A Grammar of the Greek New Testament in the Light of Historical Research* (Logos Bible Software, 2006), 353.

[4] Köstenberger, Merkle, and Plummer, *Going Deeper with New Testament Greek*, 271.

[5] Köstenberger, Merkle, and Plummer, 277.

FUTURE INDICATIVE		
DELIBERATIVE	Asks a question (real or rhetorical).	πῶς ἔτι **ζήσομεν** ἐν αὐτῇ; ("How **can we** . . . still **live** in it [= sin]?" Rom 6:2).
GNOMIC	Expresses a timeless truth.	μόλις γὰρ ὑπὲρ δικαίου τις **ἀποθανεῖται** ("For rarely **will** someone **die** for a just person" Rom 5:7).
PROGRESSIVE	An action that was being done will continue into the future.	Ἀλλὰ καὶ **χαρήσομαι** ("Yes, and **I will continue to rejoice**" Phil 1:18).

Prepositions

Definition and Description

Prepositions are extremely common. About 80 percent of the verses in the New Testament contain prepositions. Prepositions function as an aid to substantives, clarifying their case relationship. In other words, they express the connection a substantive has with a sentence. A preposition + its substantive(s) forms a prepositional phrase.

Prepositional phrases are usually adverbial but can be adjectival or substantival as well. When functioning adverbially, they specify the extent or nature of a verb. In the sentence "I reside in my house," the words "in my house" specifies the extent of the verb "reside." If a preposition takes an adjectival force, they often take a genitival case, although not universally.

There is a difference between what are called *proper prepositions* and *improper prepositions*. Proper prepositions occur both in connection with a substantive in prepositional phrases and as prefixes in compound verbs. Improper prepositions, on the other hand, occur only in prepositional phrases, never as prefixes in compound verbs. When prefixed to a verb, a proper preposition can have one of the four possible effects on the original meaning of a verb: (1) it can add meaning, (2) it can intensify meaning, (3) it can add no meaning, or 4) it can give the verb a different meaning.

Here are some examples. First, consider the verb ἀναβαίνω. The prefix ἀνα modifies the verb by adding the meaning "up" to it. Therefore, just as you would expect, this verb means "I go up." Second, in the verb κατεσθίω, the prefix κατα adds an intensifying meaning to the verb. So instead of meaning simply "I eat," it means "I devour." Third, many verbs were modified by a prefix but by the time the New Testament was written, the distinctive meaning of these verbs had been assimilated into the more general meaning of the verb. For example, ἀνοίγω means "I open," not "I rip open" or something similar. Fourth, sometimes prepositions can modify the meaning of a verb so radically that it results in a completely different idea. By looking at the makeup of the word ἀναγινώσκω, you would expect the word to mean something like, "I know up," but that is an incoherent idea. In fact, the word means "I read."

Categories and Examples[6]

FUNCTIONS OF PREPOSITIONAL PHRASES		
ADVERBIAL (MODIFYING A VERB)	αἰτείτω δὲ **ἐν πίστει** ("But let him ask **in faith**" Jas 1:6).	
ADJECTIVAL (MODIFYING A NOUN)	τῇ **κατ' εὐσέβειαν** διδασκαλίᾳ ("the teaching that promotes **godliness**" 1 Tim 6:3).	
SUBSTANTIVAL (ACTING AS A NOUN)	Μὴ ἀγαπᾶτε τὸν κόσμον μηδὲ **τὰ ἐν τῷ κόσμῳ** ("Do not love the world or **the things in the world**" 1 John 2:15 ESV).	
THE 17 PROPER PREPOSITIONS		
PREPOSITION	CASE OF OBJECT	GLOSSES
ἀνά 13x	acc	each, in turn, up
ἀντί 22x	gen	in place of, instead of
ἀπό 646x	gen	from, of
διά 667x	gen, acc	through, because of
εἰς 1,768x	acc	into, in, at
ἐκ 914x	gen	from, out of
ἐν 2,752x	dat	in, into, by
ἐπί 890x	gen, dat, acc	on, upon, against
κατά 473x	gen, acc	against, according to
μετά 469x	gen, acc	with, after
παρά 194x	gen, dat, acc	from, with, beside
περί 333x	gen, acc	concerning, around
πρό 47x	gen	before, at
πρός 700x	gen, dat, acc	for, at, to
σύν 128x	dat	with
ὑπέρ 150x	gen, acc	for, above
ὑπό 220x	gen, acc	by, under

[6] Köstenberger, Merkle, and Plummer, *Going Deeper with New Testament Greek*, 412–14; 426–27.

IMPROPER PREPOSITIONS			
PREPOSITION		CASE OF OBJECT	GLOSSES
ἅμα	10x (1x as prep.)	dat	together with
ἄνευ	3x	gen	without, without the consent of
ἄντικρυς	1x	gen	opposite, offshore from
ἀντιπέρα	1x	gen	opposite, across from
ἀπέναντι	5x	gen	opposite, in front of, across from
ἄτερ	2x	gen	apart from, without
ἄχρι(ς)	49x (44x as prep.)	gen	until, as far as
ἐγγύς	31x (12x as prep.)	gen, dat	near, close to
ἐκτός	8x (4x as prep.)	gen	outside, except
ἔμπροσθεν	48x (44x as prep.)	gen	in front of, before, in the presence of
ἔναντι	2x	gen	in front of, before, in the judgment of
ἐναντίον	8x (5x as prep.)	gen	before, in the judgment of
ἕνεκα, ἕνεκεν, εἵνεκεν	26x	gen	because of, for the sake of
ἐντός	2x (1x as prep.)	gen	within, among
ἐνώπιον	94x	gen	before, in the sight of, in the judgment of
ἔξω	63x (19x as prep.)	gen	outside, out of
ἔξωθεν	13x (3x as prep.)	gen	outside, from outside
ἐπάνω	19x (16x as prep.)	gen	above, over, on, superior to
ἐπέκεινα	1x	gen	at a more advanced point, beyond, farther on
ἔσω	9x (1x as prep.)	gen	inside
ἕως	146x (90x as prep.)	gen	until, to, up to, as far as
κατέναντι	8x (7x as prep.)	gen	opposite, in the judgment of, before
κατενώπιον	3x	gen	in the presence of, in the judgment of, before
κυκλόθεν	3x (1x as prep.)	gen	in a circle, around
κύκλῳ	8x (3x as prep.)	gen	around
μέσον	58x (1x as prep.)	gen	in the middle of
μεταξύ	9x (7x as prep.)	gen	between, among
μέχρι(ς)	17x (16x as prep.)	gen	as far as, to the point of, up to, until
ὄπισθεν	7x (2x as prep.)	gen	after, behind
ὀπίσω	35x (26x as prep.)	gen	behind, after, following
ὀψέ	3x (1x as prep.)	gen	after

IMPROPER PREPOSITIONS (CONTINUED)			
PREPOSITION		CASE OF OBJECT	GLOSSES
παραπλήσιον	1x	gen	alongside, near, close to
παρεκτός	3x (2x as prep.)	gen	apart from, except for
πέραν	23x (15x as prep.)	gen	beyond, across from, on the other side
πλήν	31x (4x as prep.)	gen	except, only, apart from
πλησίον	17x (1x as prep.)	gen	near, close by
ὑπεράνω	3x	gen	far above
ὑπερέκεινα	1x	gen	beyond
ὑπερεκπερισσοῦ	3x (1x as prep.)	gen	far beyond
ὑποκάτω	11x	gen	beneath, under, below
χάριν	9x	gen	because of, for the sake of, on behalf of
χωρίς	41x (40x as prep.)	gen	without, apart from

GUIDED PRACTICE: MARK 10:1–16 (NA28)

10:1 Καὶ ἐκεῖθεν ἀναστὰς ἔρχεται εἰς τὰ ὅρια τῆς Ἰουδαίας [καὶ] πέραν τοῦ Ἰορδάνου, καὶ
συμπορεύονται πάλιν ὄχλοι πρὸς αὐτόν, καὶ ὡς εἰώθει πάλιν ἐδίδασκεν αὐτούς.

2 Καὶ προσελθόντες Φαρισαῖοι ἐπηρώτων αὐτὸν εἰ ἔξεστιν ἀνδρὶ γυναῖκα ἀπολῦσαι,
πειράζοντες αὐτόν. 3 ὁ δὲ ἀποκριθεὶς εἶπεν αὐτοῖς· τί ὑμῖν ἐνετείλατο Μωϋσῆς; 4 οἱ δὲ εἶπαν·
ἐπέτρεψεν Μωϋσῆς βιβλίον ἀποστασίου γράψαι καὶ ἀπολῦσαι. 5 ὁ δὲ Ἰησοῦς εἶπεν αὐτοῖς·
πρὸς τὴν σκληροκαρδίαν ὑμῶν ἔγραψεν ὑμῖν τὴν ἐντολὴν ταύτην. 6 ἀπὸ δὲ ἀρχῆς κτίσεως
ἄρσεν καὶ θῆλυ ἐποίησεν αὐτούς· 7 ἕνεκεν τούτου καταλείψει ἄνθρωπος τὸν πατέρα αὐτοῦ
καὶ τὴν μητέρα [καὶ προσκολληθήσεται πρὸς τὴν γυναῖκα αὐτοῦ,][7] 8 καὶ ἔσονται οἱ δύο εἰς
σάρκα μίαν· ὥστε οὐκέτι εἰσὶν δύο ἀλλὰ μία σάρξ. 9 ὃ οὖν ὁ θεὸς συνέζευξεν ἄνθρωπος μὴ
χωριζέτω.

[7] This phrase marked off in brackets will be considered in chapter 12 on textual criticism. Please note in the answer key below that the CSB does not translate this phrase because it is unlikely to be authentic.

[10] Καὶ εἰς τὴν οἰκίαν πάλιν οἱ μαθηταὶ περὶ τούτου ἐπηρώτων αὐτόν. [11] καὶ λέγει αὐτοῖς·
ὃς ἂν ἀπολύσῃ τὴν γυναῖκα αὐτοῦ καὶ γαμήσῃ ἄλλην μοιχᾶται ἐπ' αὐτήν· [12] καὶ ἐὰν αὐτὴ
ἀπολύσασα τὸν ἄνδρα αὐτῆς γαμήσῃ ἄλλον μοιχᾶται.

[13] Καὶ προσέφερον αὐτῷ παιδία ἵνα αὐτῶν ἅψηται· οἱ δὲ μαθηταὶ ἐπετίμησαν αὐτοῖς.
[14] ἰδὼν δὲ ὁ Ἰησοῦς ἠγανάκτησεν καὶ εἶπεν αὐτοῖς· ἄφετε τὰ παιδία ἔρχεσθαι πρός με, μὴ
κωλύετε αὐτά, τῶν γὰρ τοιούτων ἐστὶν ἡ βασιλεία τοῦ θεοῦ. [15] ἀμὴν λέγω ὑμῖν, ὃς ἂν μὴ
δέξηται τὴν βασιλείαν τοῦ θεοῦ ὡς παιδίον, οὐ μὴ εἰσέλθῃ εἰς αὐτήν. [16] καὶ ἐναγκαλισάμενος
αὐτὰ κατευλόγει τιθεὶς τὰς χεῖρας ἐπ' αὐτά.

VOCABULARY AIDS (WORDS 26X TO 50X)

10:1 **Ἰουδαία** *Judea* (43x)
10:2 **ἔξεστιν** *it is lawful* (31x)
10:2 **πειράζω** *to tempt* (43x)
10:4 **βιβλίον** *book, document* (38x)
10:11, 12 **γαμέω** *to marry* (28x)
10:13 **ἅπτω** *to touch* (39x)
10:13 **ἐπιτιμάω** *to rebuke; warn* (29x)
10:14 **κωλύω** *to hinder* (26x)

VOCABULARY AIDS (25X OR LESS)

10:1 **ὅριον** *region; boundary; district* (14x)
10:1 **πέραν** *on the other side; other side* (23x)
10:1 **Ἰορδάνης** *Jordan* (15x)
10:1 **συμπορεύομαι** *to come together, go along with* (4x)
10:1 **εἴωθα** *to be accustomed* (5x)
10:3 **ἐντέλλω** *to command* (15x)
10:4 **ἀποστάσιον** *certificate of divorce, of divorce* (3x)
10:4 **ἐπιτρέπω** *allow* (18x)
10:5 **σκληροκαρδία** *hardness of heart; obstinacy* (5x)
10:6 **ἄρσην** *male* (9x)
10:6 **κτίσις** *creation* (19x)
10:6 **θῆλυς** *female* (5x)
10:7 **ἕνεκεν** *on account of, for this reason* (24x)
10:7 **καταλείπω** *to leave* (24x)
10:7 **προσκολλάω** *to join* (2x)
10:9 **συζεύγνυμι** *to join together* (2x)
10:9 **χωρίζω** *to separate, divide* (14x)
10:11, 12 **μοιχάω** *to commit adultery [with]* (4x)
10:14 **ἀγανακτέω** *to be indignant* (9x)
10:16 **ἐναγκαλίζομαι** *to take into one's arms* (2x)
10:16 **κατευλογέω** *to bless* (1x)

EXERCISE

I. Provide your translation under the Greek text above.

II. Exegetical notes and questions: read the bullet points and answer the questions below.

Verse-by-Verse Questions

10:1

a) Συμπορεύονται is a 3rd plural present middle indicative. How should this participle be classified syntactically?

10:2

b) How should εἰ be translated in the context?

c) How should πειράζοντες (nominative plural masculine present active participle) be classified syntactically?

10:4

- The Pharisees are referring to Deuteronomy 24:1–4, which says, "If a man marries a woman, but she becomes displeasing to him because he finds something indecent about her, he may write her a divorce certificate, hand it to her, and send her away from his house. If after leaving his house she goes and becomes another man's wife, and the second man hates her, writes her a divorce certificate, hands it to her, and sends her away from his house or if he dies, the first husband who sent her away may not marry her again after she has been defiled, because that would be detestable to the Lord. You must not bring guilt on the land the Lord your God is giving you as an inheritance."

10:5

d) Why is δέ used here instead of καί?

10:6

- The phrase ἄρσεν καὶ θῆλυ is part of a quotation from Genesis 1:27 (LXX). They are more technical than the normal words for man and woman. They are also more archaic and are only used in the New Testament when either quoting or referencing Genesis 1:27. This fact attests to the influence of the Greek translation of the Old Testament among the earliest followers of Jesus in the first century.

10:8

e) How is ὥστε functioning syntactically in this sentence?

10:11

- The phrase ἐπ' αὐτήν has been understood multiple ways, with the rendering "against her" representing the view of many scholars and English translations. It has also been understood as "with her," more literally as "upon her," or "going after her." The idea behind these latter options is that the second marriage is adultery because of the act of going after the second wife. "Against" is not a normal rendering for the preposition ἐπί, but in light of the similar usage in 3:24–26 and 13:8, 12, what Mark intends to convey here is probably "against her," i.e., against the first wife.

10:12

f) What class is the conditional clause ἐὰν αὐτὴ ἀπολύσασα τὸν ἄνδρα αὐτῆς γαμήσῃ ἄλλον?

10:14

g) How should the genitive τοιούτων be classified syntactically?

Additional Questions

h) How does this radical teaching on marriage (10:1–12) relate to the topic of discipleship in the Gospel of Mark?

i) How does Jesus's teaching about children (10:13–16) relate to the theme of discipleship in Mark's Gospel?

Short Summary and Contextual Impact

III. Summarize the main idea of the passage and then discuss how it fits into the surrounding narrative.

Parsing and Classification

IV. Circle the future indicatives and underline the prepositional phrases and parse them below. Then classify each one according to the categories given in the grammar review above. For the prepositional phrases, please describe how the prepositional phrase functions in the sentence (specific categories are not listed in the grammar review above). To get an idea about how to specifically classify prepositional phrases, quickly scan through the corresponding answer key (pp. 136-37 below) in advance. Provide a brief explanation for your decision.

Future Indicatives

10:7

1)

2)

10:8

1)

Prepositional Phrases

10:1

1)

2)

3)

10:5

1)

10:6

1)

10:7

1)

2)

10:8

1)

10:10

1)

2)

10:11

1)

10:14

1)

10:15

1)

10:16

1)

ANSWER KEY

I. Translation and explanations

10:1 He set out from there and went to the region of Judea and across the Jordan. Then crowds con-
verged on him again, and as was his custom he taught them again.
2 Some Pharisees came to test him, asking, "Is it lawful for a man to divorce his wife?"
3 He replied to them, "What did Moses command you?"
4 They said, "Moses permitted us to write divorce papers and send her away."[8]
5 But Jesus told them, "He wrote this command for you because of the hardness of your hearts.
6 But from the beginning of creation God made them male and female. 7 For this reason a man will
leave his father and mother 8 and the two will become one flesh. So they are no longer two, but one
flesh. 9 Therefore what God has joined together, let no one separate."[9]
10 When they were in the house again, the disciples questioned[10] him about this matter. 11 He said
to them, "Whoever divorces his wife and marries another commits adultery against her. 12 Also, if
she divorces her husband and marries another, she commits adultery."
13 People were bringing little children to him in order that he might touch them, but the disciples
rebuked them. 14 When Jesus saw it, he was indignant[11] and said to them, "Let the little children
come to me. Don't stop them, because the kingdom of God belongs to such as these. 15 Truly I tell
you, whoever does not receive the kingdom of God like a little child will never enter it." 16 After
taking them in his arms, he laid his hands on them and blessed[12] them.

II. Answers to exegetical questions

Verse-by-verse questions

a) In 10:1, συμπορεύονται should be classified as a historical present.

b) In 10:2, it is difficult to decide whether εἰ should be translated as "if" or as "whether" (thus viewed as introducing an indirect question) or not translated (thus seen as a marker for a direct question). More likely, it is introducing an indirect question and should, therefore, be translated as "if" or "whether," partly because the participial construction ("in order to test him") follows later in v. 2, which certainly cannot be part of a direct discourse.

c) In 10:2, the participle πειράζοντες is communicating the *purpose* for which the Pharisees were speaking with Jesus.

---

[8] Or "and to let her go."

[9] Or "man must not separate." Χωριζέτω is a 3rd person imperative. The translation "man must not separate" communicates the imperatival force.

[10] Literally, "were asking." Ἐπηρώτων is an imperfect verb with an imperfective aspect. The CSB somewhat obscures the imperfective aspect of this verb.

[11] Or "he became indignant." This aorist is inceptive, meaning that Jesus *became* indignant, not that he was already indignant by this point in the narrative.

[12] Here in 10:16, "blessed" is the translation of κατευλόγει, which is the imperfect active indicative third-person singular form of the verb κατευλογέω. The present-tense form has precisely the same spelling as this imperfect-tense form, but the former has an accent (circumflex) over the last syllable instead.

d) In 10:5, δέ is used instead of καί given that the former is able to mark a change in speaker from v. 4 to v. 5 (from the Pharisees in v. 4 to Jesus in v. 5).[13]

e) In 10:8, ὥστε introduces a result clause. This result clause draws an inference drawn from the OT passages just quoted, i.e., Gen 1:27 and 2:24.[14]

f) In 10:12, this clause presents a 3rd class condition. As a brief reminder, in 3rd class conditional clauses "the event in the protasis is presented somewhat more hypothetically by the speaker. It is more tentative than the 1st class conditional."[15]

g) In 10:14, the genitive τοιούτων is describing *possession.*

Additional Questions

h) In these verses (10:1–12), the radically self-giving nature of discipleship is extended to marriage. If you want to be married as a disciple of Jesus, you must give up your life, your desires, your self-centered passions and be wholly committed to your spouse until death.[16]

i) In these verses (10:13–16), Jesus teaches that the disciples should not hinder any people from coming to him, even if they are "insignificant" in the eyes of the world, such as children in first-century Judaism. In fact, not only should the disciples *welcome* children, but they must emulate their attitude and give up earthly acclaim and riches to follow Jesus in humble faith.

III. Short Summary and Contextual Impact

Summary: Since God created man and woman to be one flesh in the covenant of marriage, discipleship implies a renunciation of divorce and commitment to one's spouse. To divorce and remarry, unless on biblical grounds, would constitute adultery.[17] Children, who represent those who have no earthly status or riches and do not care for what the world values, are to be welcomed and even emulated by the disciples, who must give up earthly acclaim and follow the way of Jesus.

Contextual impact: These short passages (10:1–12 and 10:13–16) each present an additional dimension of renouncing self and embracing Jesus and his way. It does not seem like a coincidence that the episode on divorce and remarriage (10:1–12) comes right after Jesus's warning on "temptations to sin." Adultery is the sundering of a union that God made, and this sundering is the result of yielding to a temptation to sin and has a destructive communal effect for family and even beyond. In addition, the attitude of a disciple is represented in children, who have no earthly status and do not pursue what the world seeks. To welcome children with gladness and to see in them an example of what it means to follow Jesus is paramount to discipleship, for "whoever does not receive the kingdom of God like a child will never enter it" (10:15)!

---

[13] Rodney J. Decker, *Mark 9–16: A Handbook on the Greek Text*, ed. Martin M. Culy, Baylor Handbook on the Greek New Testament (Waco: Baylor University Press, 2014), 42.

[14] Cf. Decker, 43.

[15] Köstenberger, Merkle, and Plummer, *Going Deeper with New Testament Greek*, 448.

[16] Robert H. Stein, *Mark*, Baker Exegetical Commentary on the New Testament (Grand Rapids: Baker Academic, 2008), 459; cf. Mark L. Strauss, *Mark*, Zondervan Exegetical Commentary on the New Testament (Grand Rapids: Zondervan, 2014), 427–28.

[17] For a stimulating study on divorce and remarriage, see David Instone-Brewer, *Divorce and Remarriage in the Bible: The Social and Literary Context* (Grand Rapids: Eerdmans, 2002).

IV. Parsing and Classification of the Key Grammatical Concepts for the Lesson: Future Indicatives and Prepositions

Future Indicatives

10:7

1) καταλείψει: καταλείπω; 3 sg fut act ind; *leave*, *leave behind*
   - <u>*Imperatival or Gnomic*</u>: It is most likely imperatival, since Jesus draws a mandatory principle from this passage, not simply a gnomic statement.

2) προσκολληθήσεται: προσκολλάω; 3 sg fut pass ind; *adhere to closely*, *join*
   - <u>*Imperatival or Gnomic*</u>: It is most likely imperatival, since Jesus draws a mandatory principle from this passage, not simply a gnomic statement.

10:8

1) ἔσονται: εἰμί; 3 plur fut mid ind; *to be*, *is*
   - <u>*Imperatival or Gnomic*</u>: It is most likely imperatival, since Jesus draws a mandatory principle from this passage, not simply a gnomic statement.

Prepositional Phrases

10:1

1) εἰς τὰ ὅρια τῆς Ἰουδαίας: εἰς; acc; *into*, *in*, *at*
   - <u>*Location*</u>: It is describing the location that Jesus traveled to.

2) πέραν τοῦ Ἰορδάνου: πέραν; gen; *beyond*, *across from*, *on the other side*
   - <u>*Location*</u>: It is describing the location that Jesus traveled to.

3) πρὸς αὐτόν; πρός; gen, dat, acc; *for*, *at*, *to*
   - <u>*Location*</u>: It is describing the crowds approaching where Jesus was.

10:5

1) πρὸς τὴν σκληροκαρδίαν ὑμῶν; πρός; gen, dat, acc; *for*, *at*, *to*
   - <u>*Purpose*</u>: It is communicating the *purpose* for which Moses wrote the command in Deuteronomy 24, namely, as a *concession* for the hard heartedness of mankind. However, Decker argues that it should be understood as "reference," i.e., "with reference to hard-heartedness, (i.e., because of) your perversity."[18] Both views are similar in meaning, though we believe purpose fits the context slightly better.

10:6

1) ἀπὸ δὲ ἀρχῆς κτίσεως; ἀπό; gen; *from*, *of*
   - <u>*Temporal*</u>: It is describing God's creating work at the beginning of time.

---

[18] Decker, *Mark 9–16*, 42.

10:7

1) ἕνεκεν τούτου; ἕνεκα; gen; *because of, for the sake of*
   - <u>*Causal*</u>: It is describing the causal relationship between God's creation design and the implications of that design.

2) πρὸς τὴν γυναῖκα αὐτοῦ; πρός; gen, dat, acc; *for, at, to*
   - <u>*Association*</u>: It is describing the relationship between husband and wife.

10:8

1) εἰς σάρκα μίαν; εἰς; acc; *into, in, at*
   - Although εἰς could function referentially ("the two will be one with respect to the flesh"), more than likely it is a literal translation of the underlying Hebrew in Genesis 1:27. It is functioning as a replacement for a predicate nominative, which would render the translation, "The two will become one flesh."

10:10

1) εἰς τὴν οἰκίαν; εἰς; acc; *into, in, at*
   - <u>*Location*</u>: It is describing where the disciples questioned Jesus.

2) περὶ τούτου; περί; gen, acc; *concerning, around*
   - <u>*Reference*</u>: It is referring back to the entire dialogue between Jesus and the Pharisees and Jesus's conclusion, i.e., the disciples are asking Jesus about what he had just taught.

10:11

1) ἐπ' αὐτήν; ἐπί; gen, dat, acc; *on, upon, against*
   - <u>*Respect*</u>: It is describing an action with regard to the first wife. As Decker helpfully states, "The antecedent of αὐτήν is most likely the first wife ('against her'), particularly since the reference to the same person likely continues in v. 12 (αὐτή)."[19] When used in the context of a personal relationship, ἐπί + accusative could have a nuance of hostility ("against").

10:14

1) πρός με; πρός; gen, dat, acc; *for, at, to*
   - <u>*Extension*</u>: It is functioning as a preposition of *extension*, which is clear from the preceding use of ἔρχεσθαι.

10:15

1) εἰς αὐτήν; εἰς; acc; *into, in, at*
   - <u>*Extension*</u>: It is functioning as a preposition of *extension*, which is clear from the preceding use of εἰσέλθῃ.

10:16

1) ἐπ' αὐτά; ἐπί; gen, dat, acc; *on, upon, against*
   - <u>*Location*</u>: It is describing the *location* of τὰς χεῖρας. This is clear from the preceding use of τιθεὶς.

---

[19] Decker, 45.

Now, rewrite your translation of the entire passage in the GUIDED PRACTICE section, reflecting the above exegetical procedure.

REFERENCES

Danker, Frederick William, et al. *A Greek-English Lexicon of the New Testament and other Early Christian Literature*. 3rd ed. Chicago: University of Chicago Press, 2000.

Decker, Rodney J. *Mark 9–16: A Handbook on the Greek Text*. Ed. Martin M. Culy. Baylor Handbook on the Greek New Testament. Waco: Baylor University Press, 2014.

France, R. T. *The Gospel of Mark*. The New International Greek Testament Commentary. Grand Rapids: Eerdmans, 2002.

Garland, David E. *A Theology of Mark's Gospel: Good News about Jesus the Messiah, the Son of God*. Biblical Theology of the New Testament. Grand Rapids: Zondervan, 2015.

Instone-Brewer, David. *Divorce and Remarriage in the Bible: The Social and Literary Context*. Grand Rapids: Eerdmans, 2002.

Köstenberger, Andreas J., Benjamin L. Merkle, and Robert L. Plummer. *Going Deeper with New Testament Greek: An Intermediate Study of the Grammar and Syntax of the New Testament*. Rev. ed. Nashville: B&H Academic, 2020.

Robertson, A.T. *A Grammar of the Greek New Testament in the Light of Historical Research*. Logos Bible Software, 2006.

Stein, Robert H. *Mark*. Baker Exegetical Commentary on the New Testament. Grand Rapids, MI: Baker Academic, 2008.

Strauss, Mark L. *Mark*. Zondervan Exegetical Commentary on the New Testament. Grand Rapids: Zondervan, 2014.

Wallace, Daniel B. *Greek Grammar Beyond the Basics: An Exegetical Syntax of the New Testament*. Grand Rapids: Zondervan, 1996.

Williams, Joel. *Mark*. Ed. Andreas J. Köstenberger and Robert W. Yarbrough. Exegetical Guide to the Greek New Testament. Nashville: B&H Academic, 2020.

CHAPTER NINE

////////////////

MARK 10:17–31

WITH ATTENTION TO NOMINATIVES AND ADJECTIVES

GRAMMAR REVIEW:

Nominatives

Definition and Description

The nominative case specifies something with a name or designation. This differs from the genitive or dative cases which specify relationships.[1] Köstenberger, Merkle, and Plummer say the nominative case usually specifies an object or person as the subject.[2] Wallace broadens this idea by explaining that the nominative case will frequently name the main topic, but he notes that the main topic can be more than just a single word (e.g., the syntactical or grammatical subject of the sentence).[3]

Example: The student who studies diligently will succeed.

The syntactical (grammatical) subject is *the student* while the topic (semantic or logical subject) is *the student who studies diligently*. In some cases, the syntactical subject can completely match the semantic (or logical) subject; the distinction of the syntactical and semantic subject helps avoid the notion that the nominative is only used to identify the subject of a sentence.[4]

---

[1] David L. Mathewson and Elodie B. Emig, *Intermediate Greek Grammar: Syntax for Students of the New Testament* (Grand Rapids: Baker Academic, 2016), 3.

[2] Andreas J. Köstenberger, Benjamin L. Merkle, and Robert L. Plummer, *Going Deeper with New Testament Greek: An Intermediate Study of the Grammar and Syntax of the New Testament*, rev. ed. (Nashville: B&H Academic, 2020), 72.

[3] Daniel B. Wallace, *Greek Grammar Beyond the Basics: An Exegetical Syntax of the New Testament* (Grand Rapids: Zondervan, 1996), 37.

[4] Mathewson and Emig do not define the nominative in terms of a subject or main topic but instead define the nominative with a more generalized definition of simply specifying a nominal (naming) idea. They use this broad definition in light of the many functions the nominative can take on through discourse. Mathewson and Emig, *Intermediate Greek Grammar*, 3.

Categories and Examples[5]

MAJOR USES OF THE NOMINATIVE		
SUBJECT	The subject of a finite verb.	**Ἰωάννης** μαρτυρεῖ περὶ αὐτοῦ ("**John** testified about Him" John 1:15 NASB).
PREDICATE NOMINATIVE	Provides further information about the subject as a complement of a copulative verb (expressing a state of being).	ὁ λόγος **σὰρξ** ἐγένετο ("The Word became **flesh**" John 1:14).
APPOSITION	Further explains the subject by clarification, description, or identification.	Παῦλος **δοῦλος** Χριστοῦ Ἰησοῦ ("Paul, **a servant** of Christ Jesus" Rom 1:1).
OTHER USES OF THE NOMINATIVE		
ADDRESS	Used in the place of a vocative in direct address.	**Οἱ ἄνδρες**, ἀγαπᾶτε τὰς γυναῖκας ("**Husbands**, love your wives" Eph 5:25).
APPELLATION	Used in conjunction with an address or title where a case other than the nominative would be expected.	ὑμεῖς φωνεῖτέ με **ὁ διδάσκαλος** ("You call me **Teacher**" John 13:13).
ABSOLUTE	Grammatically independent use of the nominative in introductory material (such as titles, headings, salutations, or addresses).	**Παῦλος** δοῦλος θεοῦ ("**Paul**, a servant of God" Titus 1:1).
HANGING NOMINATIVE	The logical rather than syntactical subject at the beginning of a sentence.	**Ὁ νικῶν** ποιήσω αὐτὸν στῦλον ἐν τῷ ναῷ τοῦ θεοῦ μου ("**The one who conquers**, I will make him a pillar in the temple of my God" Rev 3:12 ESV).

Adjectives

Definition and Description

Adjectives primarily describe or modify a noun or substantive through agreement in case, number, and gender with the substantive or noun to which they are referring. Adjectives can also function as substantives and as adverbs. Like nouns, adjectives also occur in all three declensions.

According to Köstenberger, Merkle, and Plummer, the general use of the adjective can be broken into four major categories: "(1) predicate (modifying a copulative or 'being' verb), (2) attributive (this is the function we typically associate with an adjective), (3) substantival (functioning as a noun), and (4) adverbial (used like an adverb)."[6] The other uses outside of these major categories will be reviewed in the section below.

[5] Köstenberger, Merkle, and Plummer, *Going Deeper with New Testament Greek,* 72.
[6] Köstenberger, Merkle, and Plummer, 165.

Categories and Examples[7]

GENERAL USE OF THE ADJECTIVE[8]		
PREDICATE	An adjective that predicates a certain quality to the subject, frequently by way of a copulative (linking) verb.	***With Article***: **πιστὸς** ὁ θεός ("God is **faithful**" 1 Cor 1:9).
		Without Article: **μακάριος** ἀνὴρ οὗ οὐ μὴ λογίσηται κύριος ἁμαρτίαν ("**blessed** is the man against whom the Lord will not count his sin" Rom 4:8 ESV)
ATTRIBUTIVE	An adjective that ascribes a particular quality to a noun or substantive.	***With Article***: ὁ **ἀληθινὸς** θεός ("the **true** God" 1 John 5:20).
		Without Article: **πολλῶν** στρουθίων διαφέρετε ὑμεῖς ("you are worth more than **many** sparrows" Matt 10:31).
SUBSTANTIVAL	The adjective normally takes on the characteristics of a noun (e.g., the article) and functions as a noun or substantive in a given phrase.	σὺ εἶ **ὁ ἅγιος** ("You are **the Holy One**" John 6:69 NASB).
ADVERBIAL	Use of an adjective (usually in the neuter accusative singular) to modify a verb rather than noun.	Καὶ προελθὼν **μικρὸν** ἔπεσεν ἐπὶ πρόσωπον αὐτοῦ ("Going **a little farther**, he fell facedown" Matt 26:39).
USE OF THE ADJECTIVE TO SHOW KIND/DEGREE[9]		
POSITIVE	Focuses on the properties of a noun in terms of kind rather than degree.	ὁ νόμος **πνευματικός** ἐστιν ("the law is **spiritual**" Rom 7:14).
COMPARATIVE	Focuses on the properties of a noun in terms of degree rather than kind.	ἔρχεται ὁ **ἰσχυρότερός** μου ὀπίσω μου ("One who is **more powerful** than I am is coming after me" Mark 1:7).
SUPERLATIVE	Compares the qualities of three or more entities.	τί ἐμοὶ καὶ σοί, Ἰησοῦ υἱὲ τοῦ θεοῦ τοῦ **ὑψίστου**; ("What do you have to do with me, Jesus, Son of the **Most High** God?" Luke 8:28).
ELATIVE	Use of the comparative or superlative adjective to describe an intensification of the positive notion.	***Comparative for Elative***: **σπουδαιότερος** . . . ἐξῆλθεν ("[he] **being very diligent**, went out" 2 Cor 8:17).
		Superlative for Elative: ὄχλος **πλεῖστος** ("a **very large** crowd" Mark 4:1).

[7] Köstenberger, Merkle, and Plummer, 179–80.
[8] In the parsing and classification section below, we refer to the general use of the adjective as the "structure" of the adjective.
[9] In the parsing and classification section below, we refer to the use of the adjective to show kind/degree as the "function" of the adjective.

<table>
<tr><th colspan="3">GENERAL USE OF THE ADJECTIVE (CONTINUED)</th></tr>
<tr><td rowspan="3">SPECIAL CASES</td><td rowspan="3">Instances where popular speech and/or Semitic influence affected the use of the positive, comparative, and superlative for one another.</td><td>Positive for Comparative: καλόν σοί ἐστιν ("It is better for you" Matt 18:8).</td></tr>
<tr><td>Positive for Superlative: ἡ μεγάλη καὶ πρώτη ἐντολή ("the greatest and most important command" Matt 22:38).</td></tr>
<tr><td>Comparative for Superlative: μείζων δὲ τούτων ἡ ἀγάπη ("but the greatest of these is love" 1 Cor 13:13).</td></tr>
</table>

GUIDED PRACTICE: MARK 10:17–31 (NA[28])

10:17 Καὶ ἐκπορευομένου αὐτοῦ εἰς ὁδὸν προσδραμὼν εἷς καὶ γονυπετήσας αὐτὸν ἐπηρώτα
αὐτόν· διδάσκαλε ἀγαθέ, τί ποιήσω ἵνα ζωὴν αἰώνιον κληρονομήσω; 18 ὁ δὲ Ἰησοῦς εἶπεν
αὐτῷ· τί με λέγεις ἀγαθόν; οὐδεὶς ἀγαθὸς εἰ μὴ εἷς ὁ θεός. 19 τὰς ἐντολὰς οἶδας· μὴ φονεύσῃς,
μὴ μοιχεύσῃς, μὴ κλέψῃς, μὴ ψευδομαρτυρήσῃς, μὴ ἀποστερήσῃς, τίμα τὸν πατέρα σου καὶ
τὴν μητέρα. 20 ὁ δὲ ἔφη αὐτῷ· διδάσκαλε, ταῦτα πάντα ἐφυλαξάμην ἐκ νεότητός μου. 21 Ὁ
δὲ Ἰησοῦς ἐμβλέψας αὐτῷ ἠγάπησεν αὐτὸν καὶ εἶπεν αὐτῷ· ἕν σε ὑστερεῖ· ὕπαγε, ὅσα ἔχεις
πώλησον καὶ δὸς [τοῖς] πτωχοῖς, καὶ ἕξεις θησαυρὸν ἐν οὐρανῷ, καὶ δεῦρο ἀκολούθει μοι.
22 ὁ δὲ στυγνάσας ἐπὶ τῷ λόγῳ ἀπῆλθεν λυπούμενος· ἦν γὰρ ἔχων κτήματα πολλά.

23 Καὶ περιβλεψάμενος ὁ Ἰησοῦς λέγει τοῖς μαθηταῖς αὐτοῦ· πῶς δυσκόλως οἱ τὰ χρήματα
ἔχοντες εἰς τὴν βασιλείαν τοῦ θεοῦ εἰσελεύσονται. 24 Οἱ δὲ μαθηταὶ ἐθαμβοῦντο ἐπὶ τοῖς
λόγοις αὐτοῦ. ὁ δὲ Ἰησοῦς πάλιν ἀποκριθεὶς λέγει αὐτοῖς· τέκνα, πῶς δύσκολόν ἐστιν εἰς

τὴν βασιλείαν τοῦ θεοῦ εἰσελθεῖν· 25 εὐκοπώτερόν ἐστιν κάμηλον διὰ [τῆς] τρυμαλιᾶς
[τῆς] ῥαφίδος διελθεῖν ἢ πλούσιον εἰς τὴν βασιλείαν τοῦ θεοῦ εἰσελθεῖν. 26 οἱ δὲ περισσῶς
ἐξεπλήσσοντο λέγοντες πρὸς ἑαυτούς· καὶ τίς δύναται σωθῆναι; 27 ἐμβλέψας αὐτοῖς ὁ Ἰησοῦς
λέγει· παρὰ ἀνθρώποις ἀδύνατον, ἀλλ᾽ οὐ παρὰ θεῷ· πάντα γὰρ δυνατὰ παρὰ τῷ θεῷ.

28 Ἤρξατο λέγειν ὁ Πέτρος αὐτῷ· ἰδοὺ ἡμεῖς ἀφήκαμεν πάντα καὶ ἠκολουθήκαμέν σοι.
29 ἔφη ὁ Ἰησοῦς· ἀμὴν λέγω ὑμῖν, οὐδείς ἐστιν ὃς ἀφῆκεν οἰκίαν ἢ ἀδελφοὺς ἢ ἀδελφὰς ἢ
μητέρα ἢ πατέρα ἢ τέκνα ἢ ἀγροὺς ἕνεκεν ἐμοῦ καὶ ἕνεκεν τοῦ εὐαγγελίου, 30 ἐὰν μὴ λάβῃ
ἑκατονταπλασίονα νῦν ἐν τῷ καιρῷ τούτῳ οἰκίας καὶ ἀδελφοὺς καὶ ἀδελφὰς καὶ μητέρας
καὶ τέκνα καὶ ἀγροὺς μετὰ διωγμῶν, καὶ ἐν τῷ αἰῶνι τῷ ἐρχομένῳ ζωὴν αἰώνιον. 31 πολλοὶ
δὲ ἔσονται πρῶτοι ἔσχατοι καὶ [οἱ] ἔσχατοι πρῶτοι.

VOCABULARY AIDS (WORDS 26X TO 50X)

10:17 **ἐκπορεύομαι** *to go, proceed, depart* (33x)
10:20 **φυλάσσω** *to keep, observe, beware, guard, save* (31x)
10:21 **πτωχός** *poor, beggar, poor man, beggarly* (34x)
10:22 **λυπέω** *to be sorrowful, grieve, make sorry, offend* (26x)
10:25 **διέρχομαι** (aorist: διῆλθον) *to pass (through), go (over, through)* (41x)
10:25 **πλούσιος** *rich, wealthy* (28x)
10:27 **δυνατός** *possible, able, mighty, strong, power, capable* (32x)
10:29, 30 **ἀδελφή** *sister* (26x)
10:29, 30 **ἀγρός** *field, country, land, farm, piece of ground* (37x)

VOCABULARY AIDS (WORDS 25X OR LESS)

10:17 **προστρέχω** (aorist: προσέδραμον) *to run to, run, run out to* (3x)
10:17 **γονυπετέω** *to kneel down to, bow the knee, kneel to* (4x)
10:17 **κληρονομέω** *to inherit, become heir, obtain by inheritance* (18x)
10:19 **φονεύω** *to kill, do murder, slay* (12x)
10:19 **μοιχεύω** *to commit adultery, be in adultery* (15x)
10:19 **κλέπτω** *to steal* (13x)
10:19 **ψευδομαρτυρέω** *to bear false witness* (5x)
10:19 **ἀποστερέω** *to defraud, keep back by fraud* (6x)
10:19 **τιμάω** *to honor, respect, value* (21x)
10:20 **νεότης** *youth* (4x)
10:21, 27 **ἐμβλέπω** *to behold, look upon, see, gaze up, be able to see* (11x)
10:21 **ὑστερέω** *to lack, be behind, come short, fail, be destitute* (15x)
10:21 **πωλέω** *to sell, am sold* (22x)
10:21 **θησαυρός** *treasure, repository, storehouse* (17x)
10:21 **δεῦρο** *to come, come hither, hitherto* (9x)
10:22 **στυγνάζω** *to be shocked, sad, appalled* (2x)
10:22 **κτῆμα** *possession* (4x)
10:23 **περιβλέπω** *to look around, look round about upon* (7x)
10:23 **δυσκόλως** *with difficulty, hardly* (3x)
10:23 **χρῆμα** *money, riches* (6x)
10:24 **θαμβέω** *to be amazed, astonished* (3x)
10:24 **δύσκολος** *hard, difficult* (1x)
10:25 **εὔκοπος** *easy* (7x)
10:25 **κάμηλος** *camel* (6x)
10:25 **τρυμαλιά** *eye* (2x)

10:25 **ῥαφίς** *needle* (3x)
10:26 **περισσῶς** *the more*, *out of measure*, *exceedingly* (5x)
10:26 **ἐκπλήσσω** *to be astonished*, *amazed* (13x)
10:27 **ἀδύνατος** *impossible*, *impotent*, *could not do*, *weak* (10x)
10:30 **ἑκατονταπλασίων** *hundredfold* (2x)
10:30 **διωγμός** *persecution* (10x)

EXERCISE

I. Provide your translation under the Greek text above.

II. Exegetical notes and questions: read the bullet points and answer the questions below.

Verse-by-Verse Questions

10:17

a) How would you classify the participle ἐκπορευομένου? In a sentence or two, explain your classification.

- Regarding the epithet in 10:17, addressing someone with the title διδάσκαλε ἀγαθέ (both words are vocative) does not have any contemporary Jewish parallel, and it may suggest flattery.[10]
- The word εἷς is functioning as an indefinite pronoun (similar to τις) with the meaning "someone" or "a certain one."[11]

10:18

b) What is the classification of the accusative ἀγαθόν? Hint: The classification helps in translating λέγεις as "call, identify someone as."[12]

c) Mark has used multiple nominatives in relaying Jesus's response to the rich man: "No one is good except God alone." How are the nominatives οὐδείς and ἀγαθός functioning in this sentence? How would you classify the nominatives εἷς and ὁ θεός?

---

[10] R. T. France, *The Gospel of Mark: A Commentary on the Greek Text*, New International Greek Testament Commentary (Grand Rapids: Eerdmans, 2002), 401.

[11] Joel Williams, *Mark*, ed. Andreas J. Köstenberger and Robert W. Yarbrough, Exegetical Guide to the Greek New Testament (Nashville: B&H Academic, 2020), 170.

[12] Williams, 171, referencing *BDAG* 590b.

10:19

- All the commands Jesus lists (almost the latter half of the Ten Commandments) use the aorist subjunctive negated by μή (except the present imperative τίμα). Decker notes that there is no difference in meaning as compared to the LXX and Matthew, both of which use future indicatives negated by οὐ.[13]

10:20

d) Mark uses δέ to denote a shift in the speaker. How is the nominative article ὁ classified?

- The middle verb ἐφυλαξάμην is active in Matthew and Luke's accounts, but here in Mark this middle-voice verb may have a stronger focus on the rich man himself ("I kept myself from"; reflexive use of the middle verb).[14]

10:21

- The adverb δεῦρο is an adverb of place, but, in the NT, it often functions as an interjection preceding an imperative.[15]

10:22

- The participle λυπούμενος expresses the manner in which the rich man went away. This participle describing sorrow follows closely after στυγνάσας which carries a similar meaning, and they together serve to reinforce the rich man's shock and dismay.[16]

e) How is the participle ἔχων functioning in this context? Hint: the presence of the "to be" verb.

f) Relatedly, what is the verbal aspect of the periphrastic construction (a "to be" verb + a ptc) in the verse?

10:23

- The interrogative particle πῶς is normally used to introduce questions, but it can also be employed in exclamations (as is the case in this context).[17]

---

[13] Rodney J. Decker, *Mark 9–16: A Handbook on the Greek Text*, ed. Martin M. Culy, Baylor Handbook on the Greek New Testament (Waco: Baylor University Press, 2014), 51.

[14] France, *The Gospel of Mark*, 403.

[15] Decker, *Mark 9–16*, 53.

[16] Decker, 54.

[17] Williams, *Mark*, 172.

10:24

g) Note that this is the only verse in the Gospels where the disciples are referred to as τέκνα, and it may be a term of affection.[18] How is the nominative τέκνα classified?

10:25

h) How is the prepositional phrase εἰς τὴν βασιλείαν τοῦ θεοῦ functioning in the sentence?

10:26

- The passive σωθῆναι used by the disciples in their exclamation of shock is a parallel to "entering the kingdom of God" (10:23–25) and "inheriting eternal life" (10:17, 30).[19] The rhetorical question in v. 26 expects the answer to be "no one." In the first-century Jewish context, wealth was an indication of God's favor, and if it is impossible for a rich man to be saved, then there is no chance for anyone else (from the disciples' perspective).[20]

10:28

i) The nominative ἡμεῖς functioning as the subject of ἀφήκαμεν was not needed as the verb implicitly contains the subject. Why might Peter explicitly state ἡμεῖς? Look at the preceding context for clues.

10:29

- The phrase ἕνεκεν ἐμοῦ καὶ ἕνεκεν τοῦ εὐαγγελίου is a hendiadys (ἐν διὰ δυοῖν, "one by means of two") and bears a Christological significance of Jesus's divinity. Living for Jesus and living for the gospel are not two different things. They are one and the same.

10:30

- The phrase ἐὰν μὴ λάβῃ introduces an unusual third-class conditional clause as the protasis, and the apodosis is what was stated in 10:29. Most English translations render the conditional clause in 10:30 like a relative clause ("who will not . . .").

---

[18] France, *The Gospel of Mark*, 404.
[19] France, 405–6.
[20] France, 405.

Short Summary and Contextual Impact

III. Summarize the main idea of the passage and then discuss how it fits into the surrounding narrative.

Parsing and Classification

IV. Circle the nominatives (excluding participles) in the text and parse them below. Then classify each one according to the categories given in the grammar review above. Provide a brief explanation for your decisions. After finishing with the nominatives, repeat the same instructions with the adjectives but underline them instead (as for the adjectives in the nominative case, they must be included in both sections below [i.e., under Nominatives and also under Adjectives]). Classify adjectives according to both structure (e.g., predicate, attributive, substantival, or adverbial) and function (e.g., positive, comparative, superlative, elative, or special case) as applicable. Note that not every adjective will have a relevant functional category (you may supply N/A for function).

Nominatives (Excluding Participles)

10:17

1)

10:18

1)

2)

3)

4)

5)

10:20

1)

10:21

1)

2)

10:23

1)

10:24

1)

2)

3)

10:25

1)

10:26

1)

2)

10:27

1)

2)

3)

4)

10:28

1)

2)

10:29

1)

2)

3)

10:31

1)

2)

3)

4)

5)

Adjectives (Including Nominatives)

10:17

1)

2)

3)

10:18

1)

2)

3)

4)

10:20

1)

10:21

1)

2)

10:22

1)

10:24

1)

10:25

1)

2)

10:27

1)

2)

3)

10:28

1)

10:29

1)

10:30

1)

2)

10:31

1)

2)

3)

4)

5)

ANSWER KEY

I. Translation and explanations

10:17 As he was setting out on a journey, a man ran up, knelt down before him, and asked him,
"Good teacher, what must I do to inherit eternal life?"
18 "Why do you call me good?" Jesus asked him. "No one is good except God alone.[21] 19 You know
the commandments: Do not murder; do not commit adultery; do not steal; do not bear false witness; do not defraud; honor your father and mother."
20 He said to him, "Teacher, I have kept all these from my youth."
21 Looking at him, Jesus loved him and said to him, "You lack one thing:[22] Go, sell all you have
and give to the poor, and you will have treasure in heaven. Then come, follow me." 22 But he was
dismayed[23] by this demand, and he went away grieving, because he had many possessions.
23 Jesus looked around and said to his disciples, "How hard it is for those who have wealth to enter
the kingdom of God!"
24 The disciples were astonished at his words. Again Jesus said to them, "Children, how hard it is
to enter the kingdom of God! 25 It is easier for a camel to go through the eye of a needle than for a
rich person to enter the kingdom of God."
26 They were even more astonished, saying to one another, "Then who can be saved?"
27 Looking at them, Jesus said, "With man it is impossible, but not with God, because all things are
possible with God."
28 Peter began to tell him, "Look, we have left everything and followed you."
29 "Truly I tell you," Jesus said, "there is no one who has left house or brothers or sisters or mother
or father or children or fields for my sake and for the sake of the gospel, 30 who will not receive
a hundred times more, now at this time—houses, brothers and sisters, mothers and children, and
fields, with persecutions—and eternal life in the age to come. 31 But many who are first will be last,
and the last first."[24]

II. Answers to exegetical questions

Verse-by-Verse Questions

a) In 10:17, the participle ἐκπορευομένου is a genitive absolute (temporal). As a genitive absolute, it is setting up the scene for the reader by providing background information.

b) In 10:18, the adjective ἀγαθόν is functioning as a complement within a double accusative construction.

c) In 10:18, the word οὐδείς is a nominative subject and ἀγαθός is a predicate nominative. The nominative ὁ θεός is functioning appositionally to εἷς (subject of the elliptical statement: "**one** is good.").

d) In 10:20, the nominative article ὁ functions as a personal pronoun ("he"). It is the subject of ἔφη and represents Jesus's interlocutor, who was rich according to the subsequent information revealed in v. 22.

---

[21] This could also be translated as "No one is good except One, namely, God."
[22] More literally: "One thing you are lacking."
[23] This could also be translated as "shocked," "appalled," or "grieved."
[24] This could also be translated as "the last will be first."

e) In 10:22, the participle ἔχων is functioning as a periphrastic participle. The close proximity between the εἰμί verb (ἦν) and ἔχων (present participle) suggest that they together form a periphrastic construction. Note that the NASB, AV, and RSV take this participle to be substantival.[25]

f) In 10:22, ἔχων functions as a periphrastic participle. The imperfect tense (i.e., the periphrastic tense of the imperfect verb ἦν + the present participle ἔχων) has an imperfective aspect, which in this context signifies the state of the man's wealthiness that was an ongoing reality. This continuing wealth was what prevented this man from entering the kingdom of God (obtaining eternal life).

g) In 10:24, τέκνα is a form of direct address and is in the vocative case.

h) In 10:25, the prepositional phrase εἰς τὴν βασιλείαν τοῦ θεοῦ is describing location.

i) In 10:28, the nominative subject ἡμεῖς may emphasize that Peter and the disciples have left everything to follow Jesus in contrast to the rich man who did not. This response follows right after Jesus says it is impossible to enter the kingdom of God by human means. Peter and the disciples may be attempting to justify themselves in that they have abandoned all possessions and may now be able to enter the kingdom of God.

III. Short Summary and Contextual Impact

Summary: This passage as a whole (10:17–31) shows that "eternal life" (mentioned in vv. 17 and 30) is possible only in and through Jesus and, in so doing, highlights the peril of money. While on the road to Jerusalem, Jesus and his disciples encounter a wealthy man who, in combination with his asserted adherence to the Ten Commandments, appears to be a prime candidate for the kingdom of God. However, his self-claimed adherence to the Ten Commandments was not enough to prevent his desire for wealth, which eventually overrode his ability to follow Jesus and thus enter the kingdom. Jesus uses this person's failure to teach the paradoxical nature of entering the kingdom of God and the related reversal of human expectations.

Contextual Impact: Jesus continues to teach the disciples concerning the paradoxical nature of God's kingdom. In the preceding verses (10:13–16), the disciples learn that the kingdom of God belongs to those who receive it like children, who were viewed as lower-class and without rights in the first-century Jewish context. After Jesus reveals that the kingdom of God belongs to unlikely candidates (10:14), Mark reports about a highly likely candidate, from the perspective of Jesus's disciples, who has wealth (regarded normally as a sign of God's favor in first-century Judaism) and who has claimed to obey the Ten Commandments from his youth (10:17–20). This promising candidate's utter failure to follow the Savior serves as another teaching platform that Jesus uses to convey to his disciples how the kingdom of God is unlike how they imagine it to be (cf. 10:24 and 10:26). Jesus concludes this section with a paradoxical saying that those who are first will be last and the last will be first (10:31). The theme of being last sets the stage for the next section (10:32–45), where James and John reveal their worldly ambition to be the first, following Jesus's third passion prediction.

---

[25] Decker, *Mark 9–16*, 54.

IV. Parsing and Classification of the Key Grammatical Concepts for the Lesson: Nominatives and Adjectives

Nominatives (Excluding Participles)

10:17

1) εἷς; εἷς, μία, ἕν; masc, sg, nom; *one*
    - *Subject*: The adjective εἷς is the subject of the verb ἐπηρώτα.

10:18

1) ὁ Ἰησοῦς; Ἰησοῦς; masc, sg, nom; *Jesus*
    - *Subject*: The proper noun ὁ Ἰησοῦς is the subject of εἶπεν.

2) οὐδεὶς; οὐδείς, οὐδεμία, οὐδέν; masc, sg, nom; *no*, *no one*, *nobody*
    - *Subject*: The indefinite adjective οὐδεὶς is the subject of an implied ἐστίν.

3) ἀγαθός; ἀγαθός; masc, sg, nom; *useful*, *good*
    - *Predicate Nominative*: The adjective ἀγαθός is predicating something about the subject (οὐδείς) through an implied ἐστίν.

4) εἷς; εἷς, μία, ἕν; masc, sg, nom; *one*
    - *Subject*: The adjective εἷς is the subject of an elliptical statement: "One is good."[26]

5) ὁ θεός; θεός; masc, sg, nom; *God*
    - *Apposition*: The proper noun ὁ θεός explains εἷς without any verbal linkage.

10:20

1) ὁ; ὁ, ἡ, τό; masc, sg, nom; *the*, *this one*
    - *Subject*: The article ὁ functions as a pronoun and as the subject of ἔφη.

10:21

1) ὁ Ἰησοῦς; Ἰησοῦς; masc, sg, nom; *Jesus*
    - *Subject*: The proper noun ὁ Ἰησοῦς is the subject of ἐμβλέψας.

2) ἕν; εἷς, μία, ἕν; neut, sg, nom; *one*
    - *Subject*: The adjective ἕν is the subject of ὑστερεῖ.

10:23

1) ὁ Ἰησοῦς; Ἰησοῦς; masc, sg, nom; *Jesus*
    - *Subject*: The proper noun ὁ Ἰησοῦς is the subject of λέγει.

10:24

1) οἱ μαθηταί; μαθητής; masc, plur, nom; *disciple*, *pupil*
    - *Subject*: The noun οἱ μαθηταί is the subject of ἐθαμβοῦντο.

2) ὁ Ἰησοῦς; Ἰησοῦς; masc, sg, nom; *Jesus*
    - *Subject*: The proper noun ὁ Ἰησοῦς is the subject of λέγει.

---

[26] Decker, 51.

3) δύσκολόν; δύσκολος; neut, sg, nom; *hard, difficult*
   • <u>*Predicate Nominative*</u>: The adjective δύσκολόν is predicating something about the implied subject of ἐστιν.

10:25

1) εὐκοπώτερόν; εὔκοπος; neut, sg, nom; *easy*
   • <u>*Predicate Nominative*</u>: The adjective εὐκοπώτερόν is predicating something about the subject of ἐστιν.

10:26

1) οἱ; ὁ, ἡ, τό; masc, plur, nom; *the, this one*
   • <u>*Subject*</u>: The article οἱ is functioning as a pronoun and is the subject of ἐξεπλήσσοντο.

2) τίς; τίς, τί; masc, sg, nom; *who*, *which*, *what*
   • <u>*Subject*</u>: The interrogative pronoun τίς is functioning as a pronoun and is the subject of σωθῆναι.

10:27

1) ὁ Ἰησοῦς; Ἰησοῦς; masc, sg, nom; *Jesus*
   • <u>*Subject*</u>: The proper noun ὁ Ἰησοῦς is the subject of λέγει.

2) ἀδύνατον; ἀδύνατος; neut, sg, nom; *powerless*, *impotent*
   • <u>*Predicate Nominative*</u>: The adjective ἀδύνατον is predicating something about the implied subject of the implied verb ἐστιν.

3) πάντα; πᾶς, πᾶσα, πᾶν; neut, plur, nom; *each*, *every*, *all*
   • <u>*Subject*</u>: The adjective πάντα is the subject of the implied verb ἐστιν.

4) δυνατά; δυνατός; neut, plur, nom; *able*, *powerful*
   • <u>*Predicate Nominative*</u>: The adjective δυνατά is predicating something about πάντα (the subject of the implied verb ἐστιν).

10:28

1) ὁ Πέτρος; Πέτρος; masc, sg, nom; *Peter*
   • <u>*Subject*</u>: The proper noun ὁ Πέτρος is the subject of ἤρξατο.

2) ἡμεῖς; ἐγώ; 1st pers, plur, nom; *we*
   • <u>*Subject*</u>: The pronoun ἡμεῖς is the subject of ἀφήκαμεν.

10:29

1) ὁ Ἰησοῦς; Ἰησοῦς; masc, sg, nom; *Jesus*
   • <u>*Subject*</u>: The proper noun ὁ Ἰησοῦς is the subject of ἔφη.

2) οὐδείς; οὐδείς, οὐδεμία, οὐδέν; masc, sg, nom; *no one*, *nobody*
   • <u>*Subject*</u>: The indefinite adjective οὐδείς is the subject of ἐστιν.

3) ὅς; ὅς, ἥ, ὅ; masc, sg, nom; *who*, *which*, *that*
   • <u>*Subject*</u>: Within the relative clause, the relative pronoun, ὅς, functions as the subject of the verb ἀφῆκεν. The relative pronoun's antecedent is οὐδείς.

10:31

1) πολλοί; πολύς, πολλή, πολύ; masc, plur, nom; *many*, *much*
   - *Subject*: The adjective πολλοί is the subject of an implied ἐστιν.

2) πρῶτοι; πρῶτος; masc, plur, nom; *first*
   - *Predicate Nominative*: The adjective πρῶτοι is predicating something (through an implied ἐστιν) about πολλοί.

3) ἔσχατοι; ἔσχατος; masc, plur, nom; *last*
   - *Predicate Nominative*: The adjective ἔσχατοι is predicating something about πολλοὶ . . . πρῶτοι (subject of ἔσονται).

4) [οἱ] ἔσχατοι; ἔσχατος; masc, plur, nom; *last*
   - *Subject*: The adjective [οἱ] ἔσχατοι is the subject of an implied ἔσονται.

5) πρῶτοι; πρῶτος; masc, plur, nom; *first*
   - *Predicate Nominative*: The adjective πρῶτοι is predicating something (through an implied ἔσονται) about [οἱ] ἔσχατοι.

Adjectives (Including Nominatives)

10:17

1) εἷς; εἷς, μία, ἕν; masc, sg, nom; *one*
   - Structure: *Substantival*: The adjective εἷς is functioning as the subject (noun/substantive) of the sentence.
   - Function: *Positive*: The focus is contextually on the *kind* of εἷς (man) and not on any comparison (degree).

2) ἀγαθέ; ἀγαθός; masc, sg, voc; *good*
   - Structure: *Attributive*: The adjective ἀγαθέ is in the fourth attributive position and modifies διδάσκαλε.
   - Function: *Positive*: The focus is contextually on the *kind* of διδάσκαλε and not on any comparison (degree).

3) αἰώνιον; αἰώνιος; fem, sg, acc; *eternal*
   - Structure: *Attributive*: The adjective αἰώνιον is in the fourth attributive position and modifies ζωήν.
   - Function: *Positive*: The focus is contextually on the *kind* of ζωήν and not on any comparison (degree).

10:18

1) ἀγαθόν; ἀγαθός; masc, sg, acc; *good*
   - Structure: *Substantival*: The adjective ἀγαθόν is functioning as a complement to με in a double accusative construction which takes two substantives.
   - Function: *Positive*: The term "good" is not comparative, and ἀγαθόν does not contain any endings to indicate a comparative or superlative construction.

2) οὐδείς; οὐδείς, οὐδεμία, οὐδέν; masc, sg, nom; *no one*, *nobody*
   - Structure: *Substantival*: The indefinite adjective οὐδείς is the subject (substantive) of an implied ἐστίν.
   - Function: *N/A*: This adjective is indefinite and not comparable.

3) ἀγαθός; ἀγαθός; masc, sg, nom; *good*
   - Structure: *Predicate*: The adjective ἀγαθός is functioning as a predicate nominative in this sentence.
   - Function: *Positive*: The term "good" is not comparative, and ἀγαθός does not contain any endings to indicate a comparative or superlative construction.

4) εἷς; εἷς, μία, ἕν; masc, sg, nom; *one*
   - Structure: *Substantival*: The adjective εἷς is functioning as a subject in this sentence.
   - Function: *Positive*: The focus is contextually on the *kind* of εἷς and not on any comparison (degree).

10:20

1) πάντα; πᾶς, πᾶσα, πᾶν; neut, plur, acc; *each*, *every*, *all*
   - Structure: *Substantival*: The adjective πάντα is the direct object of the verb ἐφυλαξάμην.
   - Function: *Superlative*: Lexically the word πάντα has a superlative connotation or a connotation that is closer to a superlative notion than a positive or comparative idea.

10:21

1) ἕν; εἷς, μία, ἕν; neut, sg, nom; *one*
   - Structure: *Substantival*: The adjective ἕν is functioning as a subject of ὑστερεῖ in this sentence.
   - Function: *Positive*: The focus is contextually on the *kind* of ἕν (the one thing that is lacking) and not on any comparison (degree).

2) πτωχοῖς; πτωχός; masc, plur, dat; *poor*
   - Structure: *Substantival*: The adjective πτωχοῖς is functioning as an indirect object of δός in this sentence.
   - Function: *Positive*: The focus is contextually on the *kind* of people (poor) and not on any comparison (degree).

10:22

1) πολλά; πολύς, πολλή, πολύ; neut, plur, acc; *many*, *much*
   - Structure: *Attributive*: The adjective πολλά is in the fourth attributive position and modifies κτήματα.
   - Function: *Positive*: The focus is contextually on the *kind* of possessions (many) and not on any comparison (degree).

10:24

1) δυσκολόν: δύσκολος; neut sing nom; *difficult*
   - Structure: *Predicate*: "It is difficult" or "To enter into the kingdom of God is difficult."
   - Function: *Positive*: It emphasizes the great difficulty of wealthy people to enter heaven.

10:25

1) εὐκοπώτερόν; εὔκοπος; neut, sg, *nom*; *easy*
   - Structure: *Predicate*: The adjective εὐκοπώτερόν is predicating something about the subject (it = for a camel to go through) of ἐστιν.
   - Function: *Comparative*: The focus is contextually on the *degree* of easiness. Note the comparative ending placed on εὔκοπος.

2) πλούσιον; πλούσιος; masc, sg, acc; *rich*, *wealthy*
   - Structure: _Substantival_: The adjective πλούσιον is the accusative subject of εἰσελθεῖν.
   - Function: _Positive_: While the context presents comparison (note the particle ἤ), πλούσιον itself does not carry a comparative notion.

10:27

1) ἀδύνατον; ἀδύνατος; neut, sg, nom; *powerless*, *impotent*
   - Structure: _Predicate_: The adjective ἀδύνατον is predicating something about the implied subject of the implied verb ἐστιν.
   - Function: _N/A_: The word *impossible* is not gradable.

2) πάντα; πᾶς, πᾶσα, πᾶν; neut, plur, nom; *each*, *every*, *all*
   - Structure: _Substantival_: The adjective πάντα is the subject of the implied verb ἐστιν.
   - Function: _Superlative_: Lexically, the word πάντα has a superlative connotation, and, contextually, this saying contrasts all men to God.

3) δυνατά; δυνατός; neut, plur, nom; *able*, *powerful*
   - Structure: _Predicate_: The adjective δυνατά is predicating something about πάντα (subject from the implied verb ἐστιν).
   - Function: _Positive_: The context is focused on simply stating something to be possible and not on any comparison (more possible or less possible).

10:28

1) πάντα; πᾶς, πᾶσα, πᾶν; neut, plur, acc; *each*, *every*, *all*
   - Structure: _Substantival_: The adjective πάντα is the direct object of ἀφήκαμεν.
   - Function: _Superlative_: Lexically the word πάντα has a superlative connotation, and, in the given context, this saying contrasts the disciples (including Peter himself) with the rich man who rejected Jesus's call (10:22).

10:29

1) οὐδείς; οὐδείς, οὐδεμία, οὐδέν; masc, sg, nom; *no one*, *nobody*
   - Structure: _Substantival_: The indefinite adjective οὐδείς is the subject (substantive) of ἐστίν.
   - Function: _N/A_: This adjective is indefinite, so it does not have degrees of comparison.

10:30

1) ἑκατονταπλασίονα; ἑκατονταπλασίων; neut, plur, acc; *hundredfold*
   - Structure: _Adverbial_ (Accusative of Measure): The neuter accusative adjective ἑκατονταπλασίονα modifies the verb λάβῃ.
   - Function: _N/A_: This adjective is not comparable nor does it have degrees of comparison.

2) αἰώνιον: αἰώνιος; fem sing acc; *eternal*, *everlasting*.
   - Structure: _Attributive_: It modifies the preceding noun ζωήν, "eternal life."
   - Function: _Positive_: It describes a characteristic of life in "the coming age," namely that it is eternal.

10:31

1) πολλοί; πολύς, πολλή, πολύ; masc, plur, nom; *many*, *much*
   - Structure: *Substantival*: The adjective πολλοί is the subject of an implied ἐστιν.
   - Function: *Positive*: The focus is contextually on the *kind* of people (many) and not on any comparison (the comparative would be *more* and the superlative would be *most*).

2) πρῶτοι; πρῶτος; masc, plur, nom; *first*
   - Structure: *Predicate*: The adjective πρῶτοι is predicating something (through an implied ἐστιν) about πολλοί.
   - Function: *Superlative*: Due to the lexical nature of the word πρῶτοι.

3) ἔσχατοι; ἔσχατος; masc, plur, nom; *last*
   - Structure: *Substantival*: The adjective ἔσχατοι is the predicating something about πολλοὶ . . . πρῶτοι (subject of ἔσονται).
   - Function: *Superlative*: Due to the lexical nature of the word ἔσχατοι.

4) [οἱ] ἔσχατοι; ἔσχατος; masc, plur, nom; *last*
   - Structure: *Substantival*: The adjective [οἱ] ἔσχατοι is the subject of an implied ἔσονται.
   - Function: *Superlative*: Due to the lexical nature of the word ἔσχατοι.

5) πρῶτοι; πρῶτος; masc, plur, nom; *first*
   - Structure: *Predicate*: The adjective πρῶτοι is the predicating something (through an implied ἔσονται) about [οἱ] ἔσχατοι.
   - Function: *Superlative*: Due to the lexical nature of the word πρῶτοι.

Now, rewrite your translation of the entire passage in the GUIDED PRACTICE section, reflecting the above exegetical procedure.

REFERENCES

Danker, Frederick William, et al. *A Greek-English Lexicon of the New Testament and other Early Christian Literature*. 3rd ed. Chicago: University of Chicago Press, 2000.

Decker, Rodney J. *Mark 9–16: A Handbook on the Greek Text*. Ed. Martin M. Culy. Baylor Handbook on the Greek New Testament. Waco: Baylor University Press, 2016.

France, R. T. *The Gospel of Mark: The New International Greek Testament Commentary*. Grand Rapids: Eerdmans, 2002.

Köstenberger, Andreas J., Benjamin L. Merkle, and Robert L. Plummer. *Going Deeper with New Testament Greek: An Intermediate Study of the Grammar and Syntax of the New Testament*. Rev ed. Nashville: B&H Academic, 2020.

Mathewson, David L. and Elodie B. Emig. *Intermediate Greek Grammar: Syntax for Students of the New Testament*. Grand Rapids: Baker Academic, 2016.

Wallace, Daniel B. *Greek Grammar Beyond the Basics: An Exegetical Syntax of the New Testament*. Grand Rapids: Zondervan, 1996.

Williams, Joel. *Mark*. Ed. Andreas J. Köstenberger and Robert W. Yarbrough. Exegetical Guide to the Greek New Testament. Nashville: B&H Academic, 2020.

CHAPTER TEN

////////////////

MARK 10:32–45

WITH ATTENTION TO VERBS AND CONJUNCTIONS

GRAMMAR REVIEW

Greek Verbs[1]

Definition and Description

The Greek verb is inflected to communicate a verb's person, number, voice, and aspect. Inflection involves adding morphemes (a meaningful unit of a language) to a verb's stem by attaching prefixes (before the verbal stem), suffixes (after the verbal stem), and infixes (after the verbal stem but before the suffix). The verbal stem (obtained from the verbal root) can also undergo changes, especially when switching verbal tenses.

As a reminder, verbs can either be finite or infinite. A finite verb indicates an action or state of being while also conveying something about the subject. For example, the verb λέγω expresses both the action of speaking and who is speaking (I say: 1st person singular). Infinite verbs convey action or state of being but do not convey anything about the subject.[2] For example, the infinitive λαβεῖν conveys that something was received or taken hold of, but without the additional context, we do not know who the recipient was.

Additionally, verbs can be either transitive or intransitive. Transitive verbs take a direct object whereas intransitive verbs do not take a direct object. For example, "felt" in the sentence "I felt shame" is a transitive verb as it takes the direct object "shame." Alternatively, "live" in the sentence "I live" does not take a direct object. The verb "live" can be modified by other parts of speech like a preposition, as in, "I live in Kansas City," but the verb in the modified sentence still does not take a direct object and is thus used intransitively. Admittedly, these verbs can function as either transitive or intransitive, and context is determinative in those situations.[3]

One reward of understanding the many complexities of the Greek verbal system is the ability to determine the person, number, voice, and aspect of the verb just by looking at the verb and context.

---

[1] Mark's Gospel has the second highest ratio of verbs in the NT (245.99 per 1,000 words). It has 2,635 verbs in total, the fifth highest of any NT book.

[2] See Andreas J. Köstenberger, Benjamin L. Merkle, and Robert L. Plummer, *Going Deeper with New Testament Greek: An Intermediate Study of the Grammar and Syntax of the New Testament*, rev. ed. (Nashville: B&H Academic, 2020), 192.

[3] The verb "felt" may function intransitively, e.g., "She felt terrible about her piano performance last night." The verb "live" can be used transitively, thus taking a direct object, e.g., "He indeed lived a dramatic life."

Categories and Examples[4]

PERSON AND NUMBER (NOMINATIVE)		
	SINGULAR	PLURAL
FIRST	ἐγώ ("I")	ἡμεῖς ("we")
SECOND	σύ ("you" sg)	ὑμεῖς ("you" plur)
THIRD	αὐτός, -ή, -ό ("he," "she," "it")	αὐτοί, -αί, -ά (they)
ACTIVE VOICE		
SIMPLE	The subject directly performs the action of the verb.	ἠγάπησεν ὁ θεὸς τὸν κόσμον ("God **loved** the world" John 3:16).
CAUSATIVE	The subject is the cause behind the action of the verb.	τὸν ἥλιον αὐτοῦ **ἀνατέλλει** ("he **causes** his sun **to rise**" Matt 5:45).
REFLEXIVE	The subject performs the action to himself.	**Γύμναζε** . . . σεαυτὸν πρὸς εὐσέβειαν ("**train** yourself in godliness" 1 Tim 4:7).
MIDDLE VOICE		
REFLEXIVE	The subject performs the action *to* himself.	ἀπελθὼν **ἀπήγξατο** ("he went and **hanged** himself" Matt 27:5).
SPECIAL INTEREST	The subject performs the action *for* himself.	Μαριὰμ . . . τὴν ἀγαθὴν μερίδα **ἐξελέξατο** ("Mary **has chosen** the good portion" Luke 10:42 ESV).
PERMISSIVE	The subject allows something to be done to or for himself.	ἀναστὰς **βάπτισαι** καὶ **ἀπόλουσαι** τὰς ἁμαρτίας σου ("Get up and **be baptized**, and **wash away** your sins" Acts 22:16).
PASSIVE VOICE		
SIMPLE	The subject receives the action of the verb.	δικαιοσύνη . . . θεοῦ . . . **ἀποκαλύπτεται** ("the righteousness of God **is revealed**" Rom 1:17).
PERMISSIVE	The subject gives consent or permission regarding the action of the verb.	**πληροῦσθε** ἐν πνεύματι ("**be filled** with the Spirit" Eph 5:18 ESV).
INDICATIVE MOOD		
DECLARATIVE	An unqualified assertion or statement.	Ἐν ἀρχῇ **ἦν** ὁ λόγος ("In the beginning **was** the Word" John 1:1).
INTERROGATIVE	A question that will also be answered in the indicative mood.	σὺ τίς **εἶ**; ("Who **are** you?" John 1:19).

[4] Köstenberger, Merkle, and Plummer, 215–18; 244–45.

INDICATIVE MOOD (CONTINUED)		
CONDITIONAL	First Class: The protasis ("if" clause) of a first-class conditional sentence.	Εἰ οὖν **συνηγέρθητε** τῷ Χριστῷ, τὰ ἄνω ζητεῖτε ("So if **you have been raised** with Christ, seek the things above" Col 3:1).
	Second Class: The protasis of a second-class conditional sentence.	εἰ γὰρ **ἐπιστεύετε** Μωϋσεῖ, ἐπιστεύετε ἂν ἐμοί· περὶ γὰρ ἐμοῦ ἐκεῖνος ἔγραψεν ("For if you **believed** Moses, you would believe me, because he wrote about me" John 5:46).
COHORTATIVE	A future indicative that is used as a command.	**ἀγαπήσεις** τὸν πλησίον σου ("You **shall love** your neighbor" Jas 2:8 ESV).
POTENTIAL	Used with verbs of obligation, wish, or desire, followed by a complementary infinitive.	**Βούλομαι** οὖν νεωτέρας γαμεῖν ("I **want** younger women to marry" 1 Tim 5:14).
SUBJUNCTIVE MOOD		
PURPOSE	Follows the particle ἵνα (or ὅπως) and expresses purpose (intended result).	ἵνα **μαρτυρήσῃ** περὶ τοῦ φωτός ("[John the Baptist came] to **testify** about the light" John 1:7).
RESULT	Follows the particle ἵνα (or ὅπως) and expresses result (actual result).	τίς ἥμαρτεν, οὗτος ἢ οἱ γονεῖς αὐτοῦ, ἵνα τυφλὸς **γεννηθῇ**; ("who sinned, this man or his parents, that [as a result] he was **born** blind?" John 9:2).
CONDITIONAL	Follows the particle ἐάν or ἐὰν μή and is used in the protasis of a third-class conditional sentence.	ἐάν τις τὸν ἐμὸν λόγον **τηρήσῃ** ("if anyone **keeps** my word" John 8:51).
INDEFINITE RELATIVE	Used after the indefinite relative pronouns ὅστις (ἄν/ ἐάν) or ὃς (δ') ἄν.	πᾶς ὃς ἂν **ἐπικαλέσηται** τὸ ὄνομα κυρίου σωθήσεται ("everyone who **calls** on the name of the Lord will be saved" Acts 2:21).
INDEFINITE TEMPORAL	Used after the temporal conjunction ὅταν or after a temporal adverb or preposition (e.g., ἕως, ἄχρι, μέχρι).	ὅταν γὰρ **λέγῃ** τις ("For whenever someone **says**" 1 Cor 3:4).
HORTATORY	The author commands his audience but also includes himself in the command.	**ἐργαζώμεθα** τὸ ἀγαθὸν πρὸς πάντας ("**Let us do** good to everyone" Gal 6:10 ESV).
DELIBERATIVE	Asks a real or rhetorical question.	**ἐπιμένωμεν** τῇ ἁμαρτίᾳ, ἵνα ἡ χάρις πλεονάσῃ ("**Should we continue** in sin so that grace may multiply?" Rom 6:1).
EMPHATIC NEGATION	Expressed by the double negative οὐ μή, it strongly denies that something will happen.	οὐ μὴ **εἰσέλθητε** εἰς τὴν βασιλείαν τῶν οὐρανῶν ("you **will** never **enter** the kingdom of heaven" Matt 5:20 ESV).
PROHIBITORY	Used when two conditions are met: (1) the command is negated, and (2) the subjunctive uses the aorist tense-form.	Μὴ **νομίσητε** ὅτι ἦλθον καταλῦσαι τὸν νόμον ἢ τοὺς προφήτας ("Do not **think** that I have come to abolish the Law or the Prophets" Matt 5:17 ESV).

OPTATIVE MOOD		
VOLUNTATIVE	Expresses a prayer, benediction, blessing, or wish.	χάρις ὑμῖν καὶ εἰρήνη **πληθυνθείη** ("May grace and peace **be multiplied** to you" 1 Pet 1:2).
DELIBERATIVE	Used with indirect (rhetorical) questions.	Ἐπηρώτων δὲ αὐτὸν οἱ μαθηταὶ αὐτοῦ τίς αὕτη **εἴη** ἡ παραβολή ("And His disciples began questioning Him as to what this parable **might be**" Luke 8:9 NASB77).
POTENTIAL	Involves a fourth-class conditional clause.	εἰ καὶ **πάσχοιτε** διὰ δικαιοσύνην, μακάριοι ("even if **you should suffer** for righteousness, you are blessed" 1 Pet 3:14).
IMPERATIVE MOOD		
COMMAND	An exhortation or charge.	πάντοτε **χαίρετε** ("**Rejoice** always!" 1 Thess 5:16).
PROHIBITION	A negative command that forbids an action.	**Μὴ ἀγαπᾶτε** τὸν κόσμον ("**Do not love** the world" 1 John 2:15).
REQUEST	A command that is given to a superior and is thus weakened to a request.	εἴ τι δύνῃ, **βοήθησον** ἡμῖν ("if you can do anything . . . **help** us" Mark 9:22).
PERMISSION	Used to convey permission, allowance, or toleration.	εἰ . . . ὁ ἄπιστος χωρίζεται, **χωριζέσθω** ("if the unbeliever leaves, **let him leave**" 1 Cor 7:15).
CONDITIONAL	Like the subjunctive, an imperative can be used to state a condition.	**ἔρχου** καὶ ἴδε ("Come and see" = "**If you come**, you will see" John 1:46).
GREETING	Greetings are often expressed with a stereotyped imperative.	**χαῖρε**, ῥαββί ("**Greetings**, Rabbi!" Matt 26:49).
TENSE (ONLY IN THE INDICATIVE MOOD)		
PRESENT	λύω	"I am loosing"
FUTURE	λύσω	"I will loose"
IMPERFECT	ἔλυον	"I was loosing"
AORIST	ἔλυσα	"I loosed"
PERFECT	λέλυκα	"I have loosed"
PLUPERFECT	ἐλελυκειν	"I had loosed"
It should be noted that this chart is an oversimplification of the wide diversity of tense-form uses and that students will not always translate verbs in such a manner.		

VERBAL ASPECT		
ASPECT	**DEFINITION**	**TENSE-FORM**
IMPERFECTIVE	Action viewed as in process, ongoing	Present/ Imperfect
PERFECTIVE	Action viewed as complete, as a whole	Aorist
STATIVE	State of affairs resulting from a previous action	Perfect/ Pluperfect

VERBAL ASPECT (CONTINUED)					
ASPECTUAL CATEGORY	PAST-TIME INDICATOR	ASPECT PREFIX	LEXICAL CORE	ASPECT SUFFIX	PERSONAL ENDING
IMPERFECTIVE (PAST)	ε	—	λυ	—	ομεν
IMPERFECTIVE (NON-PAST)	—	—	λυ	—	ομεν
PERFECTIVE (PAST)	ε	—	λυ	σ	αμεν
PERFECTIVE (NON-PAST)	—	—	λυ	σ	ομεν
STATIVE (PAST)	ε	λε	λυ	κ	ειμεν
STATIVE (NON-PAST)	—	λε	λυ	κ	αμεν
MOOD	IMPERFECTIVE	PERFECTIVE	STATIVE		
INDICATIVE	λύω / ἔλυον	(λύσω) ἔλυσα	λέλυκα / ἐλελύκειν		
INFINITIVE	λύειν	(λύσειν) λῦσαι	λελυκέναι		
SUBJUNCTIVE	λύω	λύσω	λελύκω		
IMPERATIVE	λῦε	λῦσον	λέλυκε		
PARTICIPLE	λύων	(λύσων) λύσας	λελυκώς		

TELIC	Performance	Bounded actions with perceived duration	Prefers Aorist
	Punctual	Bounded actions with little perceived duration	
ATELIC	Stative	States and relationships	Prefers Present/ Imperfect
	Activity	Actions with no inherent termination	

INTERPRETING IMPERATIVES		
LEXICAL	Determination	When a verb is limited to a particular tense-form (e.g., εἰμί and οἶδα = present; ἴδε and ἰδού = aorist) or is almost always found in a particular tense-form (e.g., verbs of motion occurring in the present tense-form).
	Influence	The impact of a verb's inherent meaning on its usage in various tense-forms. Verbs that convey specific commands prefer the aorist whereas verbs that denote general instructions prefer the present.
GRAMMATICAL	Telic verbs (which naturally prefer the aorist tense) were often used to command or forbid an action on a specific occasion, whereas atelic verbs (which naturally prefer the present tense) were often used to command or forbid a general behavior.	
CONTEXTUAL	Aorist imperatives are preferred in prayers and historical narratives whereas present imperatives are preferred in epistles (except in 1 Peter).	

Conjunctions[5]

Definition and Description

Conjunctions are indeclinable words that join together words or groups of words and relate them to each other. They also highlight relationships between clauses and units of discourse. These relationships can be coordinate or equal elements being joined together or subordinate (dependent) elements that are being joined together.

Categories and Examples[6]

CONJUNCTION TYPE	COMMON CONJUNCTIONS AND GLOSSES
COPULATIVE	καί ("and," "also"); δέ ("and"); οὐδέ ("and not"); μηδέ ("and not"); τέ ("and so"); οὔτε ("and not"); μήτε ("and not").
DISJUNCTIVE	ἤ ("or"); εἴτε ("if," "whether").
ADVERSATIVE	ἀλλά ("but"); δέ ("but"); μέν ("but"); μέντοι ("nevertheless"); πλήν ("but," "except"); εἰ μή ("except"); ὅμως ("yet"); καίτοι ("yet").
INFERENTIAL	οὖν ("therefore," "so"); ἆρα ("then"); διό ("for this reason"); δή ("therefore").
EXPLANATORY	γάρ ("for").
PURPOSE	ἵνα ("in order that," "so that"); ὅπως ("that").
RESULT	ὥστε ("so that"); ὅπως ("that").
CAUSAL	ὅτι ("that," "because"); διότι ("because"); ἐπεί ("because," "since"); ἐπειδή ("because").
COMPARATIVE	ὡς ("as," "like"); ὥσπερ ("just as"); καθώς ("as," "just as"); καθάπερ ("just as").
CONDITIONAL	εἰ ("if"); ἐάν ("if"); εἴπερ ("if indeed").
CONCESSIVE	εἰ καί ("even if"); καὶ εἰ ("even if"); κἄν ("even though"); καίπερ ("although").
DECLARATIVE	ὅτι ("that"); ἵνα ("that"). Conjunctions sometimes untranslated or communicated with a dash, colon, or quotation marks.
TEMPORAL	ὅτε ("when"); ἕως ("until"); ὅταν ("whenever"); πρίν ("before").
LOCAL	οὗ ("where"); ὅπου ("where"); ὅθεν ("from where," "whence").

[5] Mark's Gospel has the highest ratio of conjunctions in the NT (154.69 per 1,000 words). It has 1,657 conjunctions in total, the fifth most of any NT book.
[6] Köstenberger, Merkle, and Plummer, 427–28.

GUIDED PRACTICE: MARK 10:32–45 (NA[28])

10:32 Ἦσαν δὲ ἐν τῇ ὁδῷ ἀναβαίνοντες εἰς Ἱεροσόλυμα, καὶ ἦν προάγων αὐτοὺς ὁ Ἰησοῦς,
καὶ ἐθαμβοῦντο, οἱ δὲ ἀκολουθοῦντες ἐφοβοῦντο. καὶ παραλαβὼν πάλιν τοὺς δώδεκα
ἤρξατο αὐτοῖς λέγειν τὰ μέλλοντα αὐτῷ συμβαίνειν 33 ὅτι ἰδοὺ ἀναβαίνομεν εἰς Ἱεροσόλυμα,
καὶ ὁ υἱὸς τοῦ ἀνθρώπου παραδοθήσεται τοῖς ἀρχιερεῦσιν καὶ τοῖς γραμματεῦσιν, καὶ
κατακρινοῦσιν αὐτὸν θανάτῳ καὶ παραδώσουσιν αὐτὸν τοῖς ἔθνεσιν 34 καὶ ἐμπαίξουσιν αὐτῷ
καὶ ἐμπτύσουσιν αὐτῷ καὶ μαστιγώσουσιν αὐτὸν καὶ ἀποκτενοῦσιν, καὶ μετὰ τρεῖς ἡμέρας
ἀναστήσεται.

35 Καὶ προσπορεύονται αὐτῷ Ἰάκωβος καὶ Ἰωάννης οἱ υἱοὶ Ζεβεδαίου λέγοντες αὐτῷ·
διδάσκαλε, θέλομεν ἵνα ὃ ἐὰν αἰτήσωμέν σε ποιήσῃς ἡμῖν. 36 ὁ δὲ εἶπεν αὐτοῖς· τί θέλετέ
[με] ποιήσω ὑμῖν; 37 οἱ δὲ εἶπαν αὐτῷ· δὸς ἡμῖν ἵνα εἷς σου ἐκ δεξιῶν καὶ εἷς ἐξ ἀριστερῶν
καθίσωμεν ἐν τῇ δόξῃ σου. 38 ὁ δὲ Ἰησοῦς εἶπεν αὐτοῖς· οὐκ οἴδατε τί αἰτεῖσθε. δύνασθε πιεῖν

τὸ ποτήριον ὃ ἐγὼ πίνω ἢ τὸ βάπτισμα ὃ ἐγὼ βαπτίζομαι βαπτισθῆναι; 39 οἱ δὲ εἶπαν αὐτῷ·
δυνάμεθα. ὁ δὲ Ἰησοῦς εἶπεν αὐτοῖς· τὸ ποτήριον ὃ ἐγὼ πίνω πίεσθε καὶ τὸ βάπτισμα ὃ ἐγὼ
βαπτίζομαι βαπτισθήσεσθε, 40 τὸ δὲ καθίσαι ἐκ δεξιῶν μου ἢ ἐξ εὐωνύμων οὐκ ἔστιν ἐμὸν
δοῦναι, ἀλλ᾽ οἷς ἡτοίμασται.

41 Καὶ ἀκούσαντες οἱ δέκα ἤρξαντο ἀγανακτεῖν περὶ Ἰακώβου καὶ Ἰωάννου. 42 καὶ
προσκαλεσάμενος αὐτοὺς ὁ Ἰησοῦς λέγει αὐτοῖς· οἴδατε ὅτι οἱ δοκοῦντες ἄρχειν τῶν ἐθνῶν
κατακυριεύουσιν αὐτῶν καὶ οἱ μεγάλοι αὐτῶν κατεξουσιάζουσιν αὐτῶν. 43 οὐχ οὕτως δέ
ἐστιν ἐν ὑμῖν, ἀλλ᾽ ὃς ἂν θέλῃ μέγας γενέσθαι ἐν ὑμῖν ἔσται ὑμῶν διάκονος, 44 καὶ ὃς ἂν
θέλῃ ἐν ὑμῖν εἶναι πρῶτος ἔσται πάντων δοῦλος· 45 καὶ γὰρ ὁ υἱὸς τοῦ ἀνθρώπου οὐκ ἦλθεν
διακονηθῆναι ἀλλὰ διακονῆσαι καὶ δοῦναι τὴν ψυχὴν αὐτοῦ λύτρον ἀντὶ πολλῶν.

VOCABULARY AIDS (WORDS 26X TO 50X)

10:32 **παραλαμβάνω** (aorist: παρέλαβον) *to take, receive, take up, take away* (49x)
10:35, 41 **Ἰάκωβος** *James* (42x)
10:37, 40 **καθίζω** *to sit, sit down, set, be set, be set down, continue, tarry* (47x)
10:38, 39 **ποτήριον** *cup* (31x)
10:40 **ἑτοιμάζω** *to prepare, make ready, provide* (41x)
10:41 **δέκα** *ten* (27x)
10:42 **προσκαλέω** *to call unto, call, call for, call to* (29x)
10:43 **διάκονος** *minister, servant, deacon* (30x)
10:45 **διακονέω** *to minister unto, serve, minister* (37x)

VOCABULARY AIDS (WORDS 25X OR LESS)

10:32 **προάγω** (aorist: προήγαγον) *to go before, bring forth, bring out* (20x)
10:32 **θαμβέω** *to be amazed, be astonished* (3x)
10:32 **συμβαίνω** (aorist: συνέβην) *to happen unto, happen, befall* (8x)
10:33 **κατακρίνω** *to condemn, cast judgement upon* (19x)
10:34 **ἐμπαίζω** *to mock* (13x)
10:34 **ἐμπτύω** *to spit upon, spit on, spit* (6x)
10:34 **μαστιγόω** *to scourge* (7x)
10:35 **προσπορεύομαι** *to come unto* (1x)
10:35 **Ζεβεδαῖος** *Zebedee* (12x)
10:37 **ἀριστερός** *left hand, left, on the left* (4x)
10:38, 39 **βάπτισμα** *baptism* (20x)
10:40 **εὐώνυμος** *left, on the left hand, left foot* (9x)
10:41 **ἀγανακτέω** *to have indignation, be much displeased* (7x)
10:42 **κατακυριεύω** *to exercise dominion over, exercise lordship over* (4x)
10:42 **κατεξουσιάζω** *to exercise authority upon* (2x)
10:45 **λύτρον** *ransom* (2x)

EXERCISE

I. Provide your translation under the Greek text above.

II. Exegetical notes and questions: read the bullet points and answer the questions below.

Verse-by-Verse Questions

10:32

- Scholars differ whether ἀναβαίνοντες is a periphrastic participle or a purposive participle modifying the verb. The verb εἰμί is close by, but it is also noteworthy that a periphrastic use of ἀναβαίνοντες with εἰμί does not usually contain an intervening phrase that highlights location.

a) Classify both occurrences of the conjunction δέ. Then, in one sentence per instance, explain why Mark chose to use δέ instead of καί.

10:33

- Related to κατακρινοῦσιν, the accusative αὐτόν specifies the one who is condemned, and the dative θανάτῳ states the type of condemnation.
- The verb ἀναβαίνομεν is classified as a futuristic present since the action is continuing and will not reach its conclusion until a certain time in the future.

10:35

- The vocative διδάσκαλε is James and John's direct address of Jesus.

b) How is ἵνα being used in this context? (Hint: it is following θέλομεν.)

- France points out that the use of indefinite language (ὃ ἐὰν αἰτήσωμέν σε) demonstrates James and John's careful and cautious way of approaching Jesus with a self-centered request.[7]

[7] R. T. France, *The Gospel of Mark: A Commentary on the Greek Text*, New International Greek Testament Commentary (Grand Rapids: Eerdmans, 2002), 415.

10:36

c) How would you classify ποιήσω syntactically?

10:37

d) How would you classify the imperative δός? How did context help your decision?

- The prepositional phrases ἐκ δεξιῶν and ἐξ ἀριστερῶν express positions of honor. Note that both δεξιῶν and ἀριστερῶν are substantives ("the right hand" and "the left hand," respectively).

10:38

- The middle verb αἰτεῖσθε has similar meaning to the active ("ask"), but the middle has interestingly been used in the context of commercial transactions.[8] The shift in voice from the active αἰτήσωμέν in v. 35 to the middle here in v. 38 has been noted by different scholars. Some say it could draw attention to the disciples' immature and selfish request.[9] Williams states that it depicts their request as a "negotiated contract" that would require a price.[10]

e) How would you classify αἰτεῖσθε syntactically?

- The verb βαπτίζω is able to take a double accusative with an object of the thing and an object of the person. The object of the thing can be a cognate accusative (as in this instance) and, thus, be preceded by "with" in the English translation.[11]

10:39

- Jesus surprisingly does not protest against the two disciples' self-assertive request. He instead confirms that they will endure suffering after the example of Jesus himself.[12]

f) Within the phrase ὁ δὲ Ἰησοῦς εἶπεν αὐτοῖς, how is the conjunction δέ functioning? Give one sentence explaining your classification.

---

[8] Joel Williams, *Mark*, ed. Andreas J. Köstenberger and Robert W. Yarbrough, Exegetical Guide to the Greek New Testament (Nashville: B&H Academic, 2020), 177.

[9] David L. Mathewson and Elodie B. Emig, *Intermediate Greek Grammar: Syntax for Students of the New Testament* (Grand Rapids: Baker Academic, 2016), 149–50.

[10] Williams, *Mark*, 177.

[11] For further explanation, see Williams, 178.

[12] Williams, 178.

10:40

- The article τό within τὸ δὲ καθίσαι ἐκ δεξιῶν μου ἢ ἐξ εὐωνύμων converts the infinitive into a substantive, and this infinitive construction then functions as the subject of ἔστιν.

g) How is δέ classified in this context? Give one sentence explaining what it is doing in this specific verse.

- The word for "left" (εὐωνύμων) is different from the word previously used by James and John (ἀριστερῶν). Most scholars say the shift is simply stylistic, but some note that εὐωνύμων literally means "of good name" or "propitious."

h) Classify the conjunction ἀλλ' (ἀλλά) and explain in one sentence what it is doing in this context.

i) Give the classification of the passive verb ἡτοίμασται.

10:41

- The article οἱ with the noun δέκα is used to distinguish a portion of the group (remaining ten disciples), so it should not be translated "the Ten" but rather "the remaining ten."

10:42

j) Notice the use of καί in the phrase καὶ προσκαλεσάμενος. How would you classify this καί?

10:43

k) Mark switches his conjunction to δέ. Classify δέ and give one sentence describing what it is doing in this context.

- The verb ἐστιν has an imperatival connotation in this context (with a sense of prohibition as negated by οὐχ).

- In 10:43 (and also in 10:44), the future indicative verb ἔσται clearly carries an imperatival force.

10:44

- Mark uses καί to parallel v. 43b with v. 44 to strengthen the common idea of paradoxical greatness (greatness in the kingdom of God is becoming least of all).
- The noun δοῦλος carries a strong notion of service because slaves are supposed to serve their masters; they do not belong to themselves but to their masters (total allegiance).

10:45

1) How is καί being used within καὶ γὰρ ὁ υἱός ?

- The noun λύτρον is used only here and in the parallel account in Matthew within the NT. Williams gives useful background information by noting that this word was utilized in contexts involving a payment to purchase freedom for those under some type of bondage (including prisoners of war, people who owed a debt, and slaves).[13]

Short Summary and Contextual Impact

III. Summarize the main idea of the passage and then discuss how it fits into the surrounding narrative.

[13] Williams, 180.

Parsing and Classification

IV. Circle the verbs in 10:37–38 and parse them below.[14] Then classify each one according to the categories given in the grammar review above as applicable (voice, mood, telic/atelic, and aspect). Provide a brief explanation for your decisions; regarding aspect, try to utilize lexical, grammatical, and contextual factors to justify your classification. After finishing the verbs in 10:37–38, underline the conjunctions in 10:32–45. Classify the conjunctions according to their functions in the text (specific categories are not fully listed in the grammar review above). To get an idea about how to classify conjunctions, quickly scan through the corresponding answer key (pp. 195–98 below) in advance. Provide a brief explanation for your decisions.

Verbs

10:37

1)

- Voice:
- Mood:
- Telic/Atelic:
- Aspect:

2)

- Voice:
- Mood:
- Telic/Atelic:
- Aspect:

3)

- Voice:
- Mood:
- Telic/Atelic:
- Aspect:

---

[14] The limitation within two verses (10:37–38) mainly intends to keep the current exercise in a manageable size. Students are encouraged to extend the scope of their verbal parsing and classification beyond the two verses, if possible.

10:38

1)

- Voice:
- Mood:
- Telic/Atelic:
- Aspect:

2)

- Voice:
- Mood:
- Telic/Atelic:
- Aspect:

3)

- Voice:
- Mood:
- Telic/Atelic:
- Aspect:

4)

- Voice:
- Mood:
- Telic/Atelic:
- Aspect:

5)

- Voice:
- Mood:

- Telic/Atelic:
- Aspect:

6)

- Voice:
- Mood:
- Telic/Atelic:
- Aspect:

7)

- Voice:
- Mood:
- Telic/Atelic:
- Aspect:

8)

- Voice:
- Mood:
- Telic/Atelic:
- Aspect:

Conjunctions

10:32

1)

2)

3)

4)

5)

10:33

1)

2)

3)

4)

5)

10:34

1)

2)

3)

4)

5)

10:35

1)

2)

3)

10:36

1)

10:37

1)

2)

3)

10:38

1)

2)

10:39

1)

2)

3)

10:40

1)

2)

3)

10:41

1)

2)

10:42

1)

2)

3)

10:43

1)

2)

10:44

1)

10:45

1)

2)

3)

4)

ANSWER KEY

I. Translation and explanations

10:32 They were on the road, going up to Jerusalem, and Jesus was walking ahead of them. The disciples were astonished, but those who followed him were afraid. Taking[15] the Twelve aside again,
he began to tell them the things that would[16] happen to him. 33 "See, we are going up to Jerusalem.
The Son of Man will be handed over to the chief priests and the scribes, and they will condemn him
to death. Then they will hand him over to the Gentiles, 34 and they will mock him, spit on him, flog
him, and kill him, and he will rise after three days."
35 James and John, the sons of Zebedee, approached him and said, "Teacher, we want you to do
whatever we ask you."
36 "What do you want me to do for you?" he asked them.
37 They answered him, "Allow us to sit at your right and at your left in your glory."
38 Jesus said to them, "You don't know what you're asking. Are you able to drink[17] the cup I drink
or to be baptized with the baptism I am baptized[18] with?"
39 "We are able," they told him.
Jesus said to them, "You will drink the cup I drink, and you will be baptized with the baptism I am
baptized with. 40 But to sit at my right or left is not mine to give; instead, it is for those for whom
it has been prepared."
41 When the ten disciples heard this, they began to be indignant with James and John. 42 Jesus
called them over and said to them, "You know that those who are regarded as rulers of the Gentiles
lord it over them, and those in high positions act as tyrants over them. 43 But it is not so among you.
On the contrary, whoever wants to become great[19] among you will be your servant, 44 and whoever
wants to be first among you will be a slave to all. 45 For even the Son of Man did not come to be
served, but to serve, and to give his life as a ransom for many."

II. Answers to exegetical questions

Verse-by-verse questions

a) In 10:32, the first δέ is used as a transitional conjunction to mark a shift in scene, whereas καί would have a more continuous connotation. The second δέ is used as an adversative (contrastive) conjunction to distinguish the inner twelve with the others who were also following Jesus. If Mark used καί, there would be a sense that it was the same group that was both astonished (ἐθαμβοῦντο) and afraid (ἐφοβοῦντο).

b) As ἵνα is following the helping verb θέλομεν in v. 35, it introduces a complementary clause that is similar to a complementary infinitive in function.

c) In v. 36, the verb ποιήσω is a deliberative subjunctive used, in this context, to ask a real question.

---

15 Παραλαβών is an aorist active participle, and "having taken" could better reflect its perfective aspect.
16 The connotation of μέλλω probably lends itself to being translated "was about to happen."
17 In this context, πίνω is used in a futuristic sense.
18 Similar to πίνω, βαπτίζομαι has a futuristic sense contextually.
19 Μέγας may be superlative in function ("greatest").

d) In v. 37, the imperative δός is an imperative of request (entreaty). Contextually, James and John are addressing Jesus, who is their superior.

e) In v. 38, the verb αἰτεῖσθε is a special interest (intensive) middle verb.

f) In v. 39, the conjunction δέ is likely contrastive. It highlights the difference between the disciples' overconfident confirmation with Jesus's response. The δέ could also be understood as noting a change in the speaker (i.e., from James and John to Jesus).

g) As in v. 40, δέ is contrastive. In this verse, it contrasts drinking and being baptized with sitting.

h) In v. 40, the conjunction ἀλλ' (ἀλλά) is contrastive. Within this context, it provides a contrast to the preceding negative (not able to grant) statement.

i) In v. 40, the verb ἡτοίμασται is a passive without agency expressed. More specifically, it is a divine passive as God is probably the unexpressed agent.

j) In v. 42, the conjunction καί is copulative (continuative) as Mark is connecting what Jesus does here with what just happened in v. 41 as two equal parts, at least according to the Evangelist's perspective.

k) In v. 43, the conjunction δέ is contrastive. Within this context, it contrasts the worldly way of ruling and leading with how the disciples ought to engage with one another (by serving and giving up of oneself for others).

l) In v. 45, καί is ascensive ("even"), highlighting Jesus as the ultimate example of service.

III. Short Summary and Contextual Impact

Summary: While following a suffering Messiah on the way to the cross, the disciples are taught that the path to glory is paradoxical as Jesus instructs them to each be a servant of all, following the example of the Son of Man, who "came not be served but to serve, that is, to give his life as a ransom for many" (10:45).

Contextual Impact: Nearing the end of the Way Discourse, Jesus gives the third passion prediction that continues to challenge the disciples' notion of Messiahship. Mark, again, reveals the disciples' blindness to the suffering and lowly Messiah by narrating James and John's request to sit with Jesus, at his right and left, in his glory (10:37) and through the remaining ten disciples' outraged reaction to the sons of Zebedee (10:41). Jesus responds to them by teaching that to be the greatest, one must become the least (10:43–44). The ultimate example of discipleship is Jesus himself, who came not to be served but to serve and to give his life (10:45). The repeated depiction of the disciples' blindness (e.g., 8:32–33, 9:33–35, and 10:35–41) prepares the reader for the final portion of the Way Discourse, where Jesus heals a blind man (10:46–52).

IV. Parsing and Classification of the Key Grammatical Concept for the Lesson: Verbs, Verbal Tense, Verbal Aspect, and Conjunctions

Verbs, Verbal Tense, and Verbal Aspect

10:37

1) εἶπαν; εἶπον; 3 plur, aor, act, ind; *to say, to tell*
   - Voice: Active: Simple
     - James and John (subject) carry out the action.
   - Mood: Indicative: Declarative
     - James and John simply say something with no qualifications.
   - Telic/Atelic: Telic: Performance
     - Action is viewed with a terminating point (the aorist here in historical genre is conveying a holistic, terminating action).
   - Aspect: Perfective
     - Lexical reasoning: no special lexical restrictions arise from the basic form of εἶπαν.
     - Contextual reasoning: the historical genre often uses the aorist.
       - The context allows a holistic view of the verb.
     - Grammatical reasoning: the indicative mood here is declarative and simply stating something from an external perspective.
2) δός; δίδωμι; 2 sg, aor, act, impv; *to give, to grant*
   - Voice: Active: Simple
     - Jesus (subject) would carry out the action.
   - Mood: Imperative: Request
     - James and John are asking Jesus (a superior) for something (so it is not a command).
   - Telic/Atelic: Telic: Performance
     - Action is viewed with a terminating point (the aorist here in historical genre is conveying a holistic, terminating action).
   - Aspect: Perfective
     - Lexical reasoning: no special lexical restrictions arise from the basic form of δός; μι verbs prefer the aorist tense.
     - Contextual reasoning: the historical genre often uses the aorist.
       - The context allows a holistic view of the request (no indicators of a continuous action).
     - Grammatical reasoning: the imperatival mood is a request depicted from an external perspective, and this verb is following after a perfective verb.
3) καθίσωμεν; καθίζω; 1 plur, aor, act, sub; *to sit, to sit down*
   - Voice: Active: Simple
     - James and John (subject) would carry out the action.
   - Mood: Subjunctive: Purpose

    - The verb follows after ἵνα stating James and John's purpose in asking.
- Telic/Atelic: Telic: Performance
    - Action is viewed with a terminating point (the aorist here in historical genre is conveying a holistic, terminating action).
- Aspect: Perfective
    - Lexical reasoning: no special lexical restrictions arise from the basic form of καθίσωμεν; μι verbs prefer the aorist tense.
    - Contextual reasoning: the historical genre often uses the aorist.
        - The context allows a holistic view of the request (no indicators of a continuous action).
    - Grammatical reasoning: the subjunctive mood states James and John's purpose from an external perspective, and this verb is following after a couple perfective verbs.

10:38

1) εἶπεν; εἶπον; 3 sg, aor, act, ind; *to say*, *to tell*
    - Voice: Active: Simple
        - Jesus (subject) carries out the action.
    - Mood: Indicative: Declarative
        - Jesus is stating, with no qualifications, the following direct discourse.
    - Telic/Atelic: Telic: Performance
        - Action is viewed with a terminating point (the aorist here in historical genre is conveying a holistic, terminating action).
    - Aspect: Perfective
        - Lexical reasoning: no special lexical restrictions arise from the basic form of εἶπεν.
        - Contextual reasoning: the historical genre often uses the aorist.
            - The context allows a holistic view of the verb.
        - Grammatical reasoning: the indicative mood here is declarative and states something from an external perspective; it is also found within a perfective context (three prior verbs were perfective).
2) οἴδατε; οἶδα; 2 plur, perf, act, ind; *to know*
    - Voice: Active: Simple
        - James and John (subject) are carrying out the action.
    - Mood: Indicative: Declarative
        - Jesus is stating, with no qualifications, that James and John do not know what they are asking.
    - Telic/Atelic: Atelic: Stative
        - James and John are depicted to be in a state of not knowing something that originated before this context and has present consequences.
    - Aspect: Stative
        - Lexical reasoning: οἴδατε is perfect tense in form but is normally understood to function like a present-tense verb due to virtually no difference between its action and the results from that action—it carries a stative aspect.

- Contextual reasoning: the lexical impact of οἴδατε surpasses contextual argumentation for aspect, but to supplement, οἴδατε is following many perfective verbs and then precedes a couple imperfective verbs (stative is often seen as a combination of imperfective and perfective).
- Grammatical reasoning: the indicative mood here is declarative and states something from an external perspective.

3) αἰτεῖσθε; αἰτέω; 2 plur, pres, mid, ind; *to ask, to demand*
   - Voice: Middle: Special Interest
     - James and John (subject) are asking something for their own interest.
   - Mood: Indicative: Declarative
     - It is stated, with no additional qualifications, that James and John are making their request. At the micro level, we may classify the verb αἰτεῖσθε as "Interrogative" in that it is part of the indirect question, τί αἰτεῖσθε ("what you are asking").
   - Telic/Atelic: Atelic: Activity
     - Action is viewed with no hint of cessation; atelic verbs prefer the present and imperfect.
   - Aspect: Imperfective
     - Lexical reasoning: no special lexical restrictions arise from the basic form of αἰτεῖσθε.
     - Contextual reasoning: αἰτεῖσθε is following a stative verb that has continuing consequences into the present. Jesus is depicted as elaborating on those present consequences with a view to their ongoing effect (imperfective aspect).
     - Grammatical reasoning: the indicative mood here is declarative and states something, but the middle voice of special interest may highlight the disciples' selfish request, which is portrayed as something ongoing or unfolding.

4) δύνασθε; δύναμαι; 2 plur, pres, mid, ind; *to be able, to be capable*
   - Voice: Middle
     - Classification into a specific category is difficult here in that the verbal idea is completed not by δύνασθε alone but, instead, by δύνασθε + the following complementary infinitives (πιεῖν and βαπτισθῆναι).
   - Mood: Indicative: Interrogative
     - Jesus is asking if James and John are able to do something.
   - Telic/Atelic: Atelic: Activity
     - Atelic verbs prefer the present and imperfect.
   - Aspect: Imperfective
     - Lexical reasoning: no special lexical restrictions arise from the basic form of δύνασθε (although μι verbs tend to prefer the aorist tense).
     - Contextual reasoning: δύνασθε is following an imperfective verb (αἰτεῖσθε) that has continuing consequences into the present. Jesus elaborates why James and John do not know, matching the continuous consequences with a question focused on ongoing effects (imperfective aspect).
     - Grammatical reasoning: the indicative mood here is interrogative, and the indicative mood matches the previous indicative verb (αἰτεῖσθε) that is also imperfective in aspect.

5) πιεῖν; πίνω; aor, act, inf; *to drink*
   - Voice: Active: Simple

    - James and John (subject) would be carrying out the action.
- Mood: Infinitive
- Telic/Atelic: Telic: Performance
    - Action is viewed with a terminating point (the aorist is conveying a holistic, terminating action); telic verbs prefer the aorist tense.
- Aspect: Perfective
    - Lexical reasoning: no special lexical restriction arises from the basic form of πιεῖν.
    - Contextual reasoning: the historical genre often uses the aorist.
        - The context allows a holistic view of the verb.
    - Grammatical reasoning: πιεῖν is a complementary infinitive that completes the idea of δύνασθε; as described above, context indicates this complementary infinitive is perfective.

6) πίνω; πίνω; 1 sg, pres, act, ind; *to drink*
- Voice: Active: Simple
    - Jesus (subject) carries out the action.
- Mood: Indicative: Declarative
    - Simply stating that Jesus drinks with no additional qualifications.
- Telic/Atelic: Atelic: Activity
    - There is no indication of termination of the verb; atelic verbs prefer the present and imperfect.
- Aspect: Imperfective
    - Lexical reasoning: no special lexical restrictions arise from the basic form of πίνω.
    - Contextual reasoning: Jesus has not drunk the cup yet, so this present tense verb has a futuristic connotation.
    - Grammatical reasoning: the indicative mood here is declarative with a futuristic bent. Given the futuristic idea driven by context, the verb πίνω in the indicative mood will not have any past time meaning and cannot be perfective.

7) βαπτίζομαι; βαπτίζω; 1 sg, pres, pass, ind; *dip*, *immerse*, *plunge*, *baptize*
- Voice: Passive: Simple
    - Jesus (subject) would receive the baptism.
- Mood: Indicative: Declarative
    - Simply stating that Jesus is to be baptized with no qualifications.
- Telic/Atelic: Atelic: Activity
    - There is no indication of termination of the verb; atelic verbs prefer the present and imperfect.
- Aspect: Imperfective
    - Lexical reasoning: no special lexical restrictions arise from the basic form of βαπτίζομαι.
    - Contextual reasoning: Jesus has not been baptized with this baptism yet, so this present tense verb has a futuristic connotation.
    - Grammatical reasoning: the indicative mood here is declarative with a futuristic bent. Given the futuristic idea driven by context, the verb βαπτίζομαι in the indicative mood will not have any past time meaning and cannot be perfective.

8) βαπτισθῆναι; βαπτίζω; aor, pass, inf; *dip*, *immerse*, *plunge*, *baptize*
   - Voice: Passive: Simple
     - James and John (subject) would receive the baptism.
   - Mood: Infinitive
   - Telic/Atelic: Telic: Performance
     - The baptism is depicted with an end in view (the aorist is conveying a holistic, terminating action); telic verbs prefer the aorist tense.
   - Aspect: Perfective
     - Lexical reasoning: no special lexical restrictions arise from the basic form of βαπτισθῆναι.
     - Contextual reasoning: the historical genre often uses the aorist. Within this context of Mark 10:35–38, many aorist verbs have been used to convey a perfective aspect.
     - Grammatical reasoning: βαπτισθῆναι is a complementary infinitive that completes the idea of δύνασθε; as described above, context indicates that this complementary infinitive is perfective.

Conjunctions

10:32

1) δέ; *but*, *and*
   - *Transitional*: Indicating a transition in scene to going on the road up to Jerusalem.

2) καί; *and*
   - *Connective*: It continues the description of the ascent to Jerusalem.

3) καί; *and*
   - *Connective*: It gives additional information about the twelve disciples.

4) δέ; *but*, *and*
   - *Contrastive*: Differentiates between the inner twelve and the crowds that were following Jesus

5) καί; *and*
   - *Connective*: It continues the story of Jesus and his disciples traveling toward Jerusalem.
   - *Transitional*: Transitioning from a general description of all three groups to an action between Jesus and the inner twelve.

10:33

1) ὅτι; *because*, *since*, *that*
   - *Content*: Introduces direct discourse of Jesus (so it is untranslated)

2) καί; *and*
   - *Connective*: Continues Jesus's discourse, linking it to their journey up to Jerusalem.

3) καί; *and*
   - *Connective*: It connects two groups that Jesus will be handed over to.

4) καί; *and*
   - *Connective*: It connects the handing over of Jesus to his being condemned by the two groups.

5) καί; *and*
   - Connective: It connects the condemnation and handing over of Jesus, adding an additional element of what the two groups will do to him.

10:34

1) καί; *and*
   - Connective: It continues the prediction of Jesus by adding that the Gentiles will mock him.

2) καί; *and*
   - Connective: It connects the spitting on Jesus to his mocking, both done by the Gentiles.

3) καί; *and*
   - Connective: It connects the flogging to the spitting and mocking, all done by the Gentiles.

4) καί; *and*
   - Connective: It connects the killing to the flogging, spitting, and mocking, all done by the Gentiles.

5) καί; *and*
   - Connective: It continues Jesus's prediction as he finishes by telling of his resurrection.

10:35

1) καί; *and*
   - Connective: It connects James and John approaching Jesus to right after Jesus's prediction.
   - Transitional: Transitioning from Jesus's prediction to James and John approaching Jesus.

2) καί; *and*
   - Connective: It connects John to James as both being sons of Zebedee.

3) ἵνα; *that, in order that*
   - Content: It gives the content of James and John's statement.

10:36

1) δέ; *but, and*
   - Transitional: It switches the speaker from James and John to Jesus.

10:37

1) δέ; *but, and*
   - Transitional: It switches the speaker from Jesus to James and John.

2) ἵνα; *that, in order that*
   - Content: It gives the content of James and John's request.

3) καί; *and*
   - Connective: It adds sitting at the left to sitting at the right.

10:38

1) δέ; *but, and*
   - Transitional: It switches the speaker from James and John to Jesus.

2) ἤ: *or*
   - Disjunctive: It distinguishes drinking from being baptized.

10:39

1) δέ; *but, and*
   - Transitional: It switches the speaker from Jesus to James and John.

2) δέ; *but, and*
   - Transitional: It switches the speaker from James and John to Jesus.
   - Adversative (Contrastive): It highlights the difference between the disciples' overconfident confirmation with Jesus's response.

3) καί; *and*
   - Connective: It connects the drinking and baptism.

10:40

1) δέ; *but, and*
   - Contrastive: It contrasts the drinking and baptizing with the sitting3)

2) ἤ: *or*
   - Disjunctive: It distinguishes the right-hand seat from the one on the left.

3) ἀλλ'; *but, yet, rather*
   - Contrastive: It gives a positive contrast to the previous negative (not able to grant) statement.

10:41

1) καί; *and*
   - Connective: It connects James and John's request and Jesus's response with the other ten disciples becoming indignant.

2) καί; *and*
   - Connective: It connects John and James as recipients of indignation.

10:42

1) καί; *and*
   - Connective: It connects the ten disciple's indignation with Jesus's response.

2) ὅτι; *because, since, that*
   - Content: It describes the content of the disciples' knowledge.

3) καί; *and*
   - Connective: It connects a parallel idea of worldly ruling.

10:43

1) δέ; *but, and*
   - Contrastive: It contrasts the worldly way of ruling and relationships with the way the disciples' relationships ought to be with one another (service and giving up one's preferences for another).

2) ἀλλ'; *but*, *yet*, *rather*
   - Contrastive: It also contrasts the worldly way of ruling and relationships with the way the disciples' relationships ought to be with one another (service and giving up one's preferences for another).

10:44

1) καί; *and*
   - Connective: It connects the parallel statement about obtaining greatness with the first statement.

10:45

1) καί; *even*
   - Ascensive: Jesus is highlighting himself as an example of serving ("for *even* the Son of Man . . .").

2) γάρ; *for*
   - Explanatory: Jesus is explaining why they should serve in such a sacrificial way.

3) ἀλλά; *but*, *yet*, *rather*
   - Contrastive: Jesus explains that he did not come to be served but to serve.

4) καί; *and*
   - Connective: Jesus is connecting his death as a ransom with his divine purpose of coming to serve others.

Now, rewrite your translation of the entire passage in the GUIDED PRACTICE section, reflecting the above exegetical procedure.

REFERENCES

Campbell, Constantine R. *Advances in the Study of Greek: New Insights for Reading the New Testament*. Grand Rapids: Zondervan, 2015.

Decker, Rodney J. *Mark 9–16: A Handbook on the Greek Text*. Ed. Martin M. Culy. Baylor Handbook on the Greek New Testament. Waco: Baylor University Press, 2016.

France, R. T. *The New International Greek Testament Commentary: The Gospel of Mark*. Grand Rapids: Eerdmans, 2002.

Köstenberger, Andreas J., Benjamin L. Merkle, and Robert L. Plummer. *Going Deeper with New Testament Greek: An Intermediate Study of the Grammar and Syntax of the New Testament*. Rev. ed. Nashville: B&H Academic, 2020.

Mathewson, David L. and Elodie B. Emig. *Intermediate Greek Grammar: Syntax for Students of the New Testament*. Grand Rapids: Baker Academic, 2016.

Wallace, Daniel B. *Greek Grammar Beyond the Basics: An Exegetical Syntax of the New Testament*. Grand Rapids: Zondervan, 1996.

Williams, Joel. *Mark*. Ed. Andreas J. Köstenberger and Robert W. Yarbrough. Exegetical Guide to the Greek New Testament. Nashville: B&H Academic, 2020.

CHAPTER ELEVEN

////////////////

MARK 10:46–52

WITH ATTENTION TO THE AORIST AND IMPERFECT TENSES

GRAMMAR REVIEW:

Aorist

Definition and Description

When authors depict an event holistically or as a summary, they will utilize the aorist tense. The event described by the aorist tends to be a snapshot describing the action without any reference to how long the action took, and it often (though not always) conveys a past-time (from the author's view) event.[1]

Köstenberger, Merkle, and Plummer helpfully comment on how the aorist functions in narrative: "In narratives, the aorist is the most commonly used tense-form in the indicative mood and as such can be viewed as the unmarked or default form. The aorist tense-form (perfective aspect) often carries the main story of the narrative where the present and imperfect tense-forms (imperfective aspect) are used to introduce significant characters, background information, or to emphasize certain features of a story."[2]

As a reminder, when translating the aorist tense-form, one must also keep in mind contextual, grammatical, and lexical factors. As Wallace notes, "The use of the aorist in any given situation depends, then, on its combination with other linguistic features."[3]

---

[1] Mathewson and Emig differ from the categories given to aorist and imperfect verbs by Wallace and Köstenberger, Merkle, and Plummer. Mathewson and Emig note that the various categories ascribed to the aorist (and imperfect below) are ill-suited, as those categories are obtained contextually (the lexical meaning of the verb, modifiers, or discourse units) and not by the tense or aspect itself. They would place these categories that are described for the aorist and imperfect, not on the tense or aspect, but on the context itself. As an example, they would say an aorist tense-form is being utilized by the author within a gnomic context instead of classifying an aorist tense-form as gnomic. See David L. Mathewson and Elodie B. Emig, *Intermediate Greek Grammar: Syntax for Students of the New Testament* (Grand Rapids: Baker Academic, 2016), 117–18; Daniel B. Wallace, *Greek Grammar Beyond the Basics: An Exegetical Syntax of the New Testament* (Grand Rapids: Zondervan, 1996), 540–52, 554–65; Andreas J. Köstenberger, Benjamin L. Merkle, and Robert L. Plummer, *Going Deeper with New Testament Greek: An Intermediate Study of the Grammar and Syntax of the New Testament*, rev. ed. (Nashville: B&H Academic, 2020), 264–69, 289–97.

[2] Köstenberger, Merkle, and Plummer, *Going Deeper with New Testament Greek*, 291.

[3] Wallace, *Greek Grammar Beyond the Basics*, 556.

Categories and Examples[4]

AORIST INDICATIVE		
CONSTATIVE	An action is portrayed in its entirety without regard to its beginning or end, or the length of time it took to accomplish the action.	**ἐβασίλευσεν** ὁ θάνατος ἀπὸ Ἀδὰμ μέχρι Μωϋσέως ("death **reigned** from Adam to Moses" Rom 5:14 ESV).
INCEPTIVE	Emphasizes the beginning of an action or a state.	**ἐπτώχευσεν** πλούσιος ὤν ("Though he was rich . . . **he became poor**" 2 Cor 8:9).
CULMINATIVE	Emphasizes the cessation of an action or state.	ἐγὼ γὰρ **ἔμαθον** . . . αὐτάρκης εἶναι ("for I **have learned** to be content" Phil 4:11).
GNOMIC	A statement that is timeless, universal, or generally true.	**ἐδικαιώθη** ἡ σοφία ἀπὸ πάντων τῶν τέκνων αὐτῆς ("wisdom **is vindicated** by all her children" Luke 7:35).
EPISTOLARY	The author writes from the perspective of the readers and thus uses the aorist instead of the expected present.	ἐγὼ Παῦλος **ἔγραψα** τῇ ἐμῇ χειρί ("I, Paul, **write** this with my own hand" Phlm 19).
FUTURISTIC	Describes an event that has not yet taken place as if it had already occurred.	**ἦλθεν** κύριος ἐν ἁγίαις μυριάσιν αὐτοῦ ("The Lord **comes** with tens of thousands of his holy ones" Jude 14).
DRAMATIC	Refers to an event that recently occurred, having present consequences.	ἡ θυγάτηρ μου ἄρτι **ἐτελεύτησεν** ("My daughter **has** just **died**" Matt 9:18 ESV).

Imperfect[5]

Definition and Description

To convey a ceaseless, incomplete, or progressing action that is usually past time (from the author's point of view), an author will likely use the imperfect tense. As opposed to the snapshot of the aorist, the imperfect describes a continuous action that may be likened to a video (records events in progression).[6]

The imperfect, along with the aorist and pluperfect, has an augment in the indicative mood. Additionally, the imperfect is used frequently in historical narrative, and it is especially prominent in Mark's Gospel.[7]

---

[4] Köstenberger, Merkle, and Plummer, *Going Deeper with New Testament Greek*, 308–9.

[5] Mark's Gospel has the highest frequency of imperfects in the NT (27.35 per 1,000 words). It has 293 imperfects in total, the third most of any NT book.

[6] See chap. 11, n. 1 for a differing perspective.

[7] Köstenberger, Merkle, and Plummer, *Going Deeper with New Testament Greek*, 266. Also, as previously mentioned, for further study on the imperfect in Mark's Gospel, please see Rodney J. Decker, "The Function of the Imperfect Tense in Mark's Gospel," in *The Language of the New Testament: Context, History, and Development*, ed. Stanley E. Porter and Andrew W. Pitts (Leiden: Brill, 2013), 347–64.

Categories and Examples[8]

IMPERFECT INDICATIVE		
PROGRESSIVE	An action in the past that is in progress from the perspective of the author.	καὶ πολλοὶ πλούσιοι **ἔβαλλον** πολλά ("Many rich people **were putting** in large sums" Mark 12:41).
INCEPTIVE	Emphasizes the beginning of an action (or state).	ἔστη καὶ **περιεπάτει** ("He stood and began to walk" Acts 3:8 ESV).
ITERATIVE	Repeated or customary action in the past.	**ἐδίδου** τοῖς μαθηταῖς [αὐτοῦ] ("**He kept giving** [the loaves] to his disciples" Mark 6:41).
TENDENTIAL	An action was begun, attempted, or proposed, but not completed.	ἐδίωκον τὴν ἐκκλησίαν τοῦ θεοῦ καὶ **ἐπόρθουν** αὐτήν ("I . . . persecuted God's church . . . and **tried to destroy** it" Gal 1:13).

[8] Köstenberger, Merkle, and Plummer, 276.

GUIDED PRACTICE: MARK 10:46–52 (NA[28])

10:46 Καὶ ἔρχονται εἰς Ἰεριχώ. Καὶ ἐκπορευομένου αὐτοῦ ἀπὸ Ἰεριχὼ καὶ τῶν μαθητῶν
αὐτοῦ καὶ ὄχλου ἱκανοῦ ὁ υἱὸς Τιμαίου Βαρτιμαῖος, τυφλὸς προσαίτης, ἐκάθητο παρὰ τὴν
ὁδόν. 47 καὶ ἀκούσας ὅτι Ἰησοῦς ὁ Ναζαρηνός ἐστιν ἤρξατο κράζειν καὶ λέγειν· υἱὲ Δαυὶδ
Ἰησοῦ, ἐλέησόν με. 48 καὶ ἐπετίμων αὐτῷ πολλοὶ ἵνα σιωπήσῃ· ὁ δὲ πολλῷ μᾶλλον ἔκραζεν·
υἱὲ Δαυίδ, ἐλέησόν με. 49 καὶ στὰς ὁ Ἰησοῦς εἶπεν · φωνήσατε αὐτόν. καὶ φωνοῦσιν τὸν τυφλὸν
λέγοντες αὐτῷ· θάρσει, ἔγειρε, φωνεῖ σε. 50 ὁ δὲ ἀποβαλὼν τὸ ἱμάτιον αὐτοῦ ἀναπηδήσας
ἦλθεν πρὸς τὸν Ἰησοῦν. 51 καὶ ἀποκριθεὶς αὐτῷ ὁ Ἰησοῦς εἶπεν· τί σοι θέλεις ποιήσω; ὁ δὲ
τυφλὸς εἶπεν αὐτῷ· ραββουνι, ἵνα ἀναβλέψω. 52 καὶ ὁ Ἰησοῦς εἶπεν αὐτῷ· ὕπαγε, ἡ πίστις
σου σέσωκέν σε. καὶ εὐθὺς ἀνέβλεψεν καὶ ἠκολούθει αὐτῷ ἐν τῇ ὁδῷ.

VOCABULARY AIDS (WORDS 26X TO 50X)

10:46	**ἐκπορεύομαι** *to go, proceed, depart* (33x)
10:46	**ἱκανός** *considerable, many, able, sufficient* (40x)
10:46, 49, 51	**τυφλός** *blind* (50x)
10:47, 48	**ἐλεέω** *to have mercy on, pity* (31x)
10:48	**ἐπιτιμάω** *to rebuke, warn, reprove, charge* (29x)
10:49	**φωνέω** *to call, call out, cry* (43x)

VOCABULARY AIDS (WORDS 25X OR LESS)

10:46	**Ἰεριχώ** *Jericho* (7x)
10:46	**Τιμαίου** *Timaeus* (1x)
10:46	**Βαρτιμαῖος** *Bartimaeus* (1x)
10:46	**προσαίτης** *beggar* (2x)
10:47	**Ναζαρηνός** *Nazarene, of Nazareth* (6x)
10:48	**σιωπάω** *to be silent* (10x)
10:49	**θαρσέω** *to be confident/courageous* (7x)
10:50	**ἀποβάλλω** (aorist: ἀπέβαλον) *to cast off* (2x)
10:50	**ἀναπηδάω** *leap up* (1x)
10:52	**ἀναβλέπω** *to receive sight* (25x)

EXERCISE

I. Provide your translation under the Greek text above.

II. Exegetical notes and questions: read the bullet points and answer the questions below.

Verse-by-Verse Questions

10:46

- Entering (ἔρχονται) and leaving (ἐκπορευομένου) Jericho in this verse serve to prepare for and highlight what follows in the narrative, i.e., Jesus's stopping for Bartimaeus, interacting with him, and healing his sight.

a) What kind of genitive is the participle ἐκπορευομένου, and how does it function here?

b) Who or what is the primary subject of ἐκπορευομένου? (Hint: the functional subject of this participle differs from the subject of the main verb.)

- The imperfect verb ἐκάθητο provides background information, as the imperfect commonly does in narrative discourse, especially by portraying Bartimaeus as one who has continually been sitting alongside the road.

10:47

- Following the adverbial, temporal participle ἀκούσας (aorist), ὅτι leads an indirect discourse that provides the content of what Bartimaeus heard. The present tense verb ἐστιν in the indirect discourse should be translated with a past tense verb in English ("it was"). This simply illustrates that the tense agreement between the governing verb/verbal (the participle ἀκούσας) and the indirect discourse is not necessarily expected in Greek.

c) Classify the infinitives κράζειν and λέγειν. Then, in one sentence, give your reasoning for that classification.

- The title υἱὲ Δαυὶδ is messianic, and the current passage is the only place in Mark where this title is directly applied to Jesus. It is used to convey Jesus as the Davidic Messiah and the one who receives and fulfills the promises that God gave to David (Cf. 2 Sam 7).

10:48

- The conjunction ἵνα is leading an indirect discourse, which provides the content of the crowd's rebuke to Bartimaeus (σιωπήσῃ, he must be quiet [subjunctive in mood and imperatival in force]).[9]

- Mark's use of πολλῷ ("much") that precedes μᾶλλον ("more") highlights the degree or extent Bartimaeus's cry intensified.[10]

d) The imperfect verb ἐπετίμων has "many" (possibly including the inner twelve) as its subject. The imperfect verb ἔκραζεν has Bartimaeus as its subject. Classify both of these imperfect verbs. In one sentence, describe how Mark is using them to portray this portion of the story.

e) The postpositive δέ follows right after ὁ to indicate a development in the story. How is this ὁ used in the sentence?

10:49

- The participle στάς is temporal ("after stopping") and portrays a dramatic event. Jesus, in v. 32 of this same chapter, was described as going ahead of the disciples on the way to Jerusalem. Here we now see the same Jesus stopping on his way for an outcast of society.

- Notice the threefold repetition of φωνέω Mark uses to emphasize Jesus's call for Bartimaeus. The verb φωνέω is not used as frequently as καλέω for the idea of inviting or summoning in Mark's Gospel.[11] This makes the three-time use of φωνέω in this verse (especially with one of them as a historical present in the middle of the current episode, which tends to draw the audience's attention to what comes next) even more noteworthy.

f) How is the articular adjective τυφλόν used here?

---

[9] Joel Williams, *Mark*, ed. Andreas J. Köstenberger and Robert W. Yarbrough, Exegetical Guide to the Greek New Testament (Nashville: B&H Academic, 2020), 182.

[10] Cf. Williams, 182.

[11] Rodney J. Decker, *Mark 9–16: A Handbook on the Greek Text*, ed. Martin M. Culy, Baylor Handbook on the Greek New Testament (Waco: Baylor University Press, 2014), 75.

10:50

g) The adverbial participles ἀποβαλών and ἀναπηδήσας are temporal. What is the role of these two adverbial participles especially in relation to the main verb (ἦλθεν)?

- A cloak was one's survival gear, especially for a beggar. Mark is illustrating the cost of discipleship through Bartimaeus's throwing off his only piece of survival gear.

10:51

- Williams and Decker rightly classify ἀποκριθείς as a redundant (pleonastic) participle, noting both ἀποκριθείς and εἶπεν involve speech.[12] In addition, it is sensible to take the redundant verbal construction (the combination of ἀποκριθείς with εἶπεν) as implying a response to the given situation rather than a direct answer to the preceding speech. The lack of direct discourse reporting Bartimaeus's speech in v. 50 appears to support this understanding.
- The indeclinable word ραββουνι functions as a vocative.[13] Students commonly used this term to address their teacher in first-century Jewish contexts.

h) The conjunction ἵνα implies an assumed governing verb, θέλω. With that understanding, how is ἵνα functioning in this sentence? How would you translate this ἵνα?

10:52

- Decker points out that the verb σῴζω has ἡ πίστις as its subject but this should not imply that Bartimaeus's faith, on its own, is what healed him. It is clear in this passage that Jesus is the agent who brought about the healing for Bartimaeus.[14]

i) How would you classify the aorist ἀνέβλεψεν and the imperfect ἠκολούθει, respectively?

- Mark's description of Bartimaeus's response with ἠκολούθει (a discipleship-sensitive verb) implies that Bartimaeus has become a disciple of Jesus.

---

[12] Williams, *Mark*, 183; Decker, *Mark 9–16*, 76.
[13] Decker, *Mark 9–16*, 77.
[14] Decker, 78.

Additional Questions

j) "Jesus" was a common name among the first-century Jews. What type of the nominative does Mark utilize to distinguish Jesus in 10:47? What would be a possible reason for Mark to use Ἰησοῦς ὁ Ναζαρηνός of all the epithets for Jesus? Respond using a few sentences. Hint: Look at the other main character of this story as well as John 1:46 for a typical first-century Jewish perspective on ὁ Ναζαρηνός.

k) The prepositional phrase παρὰ τὴν ὁδόν was mentioned only one other time in Mark's gospel, i.e., in the parable of the sower: καὶ ἐγένετο ἐν τῷ σπείρειν ὃ μὲν ἔπεσεν **παρὰ τὴν ὁδόν**, καὶ ἦλθεν τὰ πετεινὰ καὶ κατέφαγεν αὐτό ("And as he sowed, some seed fell **along the road**, and the birds came and devoured it" Mark 4:4).

The last verse of this passage (10:52) contains a prepositional phrase that has the same object with a different preposition: ἐν **τῇ ὁδῷ**. Given the usage in Mark 4:4, describe in a few sentences Bartimaeus's situation at the beginning of this section that is highlighted by παρὰ τὴν ὁδόν (v.46) and how his situation has changed by the end of this section (v. 52) as indicated by the use of ἐν τῇ ὁδῷ. Be sure to include what caused this remarkable change in your description.

Short Summary and Contextual Impact

III. Summarize the main idea of the passage and then discuss how it fits into the surrounding narrative.

Parsing and Classification

IV. Circle the aorist verbs (excluding participles and infinitives) in the text and parse them below. Then classify each one according to the categories given in the grammar review above. Provide a brief explanation for your decisions. After finishing with the aorist verbs, repeat the same instructions with the imperfect verbs but underline them instead.

Aorist

10:47

1)

2)

10:48

1)

2)

10:49

1)

2)

10:50

1)

10:51

1)

2)

3)

4)

10:52

1)

2)

Imperfect

10:46

1)

10:48

1)

2)

10:52

1)

ANSWER KEY

I. Translation and explanations

10:46 They came to Jericho. And as he was leaving Jericho with his disciples and a large crowd,
Bartimaeus (the son of Timaeus[15]), a blind beggar, was sitting by the road. **47** When he heard that it
was Jesus of Nazareth,[16] he began to cry out, "Jesus, Son of David, have mercy on me!" **48** Many
warned him to keep quiet, but he was crying out all the more, "Have mercy on me, Son of David!"
49 Jesus stopped and said, "Call him."
So they called the blind man and said to him, "Have courage! Get up; he's calling for you." **50** He
threw off his coat, jumped up, and came to Jesus.
51 Then Jesus answered him,[17] "What do you want me to do for you?"
"Rabboni," the blind man said to him, "I want to see."
52 Jesus said to him, "Go, your faith has saved you." Immediately he could see and began to follow
Jesus on the road.

II. Answers to exegetical questions

Verse-by-Verse Questions

a) In v. 46, the participle ἐκπορευομένου combined with αὐτοῦ is a genitive absolute (temporal). This genitive absolute is used to point forward to the main clause, providing background information to set the scene for what follows.

b) In v. 46, the pronoun αὐτοῦ is the primary functional subject of ἐκπορευομένου as they agree in case, number, and gender. More specifically, Jesus is the subject referred to by αὐτοῦ. Mark starts to focus in on Jesus more, as he has switched from the plural in ἔρχονται to the singular in ἐκπορευομένου despite the fact that the genitive absolute construction contains a compound subject, which includes "his disciples and a large crowd" along with Jesus.

c) In v. 47, the infinitives κράζειν and λέγειν are complementary infinitives governed by the main verb ἤρξατο ("he began"). These two infinitives complete the verbal idea introduced by ἤρξατο.

d) In v. 48, the imperfect verbs ἐπετίμων and ἔκραζεν are iterative. Mark uses the former to vividly display the crowd's repeated rebuke to Bartimaeus. However, in response, Bartimaeus repeatedly cries out all the more, as implied by the latter. Alternatively, these imperfect indicative verbs (ἐπετίμων and ἔκραζεν) might be seen as inceptive; the crowd "began" to rebuke him and, in his response, Bartimaeus "began" to cry out all the more.

e) In v. 48, the article ὁ is in the nominative case, and it is functioning as a personal pronoun that is substituting for Bartimaeus.

f) In v. 49, the adjective τυφλόν is used substantively, and it refers to Bartimaeus.

---

[15] This could be a Semitic name like *Ṭim'ay* (France, *The Gospel of Mark*, 423).
[16] It may also be rendered "Jesus the Nazarene."
[17] If ἀποκριθείς is to be translated, the verse could be rendered "Jesus responded and said . . ." though it is probably unnecessary to translate a redundant participle of speech separately.

g) In v. 50, the participles ἀποβαλών and ἀναπηδήσας intensify ἦλθεν. These participles together indicate Bartimaeus's strong and eager desire to come (ἦλθεν) to Jesus in response to his call.[18]

h) In v. 51, given the implied verb of desire, θέλω, the ἵνα clause is complementary, completing the verbal idea introduced by that implied verb. It is probably ideal to translate the ἵνα clause (ἵνα + aorist subjunctive ἀναβλέψω) as if it is a complementary infinitive ("I want **to see [again]**").[19]

i) Following εὐθύς (immediately), the verb ἀνέβλεψεν is probably a constative aorist, and the verb ἠκολούθει is likely an inceptive imperfect (v. 52).

Additional Questions

j) Mark uses ὁ Ναζαρηνός in **apposition** to Ἰησοῦς (10:47). The title ὁ Ναζαρηνός may emphasize the notion of humble beginnings as first-century Jews viewed Nazareth as insignificant. Even Nathanael, a true Israelite, questions, "Can anything good come out of Nazareth?" (John 1:46). This idea of humble beginnings coming alongside Bartimaeus, an outcast, shows how God/Jesus cares for the lowly and humble.

k) Παρὰ τὴν ὁδόν is not a favorable position. It has connotations of darkness and danger just as Jesus explains that the birds (representing Satan) immediately come to take away the word that is sown (Mark 4:4). Mark is setting the scene in 10:46 with Bartimaeus placed in an unfavorable situation that is compounded by his physical blindness; however, by the end of the passage (10:52), Bartimaeus is no longer παρὰ τὴν ὁδόν, but he is ἐν τῇ ὁδῷ following the Savior. In response to Bartimaeus's faith (v. 52), Jesus has rescued him from παρὰ τὴν ὁδόν, and Bartimaeus is now in a much more favorable position as a disciple of Jesus ἐν τῇ ὁδῷ.

III. Short Summary and Contextual Impact

Summary: Closing the Way Discourse in Mark (8:22–10:52), an unlikely candidate to become Jesus's disciple, a blind beggar, receives his sight and follows Jesus on the way to Jerusalem, to the cross.

Contextual Impact: Mark 10:46–52 concludes the Way Discourse, wherein Jesus leads his disciples on "the way" and ultimately to Jerusalem. While on the road, Jesus teaches the disciples about his true identity and mission as well as what it means to be his disciple. Mark's use of the discipleship-sensitive terms "following" (v. 52) and "the way" (vv. 46, 52) indicate to the reader that the Evangelist is continuing the theme of discipleship in the current episode. Mark reports on an unlikely disciple, the blind beggar Bartimaeus, who ends up following Jesus on "the way" to Jerusalem (v. 52) after the Son of David, the Messiah, heals his sight.

As the only two sight-healing instances in Mark's narrative and as the very passages surrounding the threefold passion-resurrection prediction cycle (8:27–10:45), 10:46–52 and 8:22–26 together form an inclusio and likely hint that the disciples' spiritual sight should be healed, which will take place after Jesus's resurrection (cf. 9:9–10). The current episode also transitions the reader into the last section of the Gospel (Mark 11–16) as it concludes the scene by portraying Bartimaeus as beginning to follow his Messiah on the way to Jerusalem.

---

[18] Decker, *Mark 9–16*, 76, referencing Ezra Palmer Gould, *A Critical and Exegetical Commentary on the Gospel according to St. Mark*, International Critical Commentary (New York: Scribner's Sons, 1922), 204.

[19] Williams, *Mark*, 183. The verb, ἀναβλέπω, could here mean either regain sight (Acts 9:12, the case of Paul) or, losing the force of ἀνά, receive sight (John 9:18, the case of the man born blind [v. 20]).

IV. Parsing and Classification of the Key Grammatical Concepts for the Lesson: Aorist and Imperfect

Aorist

10:47

1) ἤρξατο; ἄρχω; 3 sg, aor, mid, ind; *to rule, to begin*
   - *Inceptive*: In the middle voice, this verb emphasizes beginning an action.

2) ἐλέησόν; ἐλεέω; 2 sg, aor, act, impv (classified as request, i.e., a weakened "command" addressed to a superior person); *to have compassion, to have mercy*
   - *Constative*: No concern with emphasizing the beginning/end or duration of the action.

10:48

1) σιωπήσῃ; σιωπάω; 3 sg, aor, act, sub; *to keep silent, to say nothing*
   - *Constative*: No concern with emphasizing the beginning/end or duration of the action. This aorist subjunctive introduced by ἵνα is an indirect discourse and offers the content of the crowd's rebuke (ἐπετίμων) to Bartimaeus.

2) ἐλέησόν; ἐλεέω; 2 sg, aor, act, impv; *to have mercy, to have pity*
   - *Constative*: No concern with emphasizing the beginning/end or duration of the action.

10:49

1) εἶπεν; εἶπον; 3 sg, aor, act, ind; *to say, to speak*
   - *Constative*: No concern with emphasizing the beginning/end or duration of the action.

2) φωνήσατε; φωνέω; 2 plur, aor, act, impv; *to cry aloud, to speak loudly*
   - *Constative*: No concern with emphasizing the beginning/end or duration of the action.

10:50

1) ἦλθεν; ἔρχομαι; 3 sg, aor, act, ind; *to come, to go*
   - *Constative*: No concern with emphasizing the beginning/end or duration of the action.

10:51

1) εἶπεν; εἶπον; 3 sg, aor, act, ind; *to say, to speak*
   - *Constative*: No concern with emphasizing the beginning/end or duration of the action.

2) ποιήσω; ποιέω; 1 sg, aor, act, sub; *to do, to make*
   - *Constative*: No concern with emphasizing the beginning/end or duration of the action. According to the subjunctive classification, on the other hand, this verb fits the deliberative category (asking a question).

3) εἶπεν; εἶπον; 3 sg, aor, act, ind; *to say, to speak*
   - *Constative*: No concern with emphasizing the beginning/end or duration of the action.

4) ἀναβλέψω; ἀναβλέπω; 1 sg, aor, act, sub; *to look up, to gain sight, to regain sight*
   - *Constative*: No concern with emphasizing the beginning/end or duration of the action. This aorist subjunctive introduced by ἵνα functions like a complementary infinitive in relation to the implied main verb θέλω, thus specifying Bartimaeus's desire to receive sight.

10:52

1) εἶπεν; εἶπον; 3 sg, aor, act, ind; *to say*, *to speak*
   - *Constative*: No concern with emphasizing the beginning/end or duration of the action.

2) ἀνέβλεψεν; ἀναβλέπω; 3 sg, aor, act, ind; *to look up*, *to gain sight*
   - *Constative*: No concern with emphasizing the beginning/end or duration of the action.

Imperfect

10:46

1) ἐκάθητο; κάθημαι; 3 sg, impf, mid, ind; *to sit*, *to sit down*
   - *Progressive*: Provides background information by depicting Bartimaeus in a helpless situation while sitting by the road.

10:48

1) ἐπετίμων; ἐπιτιμάω; 3 plur, impf, act, ind; *to rebuke*, *to reprove*
   - *Iterative*: The crowd is depicted as rebuking Bartimaeus many times as he cries out even more (implying multiple rebukes).
   - *Inceptive*: The initial start of the crowd rebuking Bartimaeus may be in view as they respond to his initial crying out in v. 47.

2) ἔκραζεν; κράζω; 3 sg, impf, act, ind; *to cry*, *to call out*
   - *Iterative*: Bartimaeus cries out even more in reaction to the crowd's rebuke, and this would imply him crying out repeatedly.
   - *Inceptive*: Bartimaeus started crying out in a louder voice in response to the crowd's rebuke.

10:52

1) ἠκολούθει; ἀκολουθέω; 3 sg, impf, act, ind; *to follow*
   - *Inceptive*: Following εὐθύς, a sense of immediacy is in the surrounding context.
   - *Progressive*: Provides a vivid description of Bartimaeus's dedication to follow Jesus on the road to Jerusalem in a continual manner.

Now, rewrite your translation of the entire passage in the GUIDED PRACTICE section, reflecting the above exegetical procedure.

REFERENCES

Decker, Rodney J. *Mark 9–16: A Handbook on the Greek Text*. Ed. Martin M. Culy. Baylor Handbook on the Greek New Testament. Waco: Baylor University Press, 2016.

———. "The Function of the Imperfect Tense in Mark's Gospel," in *The Language of the New Testament: Context, History, and Development*, ed. Stanley E. Porter and Andrew W. Pitts. Leiden: Brill, 2013. Pages 347–64.

France, R. T. *The Gospel of Mark*. The New International Greek Testament Commentary. Grand Rapids: Eerdmans, 2002.

Köstenberger, Andreas J., Benjamin L. Merkle, and Robert L. Plummer. *Going Deeper with New Testament Greek: An Intermediate Study of the Grammar and Syntax of the New Testament*. Rev. ed. Nashville: B&H Academic, 2020.

Mathewson, David L. and Elodie B. Emig. *Intermediate Greek Grammar: Syntax for Students of the New Testament*. Grand Rapids: Baker Academic, 2016.

Wallace, Daniel B. *Greek Grammar Beyond the Basics: An Exegetical Syntax of the New Testament*. Grand Rapids: Zondervan, 1996.

Williams, Joel. *Mark*. Ed. Andreas J. Köstenberger and Robert W. Yarbrough. Exegetical Guide to the Greek New Testament. Nashville: B&H Academic, 2020.

CHAPTER TWELVE

/////////////////

TEXTUAL CRITICISM APPLIED TO THE WAY DISCOURSE

REVIEW:

Why Do We Need Textual Criticism?

For most Christians, learning more about the study of textual criticism is not high on their bucket list. In reality, many may not even know that the study of textual criticism exists. However, as students of God's Word who believe in the inspiration and inerrancy of the original autographs,[1] we must be concerned with the textual criticism of the Greek New Testament. Now, that doesn't mean that every Christian must become a text critic; rather, we simply emphasize that Bible-believing Christians cannot ignore this important discipline because of our doctrine of Scripture.

The fundamental reason we must be concerned with textual criticism in the study of the Greek New Testament is because we do not possess any of the original manuscripts, also referred to above as the autographs. Instead, we possess handwritten copies of copies of copies of copies, and so on, of the autographs, and all these copies contain differences among them. Before we discuss those differences, it is important to state that when it comes to the manuscripts available for the study of the Greek New Testament, we have "an embarrassment of riches."[2] According to a recent estimate, we have just over 5,800 Greek New Testament manuscripts.[3] These manuscripts include papyri texts, majuscules (written in all capital letters), minuscules (written in lower-case Greek), and lectionaries (texts that were adjusted for daily reading and worship practices). These manuscripts date from the second century AD all the way to the sixteenth century AD.[4]

Beyond the almost 6,000 Greek manuscripts, but if one includes early translations in Latin, Coptic, Ethiopic, and Syriac brings the total to over 30,000 manuscripts. Additionally, we have over 1 million citations of the Greek text in the early church fathers. These citations are so extensive that if all other sources/manuscripts were taken away, we could reproduce the text of the New Testament just by their citations.[5]

---

[1] Note the importance of understanding that these doctrines are only applied to the autographs, as the Chicago Statement on Biblical Inerrancy asserts, "We affirm that inspiration, strictly speaking, applies only to the autographic text of Scripture, which in the providence of God can be ascertained from available manuscripts with great accuracy. We further affirm that copies and translations of Scripture are the Word of God to the extent that they faithfully represent the original" (Article X of the Chicago Statement on Biblical Inerrancy).

[2] Daniel B. Wallace, "Laying a Foundation: New Testament Textual Criticism" in *Interpreting the New Testament Text: Introduction to the Art and Science of Exegesis*, ed. Darrell L. Bock and Buist M. Fanning, (Wheaton, IL: Crossway, 2006), 43.

[3] This number came from Dan Wallace via correspondence with Andy Naselli. The numbers are documented in Andrew David Naselli, *How to Understand and Apply the New Testament: Twelve Steps from Exegesis to Theology* (Phillipsburg, NJ: P&R, 2017), 37.

[4] The earliest fragment is a few verses from the Gospel of John known as 𝔓52. It most likely dates to the beginning of the second century (AD 100–150). That is an incredibly early date for the study of ancient documents. For more information on 𝔓52 and other papyri manuscripts, see Philip Wesley Comfort, *Encountering the Manuscripts: An Introduction to New Testament Paleography & Textual Criticism* (Nashville: B&H Academic, 2005), 55–102, especially 69.

[5] Bruce M. Metzger and Bart D. Ehrman, *The Text of the New Testament: Its Transmission, Corruption, and Restoration*, 4th ed. (New York: Oxford University Press, 2005), 126.

WHAT IS THE GOAL OF TEXTUAL CRITICISM?

For most conservative scholars, the goal of New Testament textual criticism is to recover the original text of the New Testament. As Moisés Silva notes, textual criticism is "the recovery of the original text (i.e., the text in its initial form prior to the alterations produced in the copying process)."[6] In recent years, however, there has been an effort by some scholars to alter the goal of textual criticism.[7] As Köstenberger, Merkle, and Plummer write, "These scholars have called for a study of textual variants as a window into the theological, ecclesiastical, and cultural world in which the documents were copied (and altered). The variants, thus, are a worthy end in themselves. Often this new approach has been combined with an unwarranted skepticism and sensationalistic claims about the wide influence of tendentious scribes."[8] While there may be some value in this altered aim, we still believe the primary goal of New Testament textual criticism is to recover the original text of the New Testament.

THE TYPES OF TEXTUAL VARIANTS IN THE GREEK NEW TESTAMENT

Most of our readers are likely aware of a man named Bart Ehrman. In his book *Misquoting Jesus*, he provocatively states that there are "more variations among our manuscripts than there are words in the New Testament."[9] This claim alone has undermined the faith of numerous people. Is it true? If so, what does it mean for the reliability of the New Testament? The claim is true—not barely but decidedly. We have about 138,000 words in the Greek New Testament, and, according to Peter Gurry, we have about 500,000 variants.[10] This poses a significant problem, right? Not at all.

When we discuss textual variants, we must take into account their various forms. To most textual critics, there are three different categories: (1) insignificant for the meaning of the text, (2) significant or meaningful to the text but not viable or (3) significant or meaningful and viable (i.e., it has a possible claim to authenticity).[11]

By an overwhelming majority, most textual variants fall into that first category: insignificant for the meaning of the text. This includes things like spelling changes. For instance, John's name is spelled with two νs (nu) instead of one. Or there is an added conjunction like "and" inserted into the text. The vast majority of textual variants are insignificant.

The second type (significant or meaningful but not viable) consist of a fair number of variants. These variants include examples like that found in 1 Thessalonians 2:7 where Paul writes that they became like "infants" (νήπιοι), "gentle" (ἤπιοι), or "horses" (ἵπποι) among the Thessalonians. The first two variants actually fall into the third category of being meaningful and viable. But the third variant of "horses" (ἵπποι) is only found in a few manuscripts and makes no sense contextually, therefore, it is meaningful but not viable.

Finally, the third type of variant includes those that are meaningful and viable. Only 1 percent of textual variants fall into this category. One example is found in Romans 5:1. Does Paul say, "We have peace with God," or, "Let us have peace with God"? The difference is between ἔχομεν and ἔχωμεν. The omicron would indicate the indicative mood, i.e., "we have," and the omega would indicate the subjunctive mood, i.e., "let us have." Theologically speaking, there is a significant difference between the two. It changes, in some sense, the meaning of the text.

So, in summary, Ehrman's claim is factually correct, but when these variants and their types are actually considered, the first-glance, alarming nature of that claim loses its hysteria. The truth is that we have an incredibly reliable Greek New Testament.

---

[6] Moises Silva, "Response" in David A. Black, *Rethinking New Testament Textual Criticism* (Grand Rapids: Baker Academic, 2002), 149.

[7] For example, see D. C. Parker, *The Living Text of the Gospels* (Cambridge: Cambridge University Press, 1997) or Eldon J. Epp, "The Multivalence of the Term 'Original Text' in New Testament Textual Criticism," *Harvard Theological Review* 92 (1999): 245–81.

[8] Andreas J. Köstenberger, Benjamin L. Merkle, and Robert L. Plummer, *Going Deeper with New Testament Greek: An Intermediate Study of the Grammar and Syntax of the New Testament*, rev. ed. (Nashville: B&H Academic, 2020), 35.

[9] Bart D. Ehrman, *Misquoting Jesus: The Story Behind Who Changed the Bible and Why* (New York: HarperOne, 2007), 90.

[10] Peter J. Gurry, "The Number of Variants in the Greek New Testament: A Proposed Estimate," *New Testament Studies* 62, no. 1 (2016): 97–121.

[11] For a more detailed description of these categories, see Wallace, "Laying a Foundation," 34–37.

APPROACHES TO TEXTUAL CRITICISM

Today, there are generally two main approaches to the study of New Testament textual criticism. First, there is the traditional approach. This approach is detailed on pages 27–29 of *Going Deeper with New Testament Greek*, and it focuses on the study of external and internal evidence for each variant to establish the original text.[12] This approach is very much a science and an art because though there are principles that serve as guard rails, each variant's evidence needs to be carefully thought through and considered in its own right. A more detailed review of the traditional method is beyond the scope of this chapter; however, for additional information, please see Bruce M. Metzger, *A Textual Commentary on the Greek New Testament; A Companion Volume to the United Bible Societies' Greek New Testament*, 2nd ed. (Peabody: Hendrickson Publishers, 2005), xv–xxx; Wallace, "Laying a Foundation," 45–55; Naselli, *How to Understand and Apply the New Testament*, 39–45; or Dirk Jongkind, *An Introduction to the Greek New Testament: Produced at Tyndale House, Cambridge* (Wheaton, IL: Crossway, 2019).

The second and more recent approach to New Testament textual criticism is that of the Coherence Based Genealogical Method (CBGM). The CBGM's primary objective is to provide a comprehensive hypothesis for the genealogical structure of the textual tradition.[13] As Peter M. Head helpfully summarizes:

> As a method it attempts, utilising the complete transcriptions of manuscript witnesses and the power of computer analysis, to deal with the large number of witnesses to the NT text, the problem that these witnesses are related in complex ways involving contamination, and the coincidental emergence of identical readings. . . . The CBGM uses textual agreement between transcriptions of manuscripts as a whole to identify specific genealogical relationships (or coherencies) between the texts represented in these manuscripts and the assumed initial text. Beginning with the relatively certain parts of the initial text, using computer analysis, the "textual flow" at each variant unit can be mapped and preliminary genealogical relationships can be developed.[14]

For a fuller treatment of the CBGM, see Peter J. Gurry, "How Your Greek NT Is Changing: A Simple Introduction to the Coherence-Based Genealogical Method (CBGM)," *JETS* 59, no. 4 (2016): 675–89; or Tommy Wasserman and Peter J. Gurry, *A New Approach to Textual Criticism: An Introduction to the Coherence-Based Genealogical Method*, Resources for Biblical Study, Number 80 (Atlanta, GA: SBL Press, 2017).

For the purposes of this chapter, students are expected to utilize the traditional approach in the exercises below. It is strongly recommended that students read the introduction to the critical apparatus in the NA^{28}.[15] For the exercises below, the NA^{28}'s apparatus will be used.

Summary Charts[16]

TEXT-CRITICAL CRITERIA	
EXTERNAL CRITERIA	**INTERNAL CRITERIA**
Favor the older manuscripts.	Favor the reading that best fits the literary context.
Favor the reading supported by the majority of manuscripts.	Favor the reading that corresponds best with writings by the same author.
Favor the reading best attested across manuscript families.	Favor the reading that best explains the origin of the other variants.
	Favor the shorter reading.
	Favor the more difficult reading.

[12] Köstenberger, Merkle, and Plummer, *Going Deeper with New Testament Greek*, 27–29.
[13] An introductory presentation by the developer of the CBGM, Gerd Mink, is available on the INTF website, accessed January 22, 2024, http://egora.uni-muenster.de/intf/service/downloads_en.shtml.
[14] Peter M. Head, "Editio Critica Maior: An Introduction and Assessment," *Tyndale Bulletin* 61 (2010), 143–44.
[15] Eberhard Nestle et al., *Novum Testamentum Graece*, 28th ed. (Stuttgart: Deutsche Bibelgesellschaft, 2015), 55–80.
[16] Köstenberger, Merkle, and Plummer, *Going Deeper with New Testament Greek*, 38–39.

ERRORS IN THE GREEK NEW TESTAMENT	
UNINTENTIONAL ERRORS	
TYPE	**EXPLANATION**
Errors of sight	Scribe glancing back and forth between manuscripts makes an error.
Errors of hearing	Scribe listening to dictated manuscript makes an error.
Errors of writing	Scribe makes an error in writing that cannot be attributed to a mistake in copying by sight or listening.
Errors of judgment	Scribe wrongly judges what to copy—incorporating a marginal note into the text, for example.
INTENTIONAL ERRORS	
TYPE	**EXPLANATION**
Revision of grammar and spelling	Orthographic or grammatical correction by a scribe.
Harmonization of passages	Deleting or incorporating material so that the passage corresponds with a parallel text (in the Synoptic Gospels, for example).
Elimination of difficulties	Deletion or revision of a perceived error.
Conflation of texts	Scribe incorporates two or more variant readings into his manuscript.
Adaption of liturgical tradition	Addition of liturgical material to text.
Theological or doctrinal change	Scribe omits or adds material to avoid perceived theological difficulty.

CRITICAL EDITIONS OF THE GREEK NEW TESTAMENT	
TEXT	**CHARACTERISTICS**
United Bible Society, 5th edition (UBS5)	Eclectic critical text. Notes only significant variants, but provides extensive textual data and an A, B, C, or D ranking. Edition primarily intended for pastors and translators.
Novum Testamentum Graece, 28th edition (Nestle-Aland 28 or NA^{28})	Same NT text as UBS but noting many more variants through a system of symbols incorporated into the text. Fewer textual witnesses provided than in the UBS. Aimed at the academic community.
Editio Critica Maior (ECM)	Eclectic critical text of the NT that provides comprehensive manuscript data for the first thousand years of the church. Only the Catholic Epistles, Acts, Mark, and a short volume on parallel Gospel pericopes have been completed. Material from *ECM* is gradually being incorporated into Nestle-Aland and UBS.
International Greek New Testament Project (IGNTP)	Using the *textus receptus* as a base, the IGNTP provides nearly exhaustive manuscript evidence for all ancient witnesses. Only the Gospel of Luke has been completed. Two volumes on the Gospel of John (papyri and majuscules) have been published.

TEXTUAL CRITICISM: RECOMMENDED WEBSITES	
WEBSITE	**CONTENTS**
csntm.org	Center for the Study of New Testament Manuscripts. Executive Director, Dan Wallace
nobts.edu/cntts	H. Milton Haggard Center for New Testament Textual Studies, New Orleans Baptist Theological Seminary
evangelicaltextualcriticism.blogspot.com	Forum to discuss biblical manuscripts and textual history from an evangelical perspective

EXERCISE

I. Work through the selected textual variants below seeking to establish the original reading of the text. Think through the external and internal evidence for each variant, and give an explanation for the reading chosen. Below is a thorough example from the book of Philippians. This example will demonstrate the issues you need to think through when examining a textual variant. We are not expecting you to reproduce this much material for your answers; its thoroughness is to help you see the rationale that goes into textual criticism. As a reminder, we use the NA[28]'s apparatus in the exercises below.

Example

Philippians 3:12 "Οὐχ ὅτι ἤδη ἔλαβον ⸆ ἢ ἤδη τετελείωμαι, διώκω δὲ εἰ καὶ καταλάβω, ἐφ' ᾧ καὶ κατελήμφθην ὑπὸ Χριστοῦ Ἰησοῦ."
The text variant under consideration is the omission or inclusion of ἢ ἤδη δεδικαίωμαι in Philippians 3:12.

External Evidence (Taken from the NA[28] Critical Apparatus)

ἢ ἤδη δεδικαίωμαι: 𝔓[46] D*.c (F G) ar (b; Ir[lat]) Ambst. If this variant were included, the verse would thus read: "Οὐχ ὅτι ἤδη ἔλαβον ἢ ἤδη δεδικαίωμαι ἢ ἤδη τετελείωμαι, διώκω δὲ εἰ καὶ καταλάβω, ἐφ' ᾧ καὶ κατελήμφθην ὑπὸ Χριστοῦ Ἰησοῦ."
–: ℵ* D* F G 326. 2464. 2495 lat sy[p]. (The UBS Textual Commentary by Metzger includes: A B K P Ψ 33 81 614 1739 Clement). The verse would thus read as it appears above: "Οὐχ ὅτι ἤδη ἔλαβον ἢ ἤδη τετελείωμαι, διώκω δὲ εἰ καὶ καταλάβω, ἐφ' ᾧ καὶ κατελήμφθην ὑπὸ Χριστοῦ Ἰησοῦ."

Summary of External Evidence

Discerning the weight of external evidence can be difficult for the novice textual critic because most beginners are ignorant of when manuscripts are dated and which manuscripts are more consequential than others. So, as one learns, it is generally best to consult the work of scholars who can help guide one through the manuscript evidence. Concerning our example above, the best external evidence for the reading "ἢ ἤδη δεδικαίωμαι" is the 2nd century papyri text 𝔓[46]. Aside from 𝔓[46], the next best source is the sixth–seventh century corrected text of D (06). Concerning this text, it is significant that the uncorrected text of D supports the omission. One other text that is worth mentioning is the Latin translation of Irenaeus which dates around the close of the fourth century. In other words, aside from 𝔓[46], there is not overwhelming early external support for the addition. As for the omission, the external evidence is far more impressive and extensive. First, the omission is supported by ℵ and B. These two manuscripts alone carry significant weight in the Pauline corpus. Aside from D* and other later manuscripts, Clement is significant because his text dates before 215. As far as date goes (even though ℵ and B could carry an earlier text), Clement is the earliest text supporting the omission.

Internal Evidence

The most obvious question when it comes to the internal evidence is "how could a scribe either add or omit an entire phrase?" While scribal omission is not incredibly infrequent, it is still a valid question. One plausible reason a scribe could have omitted the phrase is due to homoeoarcton.

With a slip of the eye, the scribe simply passed over the phrase. However, beyond this reasoning there does not appear to be another suitable explanation for the omission of the phrase.

When it comes to the addition of the phrase, the options are not much more extensive. The most rational explanation is that the phrase "ἢ ἤδη δεδικαίωμαι" was added by a reverent copyist "who imagined that the Divine side of sanctification was left too much out of sight."[17] Another reason the UBS left the phrase out was that "the addition of the clause destroys the balance of the four-part structure of the sentence."[18] A final note would be the effect on theology if the phrase were original. If Paul was saying that he had not already been justified, then he would contradict his view of justification elsewhere. One example comes from Romans 5:1, where Paul says, "Therefore, having been justified by faith, we have peace with God." In Pauline theology, justification happens at the moment of faith. However, some may argue that this contradiction would actually give support to the phrase being original. In one of his books, Ehrman argued that proto-orthodox scribes of the second and third centuries were prone to alter the text of the New Testament for polemical reasons.[19] Hence, he would likely state that 𝔓[46] has the original reading. In his reasoning, scribes would have been uncomfortable with the apparent contradiction with other Pauline theology; therefore, they eliminated the phrase. While Ehrman's thesis proves true in several places, in this case, it would be far reaching to assume that Paul would knowingly contradict himself on such a pivotal doctrine as justification.

Summary of Internal Evidence

If "ἢ ἤδη δεδικαίωμαι" is original, then homoeoarcton is the best explanation for its omission in most manuscripts. If the omission is original, then the phrase was likely added by an early pious scribe who wanted to elaborate further (though wrongly) on Paul's thought.

Conclusion

Due to the disruption in the four-part structure of the sentence and the seeming contradiction in Pauline theology, the omission found in א, A, B, et al. is the most likely reading. Namely, the text should read as it stands in the NA[28]: "Οὐχ ὅτι ἤδη ἔλαβον ἢ ἤδη τετελείωμαι, διώκω δὲ εἰ καὶ καταλάβω, ἐφ' ᾧ καὶ κατελήμφθην ὑπὸ Χριστοῦ Ἰησοῦ."

Select Textual Variants from The Way Discourse

Look up the following passages below in the NA[28]. Look for the text critical symbol in the text of the verses listed. Then, use the apparatus below the text to discern the textual variants in consideration.

8:26

1) 8:26 has alternate readings in a large number of manuscripts which provide additional instructions from Jesus to the healed man about not entering the village. Which reading do you think is most likely original? What (external and internal) evidence led you to this conclusion?

---

[17] Henry A. Kennedy, "Philippians," in *The Expositor's Greek Testament*, ed. W. Robertson Nicoll, 5 vols. (New York: Hodder & Stoughton, 1956), 3:457.

[18] Bruce M. Metzger, *A Textual Commentary on the Greek New Testament*, 2nd ed. (Stuttgart: Deutsche Bibelgesellschaft, 1994), 548.

[19] See Bart D. Ehrman, *The Orthodox Corruption of Scripture: The Effect of Early Christological Controversies on the Text of the New Testament* (New York: Oxford University Press, 1993).

8:28

1) Why is ὅτι in brackets? What is the difference in translation if it is included or excluded?

9:24

1) In 9:24, the father of the child either "cried out" or "cried out with tears." Which reading do you think is most likely original? What led you to this conclusion?

9:29

1) At the end of v. 29, καὶ νηστεία is appended. Which rendering do you think is most likely original? What led you to this conclusion?

10:1

1) Notice the textual signs around καὶ πέραν. Which reading do you think is most likely original? What led you to that conclusion?

10:7

1) Notice the textual signs around καὶ προσκολληθήσεται πρὸς τὴν γυναῖκα αὐτοῦ. What reading do you think is most likely original? What led you to that conclusion?

10:13

1) Notice the textual signs around ἐπετίμησαν αὐτοῖς. What reading do you think is most likely original? What led you to that conclusion?

10:34

1) Notice the textual signs around μετὰ τρεῖς ἡμέρας. What reading do you think is most likely original? What led you to that conclusion?

ANSWER KEY

I. Evaluation of Select Textual Variants from The Way Discourse

8:26

1) In v. 26, when considering alternate manuscript readings, the shorter version, as reflected in NA^{28}, is preferred. Externally, it is a bit difficult, but ℵ^{2} has the shorter version (ℵ* has μη instead of μηδέ, but still lacks the longer command), as does B. Internally, the longer versions are best explained as attempts to clarify why Jesus gave the command to not enter the village. Shorter renderings are generally preferred, as are those that most easily explain the rise of the variants. It is less likely that an explanation of motive would have been dropped than that it would have been added.

8:28

1) In v. 28, ὅτι is in brackets because the editors of NA^{28} believe there is a great degree of uncertainty about its authenticity. The translation is not impacted either way, though, because ὅτι is probably just introducing direct discourse and can be left untranslated, functioning like quotation marks in English.

9:24

1) Though there is a decent amount of external evidence for the reading "cried out with tears" (A^{c} C^{3} D K N Γ Θ $f^{1.13}$ 33. 565. 579. 892. 1241. 1424. *l* 2211 𝔐 lat sy$^{(p).h}$ bo^{pt}) the external evidence for excluding "with tears" appears to be stronger (primarily because of the agreement between 𝔓^{45} ℵ A* B C*). This expanded reading likely represents "a natural heightening of the narrative introduced by copyists and correctors (cf. corrections in A and C)." Metzger goes on to say, "Certainly if the phrase were present originally in the text, no adequate reason can be found to account for its deletion."

9:29

1) There is strong external evidence which suggests καὶ νηστεία should be appended. This longer reading is found in 𝔓^{45vid}, ℵ^{2}, A, 𝔐, and so on. However, the shorter reading is supported by ℵ* and B, and it is easier to explain the addition of the requirement to fast than to explain its deletion. Also, Jesus expressly said his disciples would not be fasting so long as he was with them (Mark 2:18–22). So, the shorter version, as represented in NA^{28}, is likely the original rendering.

10:1

1) The apparatus in the NA^{28} shows the following manuscripts in support of their decision: ℵ B C* L Ψ 0274. 892 co. That being said, δια του περαν is supported by A K N Γ 700 𝔐 sy^{h}. Finally, περαν has many witnesses in support of it as well: C^{2} D W Δ Θ $f^{1.13}$ 28. 565. 579. 1241. 1424. 2542 latt sy$^{s.p}$. This is a very difficult textual variant to solve. Judging by external evidence, the reading adopted by the NA^{28} has the most consistent witness earlier than the fifth century, including Codex Sinaiticus (ℵ) and Codex Vaticanus (B) (arguably the most important manuscripts in the world), as well as the whole Coptic tradition. But the other readings are not without early witnesses. Particularly, περαν is supported by D, W, and $f^{1.13}$, all quite compelling witnesses, in addition to the entire Latin tradition. δια του περαν is supported by Codex Alexandrinus (A), but that is the only fifth century manuscript in which it is found. That being said, it is supported by the Majority text as well as the entire Syriac tradition. Internally, the reading adopted by the NA^{28} is certainly the most difficult reading. It is hard to make sense of the geography (though not impossible). περαν is only marginally easier to understand, but δια του περαν solves the issue. This makes it very likely that δια του περαν was added later due to the confusing geography. It is not possible right now to conclusively say whether or not καὶ πέραν or simply πέραν is the correct reading, but considering that καὶ πέραν has the most consistent early testimony and the support of the entirety of the Coptic tradition and judging it to be the most difficult reading geographically, the NA^{28} probably reads correctly here.

10:7

1) The question concerning this phrase is whether it was added to make the text match Genesis 2:24 and Matthew 19:5 or it was accidentally omitted because of homoeoarcton (the scribe's eye accidently went from καί to καί). The external evidence is largely balanced with the inclusion having support from D K W Γ Θ f^{13} 28. 565. 700. 892[c]. 1241. 1424. 2542, and the negation having support from ℵ B Ψ 892* sy[s]. The internal evidence tips the hand slightly to the phrase's inclusion because if it were omitted, then the οἱ δύο in v. 8 could be referring to the father and mother. The phrase's addition ensures that οἱ δύο is, in fact, referring to the husband and wife. However, this reasoning will not be compelling to all.

10:13

1) The reading επετιμων τοις προσφερουσιν has decent external support from A D K N W Γ Θ $f^{1.13}$ 28. 565. 700. 1241. 1424. 2542. *l* 844 𝔐 lat sy; Bas (τοῖς φέρουσιν is also an option but its external evidence is less impressive: Θ $f^{1.13}$ 1424; + αυτα Γ). However, the reading found in the NA[28], ἐπετίμησαν αὐτοῖς, enjoys the most impressive external evidence of ℵ B C L Δ Ψ 579. 892 c k sa[mss] bo. Internally, it would make more sense for the scribes to add information concerning who was being rebuked. Therefore, the NA[28]'s reading of ἐπετίμησαν αὐτοῖς is most likely original.

10:34

1) Does Mark keep with his typical use of μετὰ τρεῖς ἡμέρας, as seen in 8:31 and 9:31? Or has he perhaps used the seemingly more standard way of using the dative τῇ τρίτῃ ἡμέρᾳ, as seen in Matthew 20:19 and Luke 18:33? Both the external evidence (ℵ B C D L Δ Ψ 579. 892 it sy[hmg] co) and the internal evidence (the fact that Mark has already used μετὰ τρεῖς ἡμέρας twice previously) indicate that μετὰ τρεῖς ἡμέρας is likely the original reading.

REFERENCES

Black, David A. *Rethinking New Testament Textual Criticism*. Grand Rapids: Baker Academic, 2002.

Bock, Darrell L., and Buist M. Fanning, eds. *Interpreting the New Testament Text: Introduction to the Art and Science of Exegesis*. Wheaton, IL: Crossway, 2006.

Comfort, Philip W. *Encountering the Manuscripts: An Introduction to New Testament Paleography & Textual Criticism*. Nashville: B&H Academic, 2005.

Gurry, Peter J. "How Your Greek NT Is Changing: A Simple Introduction to the Coherence-Based Genealogical Method (CBGM)." *JETS* 59, no. 4 (2016): 675–89.

———. "The Number of Variants in the Greek New Testament: A Proposed Estimate." *New Testament Studies* 62, no. 1 (2016): 97–121.

Head, Peter M. "Editio Critica Maior: An Introduction and Assessment." *TynBul* 61 (2010): 131–52.

Jongkind, Dirk. *An Introduction to the Greek New Testament: Produced at Tyndale House, Cambridge*. Wheaton, IL: Crossway, 2019.

Metzger, Bruce M. *A Textual Commentary on the Greek New Testament; A Companion Volume to the United Bible Societies' Greek New Testament*. 2nd ed. Peabody, MA: Hendrickson Publishers, 2005.

Metzger, Bruce M., and Bart D. Ehrman. *The Text of the New Testament: Its Transmission, Corruption, and Restoration*. 4th ed. New York: Oxford University Press, 2005.

Wasserman, Tommy, and Peter J. Gurry. *A New Approach to Textual Criticism: An Introduction to the Coherence-Based Genealogical Method*. Resources for Biblical Study, Number 80. Atlanta: SBL Press, 2017.

CHAPTER THIRTEEN

GREEK DIAGRAMMING

Our assumption in writing this chapter is that most of our readers will not be that familiar with grammatical diagramming (perhaps even your professors will not be that familiar!). In fact, some of your professors may even be tempted to have you skip this chapter altogether. However, our plea would be that you would work through this chapter thoughtfully and carefully. You may just find that this is, perhaps, the most important chapter in this workbook.

WHAT IS THE POINT OF DIAGRAMMING?

Learning how to diagram the Greek text can have a significant impact on one's ability to rightly divide the Word of Truth (2 Tim 2:15). Diagramming forces the student of God's Word to slow down and to think carefully about syntax. How do all the parts of a sentence relate to one another? What does the grammar reveal to be the main argument of a particular text? What are the secondary or supporting arguments of a text? Diagramming helps to reveal what the author meant for his/her readers to take away from the text. As Douglas Huffman notes, "The goal of any kind of diagramming is always the same: to better grasp the author's flow of thought." Since none of us are Koine Greek speakers, we need to think carefully about the structure of the Greek sentences we read so that we can more precisely determine their message and content. Diagramming helps us do precisely that. Though you may have had bad experiences diagramming sentences in your seventh grade English class, we believe that learning how to diagram the Greek text will have profound dividends for your life and ministry. Therefore, our encouragement would be to give diagramming a fresh look and to commit yourself to learning how to do it well. Your future self in ministry will thank you!

AN OVERVIEW OF THE THREE TYPES OF DIAGRAMMING

Sentence Diagramming

There are three main types of diagramming. Our advice would be to give each one a try and decide which one suits you best. Typically, the first thing that comes to mind when one hears the word diagramming is sentence diagramming (also known as line diagramming). This is the type of diagramming that most English students learn at one time or another to better discern the different parts of speech and how they function together.

Line diagramming can be very valuable; however, we also believe that of the three models we will review in this chapter, it is the least important for you to invest time and energy in. There are two reasons for this. First, sentence diagramming can get complicated quickly and take a lot of time to think through. Second, it is more focused on understanding how the different parts of speech function together at the sentence level than it is tracing the argument in the text. While there is great value in understanding the nuances of how the different parts of speech function together in a particular Greek sentence, we believe it is more valuable to trace the argument of the author.

With that being said, we do believe students should at least be exposed to sentence diagramming and learn the basics of how to do it. An exhaustive treatment of line diagramming is beyond the scope of this chapter. For a helpful and in-depth introduction, please see either Lee L. Kantenwein, *Diagrammatical Analysis* (Winona Lake, IN: BMH Books, 1979) or Eric Sowell, *An Intermediate Guide to Greek Diagramming*, Koine Works Diagramming (Lexel Software, n.d.), https://www.inthebeginning.org/e-diagrams/documents/intermediategreektodiagramming.pdf. For our purposes, we will start with the basics. First, begin by finding the subject and the verb of the sentence. Sometimes the subject will be implied. You can either fill in the subject that is implied by using parentheses (I), or you can put (X) to designate the subject. Once you locate the subject and the verb, place them on a horizontal line separated by a vertical line going all the way through. Second, locate the object of the verb and place it on the horizontal line after the verb. Separate the object from the verb with a vertical line that stops when it touches the horizontal line.[1]

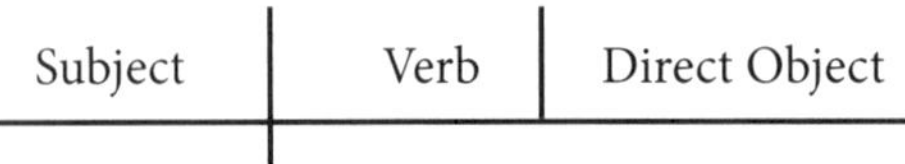

Third, look for any dependent elements in the sentence, such as prepositional phrases, adverbs, modifiers, and so on. Connect these to the base line according to what they are modifying.[2] There are specific ways to connect these dependent elements to the base line that communicates the way the word is functioning in the sentence. For example, infinitives are connected to the base line using stilts.

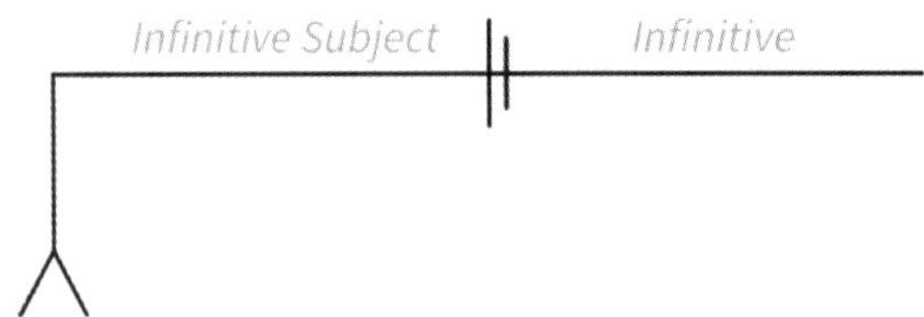

Or consider how predicate nominatives are demonstrated by a reverse slash mark on the baseline

[1] This graphic is provided by Andreas J. Köstenberger, Benjamin L. Merkle, and Robert L. Plummer, *Going Deeper with New Testament Greek: An Intermediate Study of the Grammar and Syntax of the New Testament*, rev. ed. (Nashville: B&H Academic, 2020), 458.

[2] Köstenberger, Merkle, and Plummer, 458.

The chart below is a helpful summary and guide demonstrating how to diagram each part of the Greek sentence.[3] For the exercises below, students will need to refer back to this chart as they seek to diagram the Greek text. Like most things, there is a steep learning curve; however, the more you practice diagramming, the easier and more intuitive the process becomes.

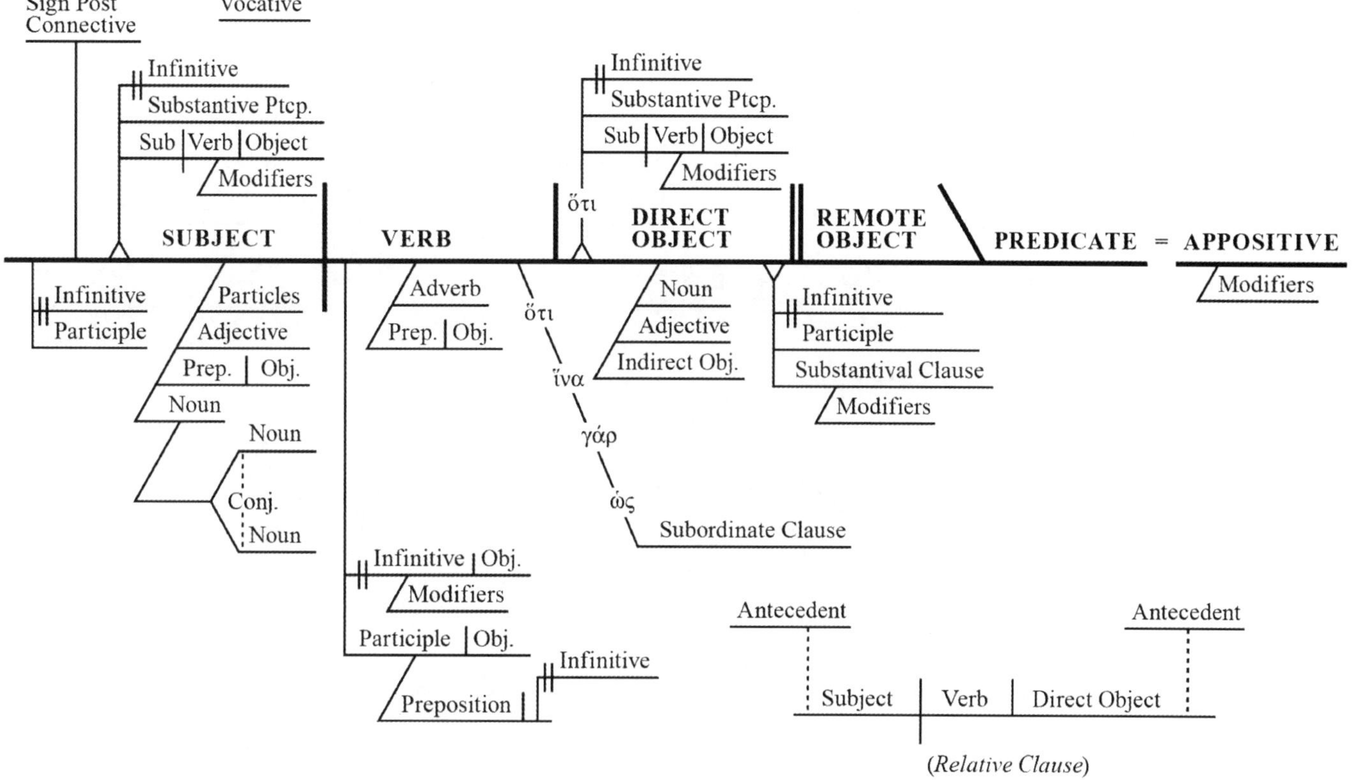

[3] Köstenberger, Merkle, and Plummer, 459. This chart originally came from Denny Burk's summary of John D. Grassmick's diagramming method.

Here is an example of sentence diagramming from 1 Cor 1:1–3:[4]

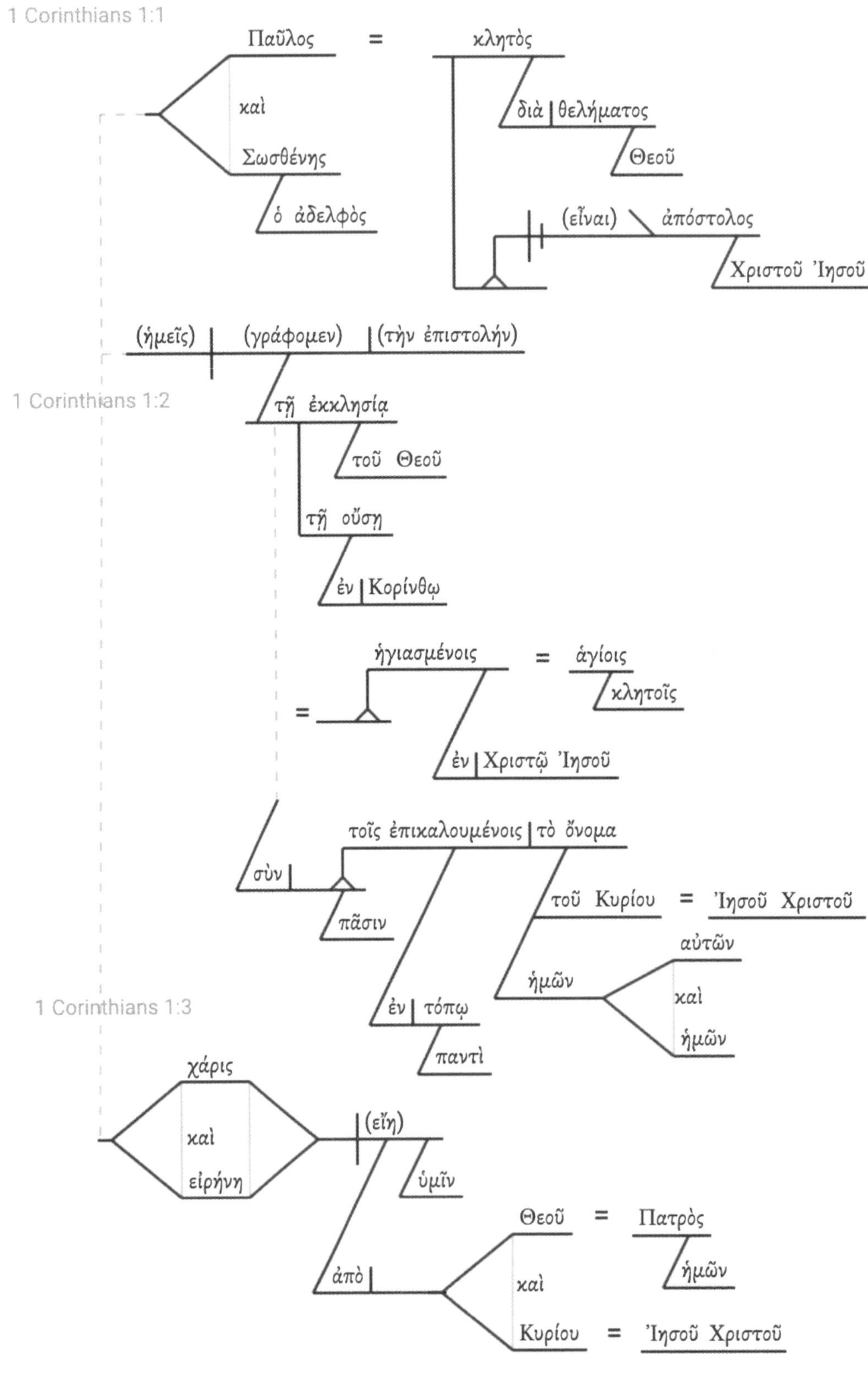

[4] Though mostly similar, some software programs adjust the specific format for diagramming certain parts of speech. For example, in the first graphic above, which gave an overview of line diagramming, the indirect object is diagrammed with an angle bracket that is identical to the noun and adjective. However, BibleArc, as seen immediately above, uses an angle bracket for the indirect object as well, but theirs has a small line proceeding from the front of the bracket (cf. 1 Cor 1:2 above with τῇ ἐκκλησίᾳ).

Arcing

With the next two methods of diagramming (arcing and phrasing), the focus shifts to tracing the argument of the author. As students of Scripture, we should make this our primary goal as we study God's Word. Andy Naselli tells us how rewarding this process can be:

> The New Testament is not a list of unrelated bullet points. It's not pearls on a string. No, the New Testament authors *argue*. They assert truths and support those truths with reasons and evidence. They attempt to persuade others to share their views. Their arguments are always profound and sometimes complex. Connectives such as *but*, *therefore*, and *because* can be hugely important to understanding what an author is arguing. Tracing the argument is not dull. It makes your heart sing . . . .
>
> The most thrilling part for me about knowing Greek is being able to sit down with the Greek text and work through it clause by clause, phrase by phrase, asking, "What's the main argument in this paragraph? What are the supporting arguments? How does this phrase relate to that one?" As I rigorously and methodically work through paragraphs, I come away with a firsthand knowledge of the text and a confidence about what it means that I couldn't get any other way.[5]

We wholeheartedly agree. In light of this, arcing is a great way to trace the argument of the author of Scripture and the arcing diagrams help illustrate that argument. As with phrasing, arcing forces the student of Scripture to think carefully about the relationships of propositions within the text, and the diagrams illustrate those relationships for quicker recall and retention.

To begin arcing, you first need to recognize that each text will have a main point. The additional propositions in the text will support, clarify, elaborate, contrast, etc. that main point. John Piper provides some helpful guidance:

> A unit of biblical text has a "main point," and the rest of the propositions in the unit are either coordinate with it and with one another or are subordinate to it and possibly to others. Coordinate relationships are not usually seen as explaining or arguing for one another. They each make their own contribution but without explanatory or argumentative relation to the others. However, within the subordinate relationships, propositions do explain or argue. We usually call this "supporting." Thus, a proposition can support another proposition by explaining it in some way or arguing for it in some way.[6]

To begin the process of discerning the main point in a text, one must first discern the number of propositions in the passage you are studying. To illustrate, let's work through the example of John 3:16.

It says, οὕτως γὰρ ἠγάπησεν ὁ θεὸς τὸν κόσμον, ὥστε τὸν υἱὸν τὸν μονογενῆ ἔδωκεν, ἵνα πᾶς ὁ πιστεύων εἰς αὐτὸν μὴ ἀπόληται ἀλλ’ ἔχῃ ζωὴν αἰώνιον.

This sentence has four propositions. Using BibleArc.com, we could separate the propositions as follows.

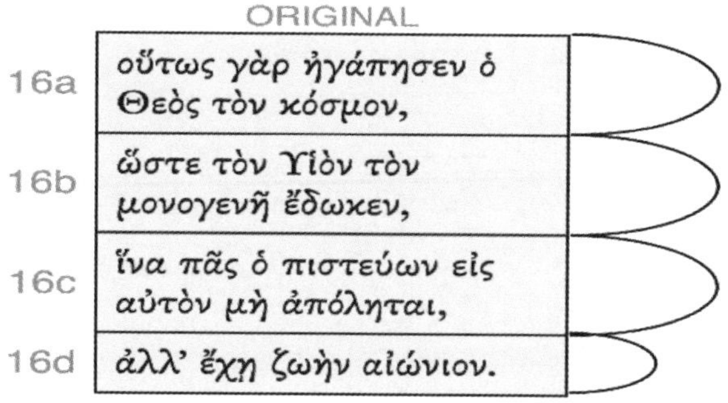

	ORIGINAL
16a	οὕτως γὰρ ἠγάπησεν ὁ Θεὸς τὸν κόσμον,
16b	ὥστε τὸν Υἱὸν τὸν μονογενῆ ἔδωκεν,
16c	ἵνα πᾶς ὁ πιστεύων εἰς αὐτὸν μὴ ἀπόληται,
16d	ἀλλ’ ἔχῃ ζωὴν αἰώνιον.

After discerning the number of propositions, the next step is to discern how the propositions relate to one another. There are numerous ways that propositions can relate to one another including: question-answer, action-result, action-purpose, situation-response, positive-negative, and so on.

An important hint at discerning the nature of these relationships is to observe any conjunctions in the text. For example, consider the relationship of action-result. This relationship describes an action and the result of that action. In this type of relationship, the conjunctions "that" or "so that" are frequently used. Discerning how the propositions relate to one another will help you to see the main point of the author.

---

[5] Andrew David Naselli, *How to Understand and Apply the New Testament: Twelve Steps from Exegesis to Theology* (Phillipsburg, NJ: P&R, 2017), 123, italics original.

[6] John Piper, *Reading the Bible Supernaturally: Seeing and Savoring the Glory of God in Scripture* (Wheaton, IL: Crossway, 2017), 396.

Back to John 3:16.[7] We observe that 16a and 16b have an action-result relationship: God so loved the world (action) *that* he gave his son (result). Next, 16c reveals the purpose of that action-result relationship (note the ἵνα), "in order that all who believe in him might not perish." There is also a contrast present in 16c and 16d which is marked by a negative sign ("might not perish") and a positive sign ("have eternal life") and by their coordinating conjunction, "but." Finally, 16a–b and 16c–d are demonstrating an action-purpose relationship.

Though it is harder to illustrate with just one verse of arcing, the main point is 16a, "God so loved the world." The rest of the propositions explain just how great that love is by describing the result and purpose of that love, that is, that God sent his only begotten Son in order that believing sinners might have eternal life.

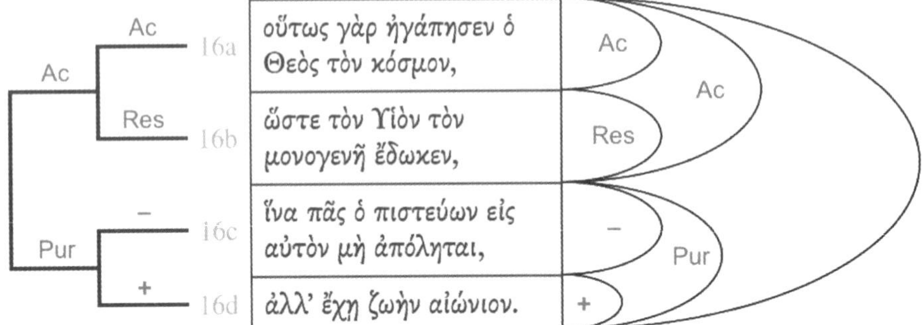

There are courses available on BibleArc.com that you can take to better understand how to arc. Once again, the more you do it, the more intuitive it will become. The following graphics on arcing were produced by John Piper in his book *Reading the Bible Supernaturally*.[8] They are a helpful summary of the different relationships that propositions can have within an argument. As you work through the exercise below, it will be important to consult these graphics to help you think through the various possibilities in how the propositions relate to one another.

7 The translations in this section are our own.

8 Piper, *Reading the Bible Supernaturally*, 410–11.

Type		Name/Symbol	Definition	Some Key Words	Examples	Notes		Symbol	
COORDINATE	(one proposition does not support the other, but each makes its own contribution in the whole)	Series (S)	Each proposition makes its own independent contribution to the whole.	and, moreover, furthermore, neither, nor, etc. (καί, δέ, τε, οὔτε, οὔδε, υήτε, υηδέ)	The sun will be darkened, and the moon will not give its light, and the stars will fall from heaven, and the powers of the heavens will be shaken. (Matt. 24:29; also 7:8; Rom. 12:12)	Arcing: A schematic way of representing the kinds of relationships between all propositions in any coherent writing, leading to a summary of the argument which shows the role of each part in play in the argument.	main clauses coexisting	29a b c d S S S	WRITTEN BETWEEN ARCS
		Progression (P)	Like series, but each proposition is a further step toward a climax.	and, moreover, furthermore, etc. (καί, δέ, τε, οὔτε, οὔδε, υήτε, υηδέ)	Those whom he predestined he also called; and those whom he called he also justified, and those whom he justified he also glorified. (Rom. 8:30; also Mark 4:28; 1 Pet. 1:5–7)		main clauses climaxing	30a b c P P	
		Alternative (A)	Each proposition expresses a different possibility arising from a situation.	or, but, while, on the other hand, etc. (ἀλλά, δέ, ἤ, μέν . . . δέ)	Some were convinced . . . but others disbelieved. (Acts 28:24; also John 10:21, 22; Matt. 11:3)	General Notes: 1. Never cross arcs; some other option is always possible. 2. There will inevitably be some overlap in categories. Try hard to get the category which best fits. 3. Do your arcing in pencil or on the computer; you will inevitably erase and change things as you go along. 4. How do you know when to join two arcs together instead of two others? Remember that the supporting arc (in subordinate relationships) should modify the supported arc as a whole, including everything in it.	main clauses contrasting	24a b A	
SUBORDINATE RELATIONSHIPS	SUPPORT BY RESTATEMENT	Action-Manner (Ac/Mn)	The statement of an action, and then a statement which indicates the way or manner in which this action is carried out.	in that, by, etc. (In Greek this relationship is often introduced by an adverbial participle of means or manner.)	God has not left himself without a witness in that he gave you from heaven rains and fruitful seasons. (Acts 14:17; also Phil. 2:7; Acts 16:16; 17:21)		main clause modal clause	17a Ac b Mn	SYMBOLS ARE WRITTEN INSIDE THE ARCS
		Comparison (Cf)	The relationship between a statement and one showing what it is like.	even as, as . . . so, like, just as (ὡς, καφώς, οὕτως, ὥσπερ)	As the Father has sent me, even so I am sending you. (John 20:2; also 1 Cor. 11:1; 1 Thess. 2:7)		main clause comparative clause	21a Cf b	
		Negative-Positive (-/+)	The relationship between two alternatives, one of which is denied so that the other is enforced. It is also the relationship implicit in contrasting statements.	not . . . but (οὐ, μή, ἀλλά, δέ)	Do not be foolish, but understand what the will of the Lord is. (Eph. 5:17; also Heb. 2:16; Eph. 5:18) Cf. 1 Cor. 4:10 for an example of contrast: "We are fools for Christ's sake, but you are wise in Christ."	Ask: "How does this proposition relate to that one?" 1. Divide 2. Assign 3. Summarize	main clause adversative clause	17a - b +	
		Idea-Explanation (Id/Exp)	The relationship between a statement and one clarifying its meaning. The clarifying proposition may define only one word of the previous proposition.	that is (τοῦτ, ἐστίν)	Jacob supplanted me these two times; he took away my brithright and now he has taken away my blessing. (Gen.27:36; also 1 Cor. 10:4)	Used when clarifying the meaning of a word, phrase, or sentence; however, if author is speaking of an action and giving details about it, use Ac-Mn instead.	main clause epexegetical clause	36a Id b c Exp	
		Question-Answer (Q/A)	Statement of question and answer to that question.	look for the question mark	What does the Scripture say? "Abraham believed God . . ." (Rom. 4:3; also Rom. 6:1; Ps. 24:3, 4)	Note: rhetorical questions can be rephrased into statements and arced as statements.	interrogative clause main clause	3a Q b A	

Type		Name/Symbol	Definition	Some Key Words	Examples	Notes		Symbol
SUBORDINATE RELATIONSHIPS	SUPPORT BY DISTINCT STATEMENT	Ground (G)	The relationship between a statement and the argument or reason for the statement (supporting proposition follows).	for, because, since, etc. (γάρ, ὅτι, ἔπεί, ἐπειδή, διότι)	Blessed are the poor in spirit, for theirs is the kingdom of heaven. (Matt. 5:3; also 1 Cor. 7:9; Phil. 2:25–26)	BE CAREFUL NOT TO MIX THESE TWO UP! In Ground, the conclusion comes first.	main clause causal clause	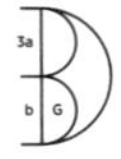 3a b G
		Inference (I)	The relationship between a statement and the argument or reason for the statement (supporting proposition precedes).	therefore, wherefore, consequently, accordingly, etc. (οὖν, διό, ὥστε)	The end of all things is at hand; therefore be sensible and sober in prayer. (1 Pet. 4:7; also Rom. 6:11–12; Matt. 23:3; 1 Pet. 5:5b–6)	In Inference, the conclusion comes second.	main clause result clause	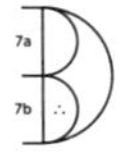 7a 7b ∴
		Action-Result (Ac/Res)	The relationship between an action and a consequence or result which accompanies that action.	so that, that, with the result that (ὥστε)	There arose a great storm on the sea, so that the boat was being swamped by the waves. (Matt. 8:24; also John 3:16; James 1:11)		main clause result clause	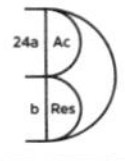 24a Ac b Res
		Action-Purpose (Ac/Pur)	The relationship between an action and the one that is intended to come as a result.	in order that, so that, that, with a view to, to the end that, lest (ἵνα, ὅπως, ἵνα . . . μή)	Humble yourselves under God's mighty hand that he may lift you up. (1 Pet. 5:6; also Rom. 1:11; Mark 7:9)		main clause purpose clause	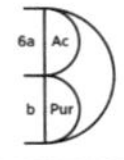 6a Ac b Pur
		Conditional (If/Tn)	This is like Action-Result except that the existence of the action is only potential.	if . . . then, provided that, except, etc. (εἰ, ἔάν)	If you are led by the Spirit, you are not under the law. (Gal. 5:18; also Gal. 6:1; John 15:14)		main clause conditional clause	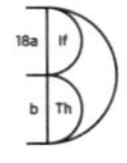 18a If b Th
		Temporal (T)	The relation between the main proposition and the occasion when it occurs.	when, whenever, after, before, etc. (ὅτε, ὅταν)	When you fast, do not look gloomy. (Matt. 6:16; also James 1:2; Luke 6:22)	The author chooses to emphasize the occasion rather than the cause even though the occasion may be the cause.	main clause temporal clause	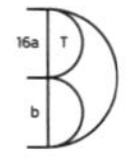 16a T b
		Locative (L)	The relationship between a proposition and the place where it is true.	where, wherever, etc. (ὅτου, οὗ)	Where two or three are gathered together in my name, there am I in the midst of them. (Matt. 18:20; also 2 Cor. 3:17; Ruth 1:16)		main clause locative clause	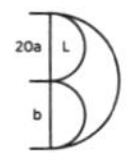 20a L b
		Bilateral (BL)	A bilateral proposition supports two other propositions, one preceding and one following.	See conjunctions for other relationships that support.	Let the nations be glad and sing for joy, for you judge the peoples with equity and guide the nations upon the earth. Let the peoples praise you, O God. (Ps. 67:4–5; also Rom. 2:1b–2)	Note that "BL" tells that there is a relationship in each direction and that the "G" and ⊠ specify exactly what the relationships are.		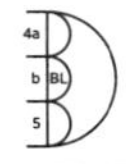 4a b BL 5
	SUPPORT-CONTRARY STATEMENT	Concessive (Csv)	The relationship between a main clause and a contrary statement.	although . . . yet, although, yet, nevertheless, but, however (καίπερ, εἰ, καί, ἐὰν, καί)	Although he was a Son, he learned obedience from what he suffered. (Heb. 5:8; also 1 Cor. 4:15; 9:13–15)	The concessive clause "supports" the main clause because it highlights the strength of the main clause which stands despite the obstacle of the concessive clause.	main clause concessive clause	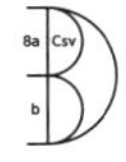 8a Csv b
		Situation-Response (Sit/R)	The relationship between a situation in one clause and a response in another.		How often would I have gathered your children together as a hen gathers her brood under her wings, and you were not willing. (Matt. 23:37; also John 7:21)	The relationship between the two clauses can either be what would be expected or a surprise, depending on the response of one's will.		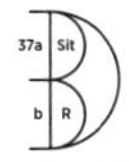 37a Sit b R

SYMBOLS ARE WRITTEN INSIDE THE ARCS

Phrasing

Phrasing, as mentioned above, is another method to visibly trace the argument of the author of Scripture. Personally, phrasing is our favorite way to diagram the Greek text. To us, it is more intuitive and quicker for discerning the argument of the passage at hand. Douglas Huffman concurs when he writes:

> The use of phrase diagramming for outlining passages of Scripture requires the use of the original languages of Greek (for the New Testament) and Hebrew and Aramaic (for the Old Testament). Too often, those trained in these original languages find life in professional preaching and teaching careers or in lay teaching opportunities to be too busy to keep up their skills in working with these languages. The time demands of life and ministry are too much and the convenience of depending upon modern translations too tempting. The idea of taking valuable, fought-over time to diagram a sentence in the original language seems too much of a luxury and not time efficient enough to wedge into one's schedule.
>
> But phrase diagramming is much *easier* than technical grammatical diagramming and much *clearer* in its structure and end product because the words that function most closely together are left together on one line. Consequently phrase diagramming is much *quicker* than technical diagramming and more *directly related* to creating a useful lesson/sermon outline. An hour (or less) of diagramming, will produce an outline by which to preach/teach a particular passage of Scripture.[9]

For a more exhaustive treatment of phrasing, please see Naselli's *How to Understand and Apply the New Testament*, pages 136–57, Huffman's *The Handy Guide to New Testament Greek*, pages 83–106, or Schreiner's *Interpreting the Pauline Epistles*, pages 97–124.

For our purposes, William Mounce offers three main principles to keep in mind when learning how to phrase diagram:

- The more dominant phrases are further to the left on the page.
- Subordinate ideas are indented, placed under (or over) the concept to which they are related.
- Parallel ideas are indented the same distance from the left.[10]

Once again, we recommend using BibleArc.com to phrase diagram, but it can also be done with pencil and paper or with a Microsoft Word document. To begin, separate the verses under consideration into their natural phrases or propositions. We will demonstrate using John 3:16 again. The first step should look like this:

Next, identify the main clauses and subordinate clauses and indent the subordinate clauses to the right. Huffman is helpful when he notes that "a clause is likely to be subordinate (but not necessarily) if it has one or more of the following features:

- if it begins with a subordinate conjunction,
- if it begins with a relative pronoun,
- it its controlling verb is in the subjunctive mood, or
- if its controlling verb is an infinitive or participle."[11]

οὕτως γὰρ ἠγάπησεν ὁ Θεὸς τὸν κόσμον,	3:16
ὥστε τὸν Υἱὸν τὸν μονογενῆ ἔδωκεν,	b
ἵνα πᾶς ὁ πιστεύων εἰς αὐτὸν μὴ ἀπόληται,	c
ἀλλ᾽ ἔχῃ ζωὴν αἰώνιον.	d

[9] Huffman, *The Handy Guide to New Testament Greek*, 85.

[10] William D. Mounce, *A Graded Reader of Biblical Greek: Exegetical Discussion*, ed. Verlyn D. Verbrugge (Grand Rapids: Zondervan, 1996), xv.

[11] Huffman, *The Handy Guide to New Testament Greek*, 91.

When you indent the subordinate clauses, you want to line them up under the verb or noun that they modify. So, back to John 3:16, the next step would look like this:

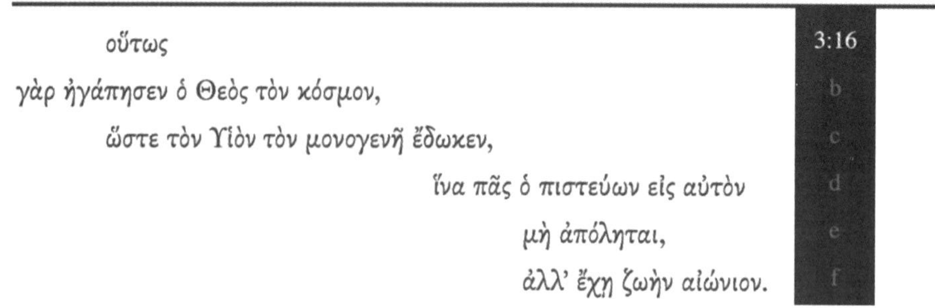

Next, add arrows and labels to help communicate the relationships between the clauses. In this step, you can add as much detail as you desire to help you think through the relationships of the text under consideration. Here is how this would look for John 3:16:[12]

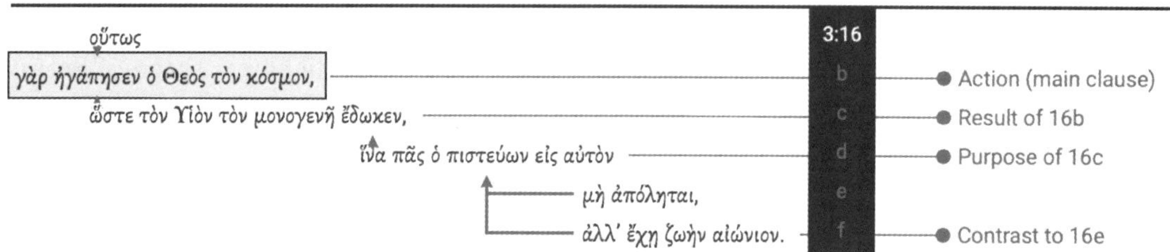

As it is easy to see, phrasing clearly demonstrates the relationships between the various propositions in the text. In our experience, phrasing is the simplest and most effective way to diagram the Greek text with the hope of discerning the argument of the author. Our encouragement is that you give each of the three diagramming methods a test drive, figure out which one works best for you, and then practice it regularly.

Summary Charts[13]

METHODS FOR ANALYZING A TEXT'S STRUCTURE		
METHOD	**STRENGTH(S)**	**WEAKNESS(ES)**
LINE DIAGRAMMING	Good for dealing exhaustively with syntactical connections at the sentence level and below.	Poor at showing relationship between sentences and larger discourse units.
ARCING/BRACKETING	Extremely detailed method for labeling the function of phrases and clauses in an author's flow of thought.	Method takes several hours to learn. Categories of modern discourse analysis not fully employed.
PHRASE DIAGRAMMING	Simple "indentation" method which allows the student to plot quickly a biblical author's flow of thought.	Not good for detailed syntactical study at sentence level and below.

[12] Andy Naselli offers a phrase diagram of this verse on page 142 of *How to Understand and Apply the New Testament*. We compared our diagram to his and found his section on phrasing especially helpful.

[13] Köstenberger, Merkle, and Plummer, *Going Deeper with New Testament Greek*, 469.

EXERCISE

Three diagramming methods applied to Mark 8:34–38

I. Sentence Diagram: In the blank space below, provide a sentence diagram of Mark 8:34–38. Refer back to the summary chart which details the various grammatical relations as much as needed. Please attempt to produce the diagram on your own before you consult the answer key. The more you think through the diagram on your own, the more you will benefit and grow in your diagramming skills.

8:34 Καὶ προσκαλεσάμενος τὸν ὄχλον σὺν τοῖς μαθηταῖς αὐτοῦ εἶπεν αὐτοῖς· εἴ τις θέλει ὀπίσω μου
ἀκολουθεῖν, ἀπαρνησάσθω ἑαυτὸν καὶ ἀράτω τὸν σταυρὸν αὐτοῦ καὶ ἀκολουθείτω μοι. **35** ὃς γὰρ
ἐὰν θέλῃ τὴν ψυχὴν αὐτοῦ σῶσαι ἀπολέσει αὐτήν· ὃς δ᾽ ἂν ἀπολέσει τὴν ψυχὴν αὐτοῦ ἕνεκεν
ἐμοῦ καὶ τοῦ εὐαγγελίου σώσει αὐτήν. **36** τί γὰρ ὠφελεῖ ἄνθρωπον κερδῆσαι τὸν κόσμον ὅλον
καὶ ζημιωθῆναι τὴν ψυχὴν αὐτοῦ; **37** τί γὰρ δοῖ ἄνθρωπος ἀντάλλαγμα τῆς ψυχῆς αὐτοῦ; **38** ὃς
γὰρ ἐὰν ἐπαισχυνθῇ με καὶ τοὺς ἐμοὺς λόγους ἐν τῇ γενεᾷ ταύτῃ τῇ μοιχαλίδι καὶ ἁμαρτωλῷ,
καὶ ὁ υἱὸς τοῦ ἀνθρώπου ἐπαισχυνθήσεται αὐτόν, ὅταν ἔλθῃ ἐν τῇ δόξῃ τοῦ πατρὸς αὐτοῦ μετὰ
τῶν ἀγγέλων τῶν ἁγίων.

II. Arc Diagram: In the blank space below, provide an arc diagram of Mark 8:34–38. Refer back to Piper's charts, which details the various propositional relationships as much as needed. Please attempt to produce the arc diagram on your own before you consult the answer key. The more you think through the diagram on your own, the more you will benefit and grow in your diagramming skills.

8:34 Καὶ προσκαλεσάμενος τὸν ὄχλον σὺν τοῖς μαθηταῖς αὐτοῦ εἶπεν αὐτοῖς· εἴ τις θέλει ὀπίσω
μου ἀκολουθεῖν, ἀπαρνησάσθω ἑαυτὸν καὶ ἀράτω τὸν σταυρὸν αὐτοῦ καὶ ἀκολουθείτω μοι.
35 ὃς γὰρ ἐὰν θέλῃ τὴν ψυχὴν αὐτοῦ σῶσαι ἀπολέσει αὐτήν· ὃς δ' ἂν ἀπολέσει τὴν ψυχὴν αὐτοῦ
ἕνεκεν ἐμοῦ καὶ τοῦ εὐαγγελίου σώσει αὐτήν. **36** τί γὰρ ὠφελεῖ ἄνθρωπον κερδῆσαι τὸν κόσμον
ὅλον καὶ ζημιωθῆναι τὴν ψυχὴν αὐτοῦ; **37** τί γὰρ δοῖ ἄνθρωπος ἀντάλλαγμα τῆς ψυχῆς αὐτοῦ;
38 ὃς γὰρ ἐὰν ἐπαισχυνθῇ με καὶ τοὺς ἐμοὺς λόγους ἐν τῇ γενεᾷ ταύτῃ τῇ μοιχαλίδι καὶ ἁμαρτωλῷ,
καὶ ὁ υἱὸς τοῦ ἀνθρώπου ἐπαισχυνθήσεται αὐτόν, ὅταν ἔλθῃ ἐν τῇ δόξῃ τοῦ πατρὸς αὐτοῦ μετὰ
τῶν ἀγγέλων τῶν ἁγίων.

III. Phrase Diagram: In the blank space below, provide a phrase diagram of Mark 8:34–38. Please attempt to produce the diagram on your own before you consult the answer key. The more you think through the diagram on your own, the more you will benefit and grow in your diagramming skills.

8:34 Καὶ προσκαλεσάμενος τὸν ὄχλον σὺν τοῖς μαθηταῖς αὐτοῦ εἶπεν αὐτοῖς· εἴ τις θέλει ὀπίσω
μου ἀκολουθεῖν, ἀπαρνησάσθω ἑαυτὸν καὶ ἀράτω τὸν σταυρὸν αὐτοῦ καὶ ἀκολουθείτω μοι.
35 ὃς γὰρ ἐὰν θέλῃ τὴν ψυχὴν αὐτοῦ σῶσαι ἀπολέσει αὐτήν· ὃς δ᾽ ἂν ἀπολέσει τὴν ψυχὴν αὐτοῦ
ἕνεκεν ἐμοῦ καὶ τοῦ εὐαγγελίου σώσει αὐτήν. 36 τί γὰρ ὠφελεῖ ἄνθρωπον κερδῆσαι τὸν κόσμον
ὅλον καὶ ζημιωθῆναι τὴν ψυχὴν αὐτοῦ; 37 τί γὰρ δοῖ ἄνθρωπος ἀντάλλαγμα τῆς ψυχῆς αὐτοῦ;
38 ὃς γὰρ ἐὰν ἐπαισχυνθῇ με καὶ τοὺς ἐμοὺς λόγους ἐν τῇ γενεᾷ ταύτῃ τῇ μοιχαλίδι καὶ ἁμαρτωλῷ,
καὶ ὁ υἱὸς τοῦ ἀνθρώπου ἐπαισχυνθήσεται αὐτόν, ὅταν ἔλθῃ ἐν τῇ δόξῃ τοῦ πατρὸς αὐτοῦ μετὰ
τῶν ἀγγέλων τῶν ἁγίων.

Three diagramming methods applied to Mark 10:42–45

IV. Sentence Diagram: In the blank space below, provide a sentence diagram of Mark 10:42–45.

10:42 καὶ προσκαλεσάμενος αὐτοὺς ὁ Ἰησοῦς λέγει αὐτοῖς· οἴδατε ὅτι οἱ δοκοῦντες ἄρχειν τῶν
ἐθνῶν κατακυριεύουσιν αὐτῶν καὶ οἱ μεγάλοι αὐτῶν κατεξουσιάζουσιν αὐτῶν. **43** οὐχ οὕτως
δέ ἐστιν ἐν ὑμῖν, ἀλλ᾽ ὃς ἂν θέλῃ μέγας γενέσθαι ἐν ὑμῖν ἔσται ὑμῶν διάκονος, **44** καὶ ὃς ἂν
θέλῃ ἐν ὑμῖν εἶναι πρῶτος ἔσται πάντων δοῦλος· **45** καὶ γὰρ ὁ υἱὸς τοῦ ἀνθρώπου οὐκ ἦλθεν
διακονηθῆναι ἀλλὰ διακονῆσαι καὶ δοῦναι τὴν ψυχὴν αὐτοῦ λύτρον ἀντὶ πολλῶν.

V. Arc Diagram: In the blank space below, provide an arc diagram of Mark 10:42–45.

10:42 καὶ προσκαλεσάμενος αὐτοὺς ὁ Ἰησοῦς λέγει αὐτοῖς· οἴδατε ὅτι οἱ δοκοῦντες ἄρχειν τῶν
ἐθνῶν κατακυριεύουσιν αὐτῶν καὶ οἱ μεγάλοι αὐτῶν κατεξουσιάζουσιν αὐτῶν. 43 οὐχ οὕτως
δέ ἐστιν ἐν ὑμῖν, ἀλλ' ὃς ἂν θέλῃ μέγας γενέσθαι ἐν ὑμῖν ἔσται ὑμῶν διάκονος, 44 καὶ ὃς ἂν
θέλῃ ἐν ὑμῖν εἶναι πρῶτος ἔσται πάντων δοῦλος· 45 καὶ γὰρ ὁ υἱὸς τοῦ ἀνθρώπου οὐκ ἦλθεν
διακονηθῆναι ἀλλὰ διακονῆσαι καὶ δοῦναι τὴν ψυχὴν αὐτοῦ λύτρον ἀντὶ πολλῶν.

VI. Phrase Diagram: In the blank space below, provide a phrase diagram of Mark 10:42–45.

10:42 καὶ προσκαλεσάμενος αὐτοὺς ὁ Ἰησοῦς λέγει αὐτοῖς· οἴδατε ὅτι οἱ δοκοῦντες ἄρχειν τῶν
ἐθνῶν κατακυριεύουσιν αὐτῶν καὶ οἱ μεγάλοι αὐτῶν κατεξουσιάζουσιν αὐτῶν. **43** οὐχ οὕτως
δέ ἐστιν ἐν ὑμῖν, ἀλλ᾽ ὃς ἂν θέλῃ μέγας γενέσθαι ἐν ὑμῖν ἔσται ὑμῶν διάκονος, **44** καὶ ὃς ἂν
θέλῃ ἐν ὑμῖν εἶναι πρῶτος ἔσται πάντων δοῦλος· **45** καὶ γὰρ ὁ υἱὸς τοῦ ἀνθρώπου οὐκ ἦλθεν
διακονηθῆναι ἀλλὰ διακονῆσαι καὶ δοῦναι τὴν ψυχὴν αὐτοῦ λύτρον ἀντὶ πολλῶν.

ANSWER KEY

Three diagramming methods applied to Mark 8:34–38

I. Sentence diagram[14] of Mark 8:34–38.[15]

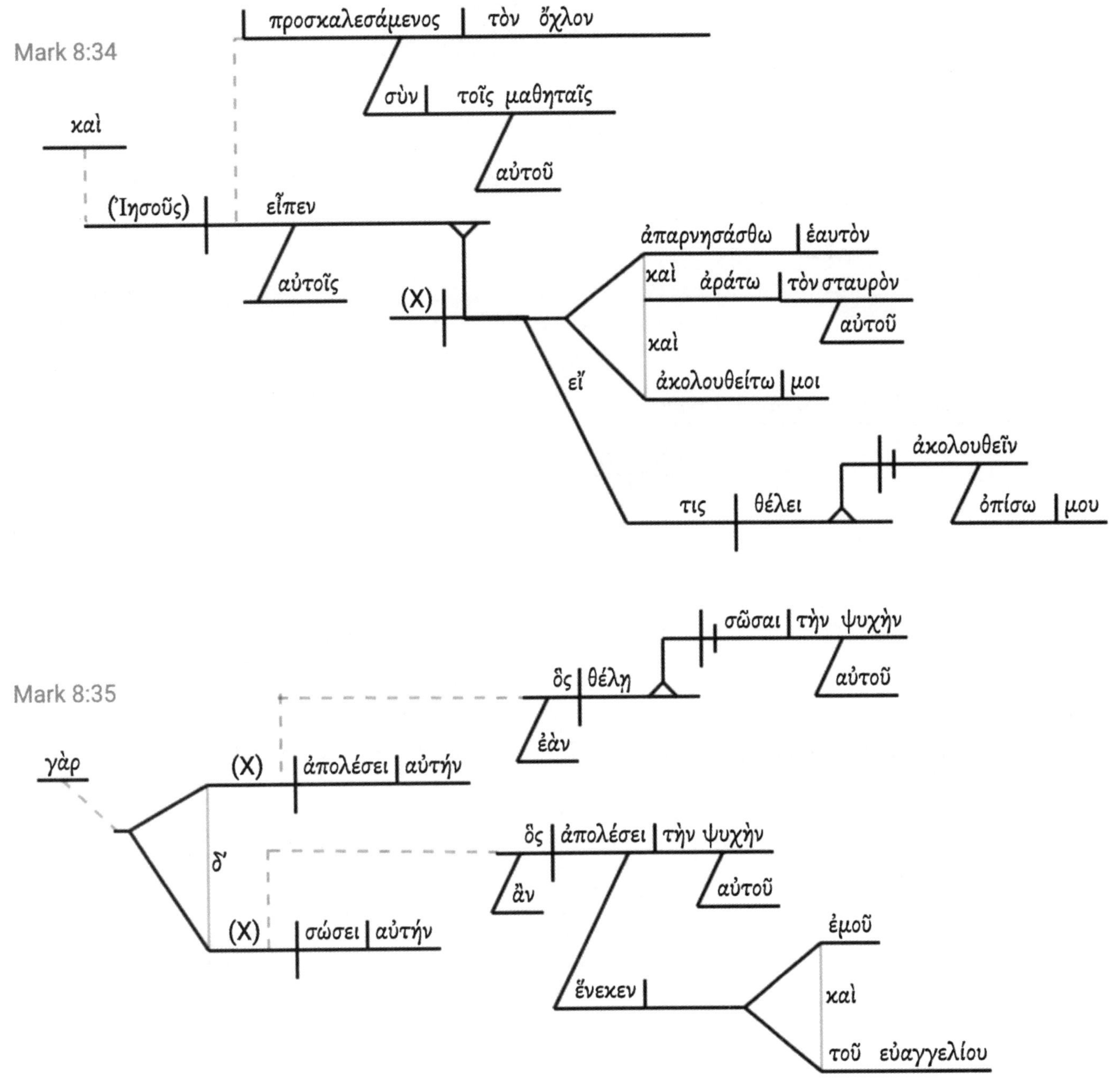

[14] Our sentence diagrams were greatly helped by Randy A. Leedy, *SBL Greek New Testament Sentence Diagrams* (Bellingham, WA: Faithlife, 2020).

[15] Even though in chapter 3 of the current workbook we demarcated this text by including Mark 9:1 with the end of Mark 8 (we, thus, agreed with most commentators on the boundary of the pericope), for the sake of diagramming, we did not include 9:1, given that it functions more as a transitional component and its logical connection to 8:34–38 is not fully clear. On a separate note, Mark 8:36 reads "κερδῆσαι" in the NA[28]. Since BibleArc comes standard with the SBL text, this explains the slight textual difference. Either is accepted for the sake of the exercise, but the text of the NA[28] is preferred.

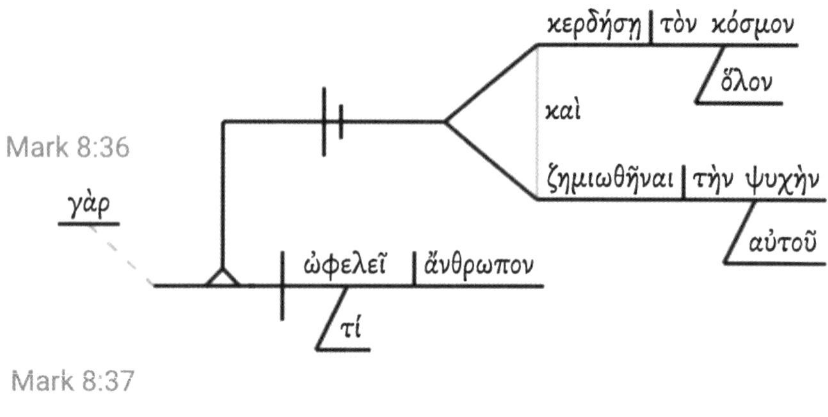
Mark 8:36
γὰρ
κερδήσῃ
τὸν κόσμον
ὅλον
καὶ
ζημιωθῆναι
τὴν ψυχὴν
αὐτοῦ
ὠφελεῖ
ἄνθρωπον
τί

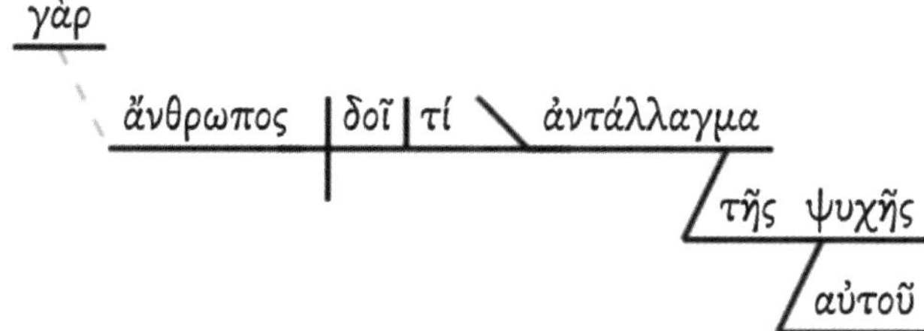
Mark 8:37
γὰρ
ἄνθρωπος
δοῖ
τί
ἀντάλλαγμα
τῆς ψυχῆς
αὐτοῦ

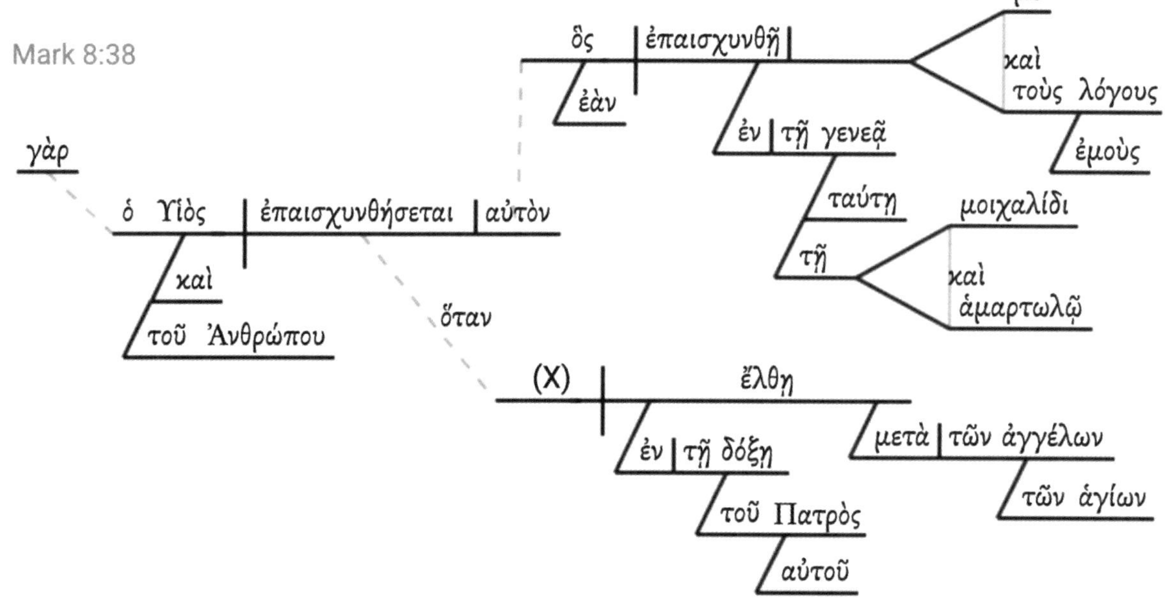
Mark 8:38
γὰρ
ὁ Υἱὸς
ἐπαισχυνθήσεται
αὐτὸν
καὶ
τοῦ Ἀνθρώπου
ὃς
ἐπαισχυνθῇ
ἐὰν
με
καὶ
τοὺς λόγους
ἐμοὺς
ἐν
τῇ γενεᾷ
ταύτῃ
τῇ
μοιχαλίδι
καὶ
ἁμαρτωλῷ
ὅταν
(X)
ἔλθῃ
ἐν
τῇ δόξῃ
τοῦ Πατρὸς
αὐτοῦ
μετὰ
τῶν ἀγγέλων
τῶν ἁγίων

II. Arc diagram of Mark 8:34–38.[16]

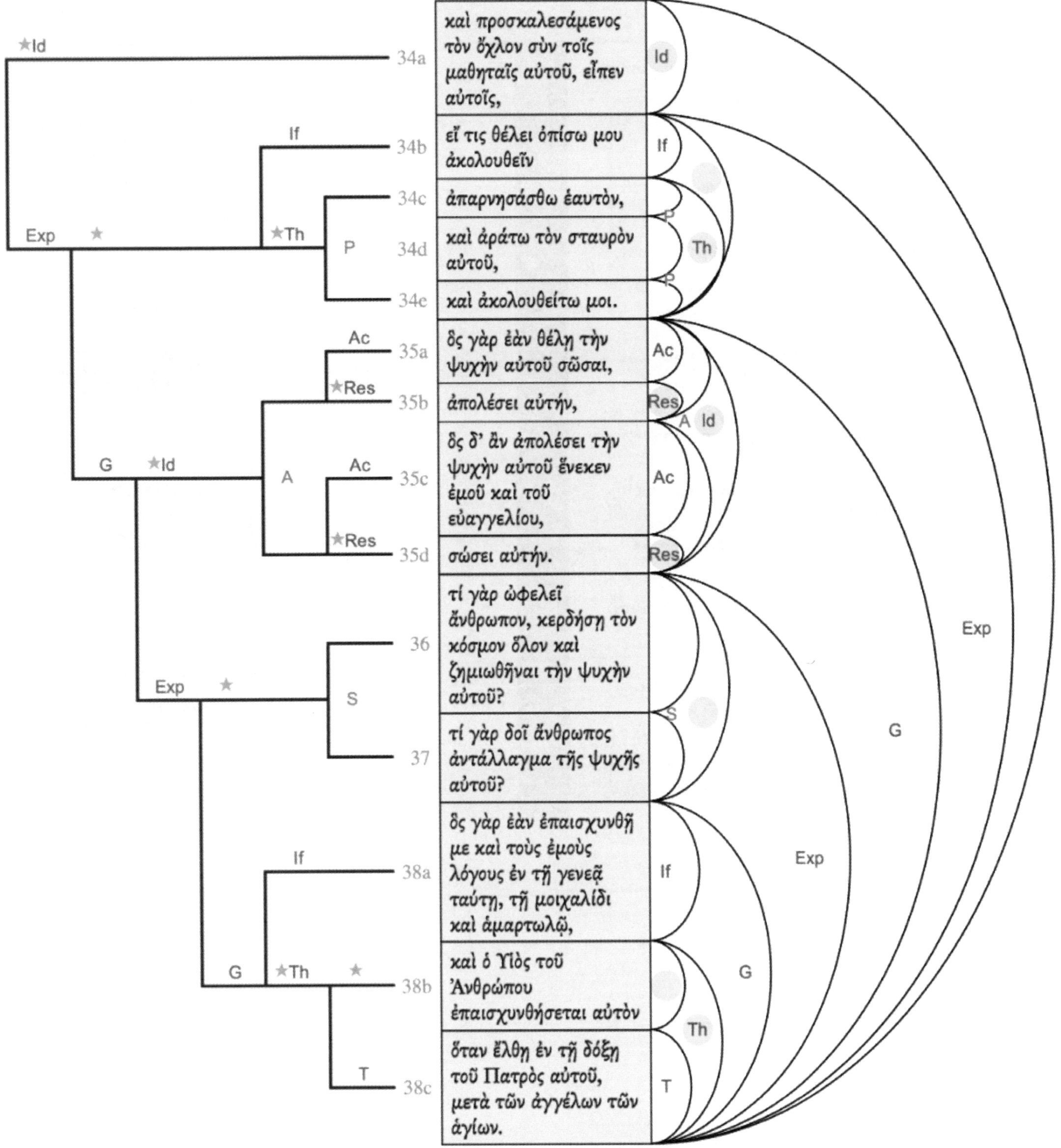

[16] We are grateful for Brent Karding from BibleArc.com, who graciously checked our arcs and provided helpful feedback.

III. Phrase diagram of Mark 8:34–38.

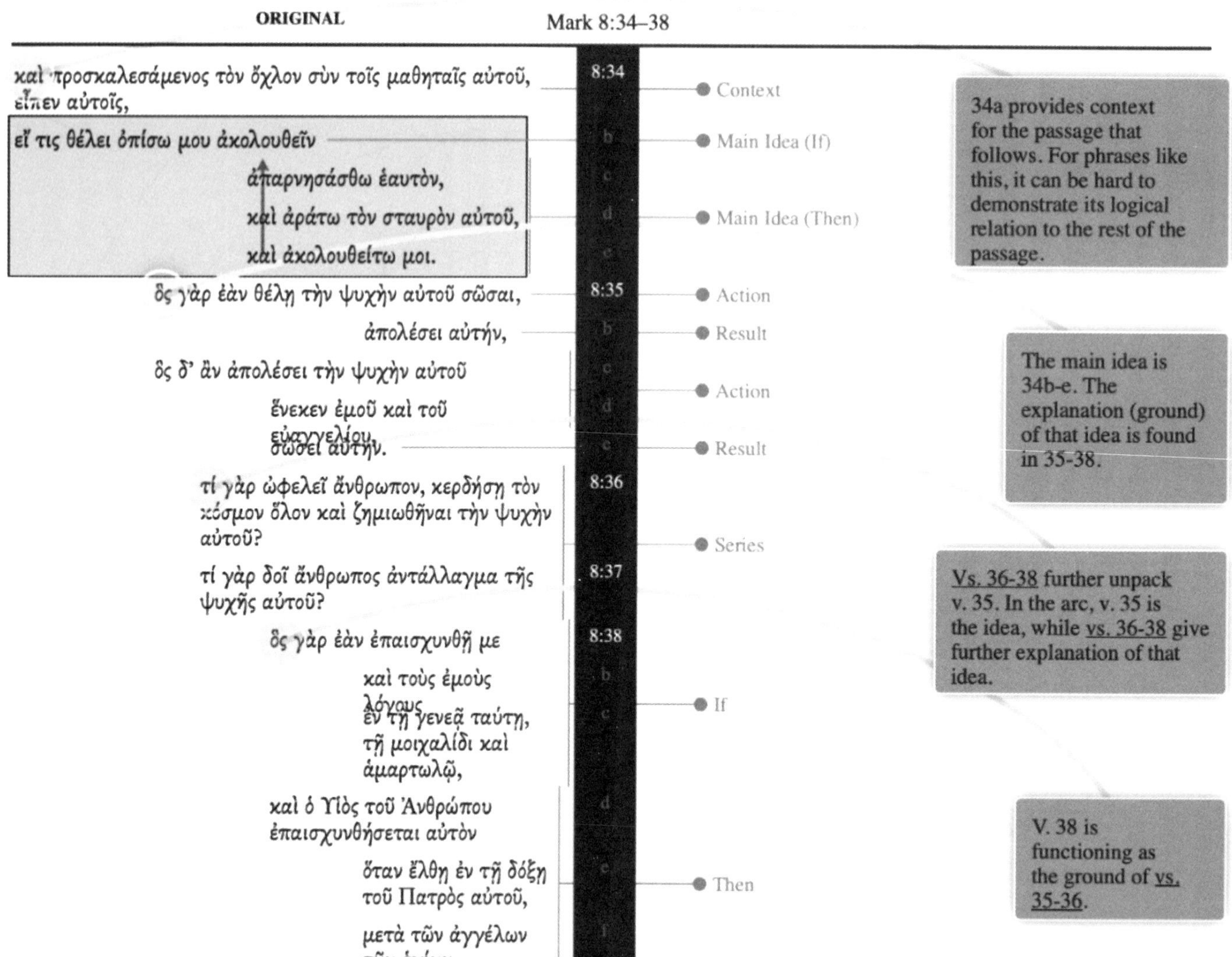

Three diagramming methods applied to Mark 10:42–45

IV. Sentence diagram of Mark 10:42–45

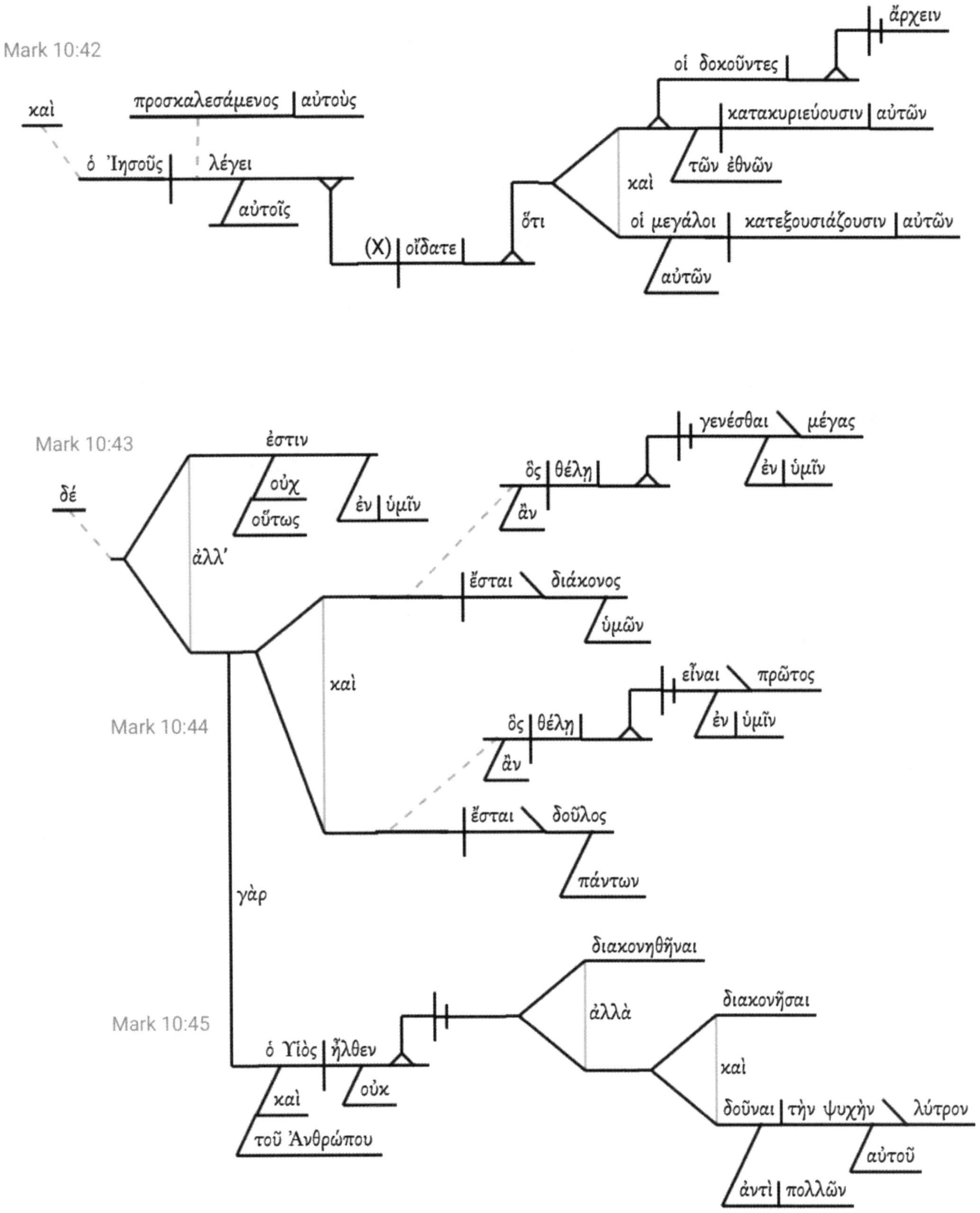

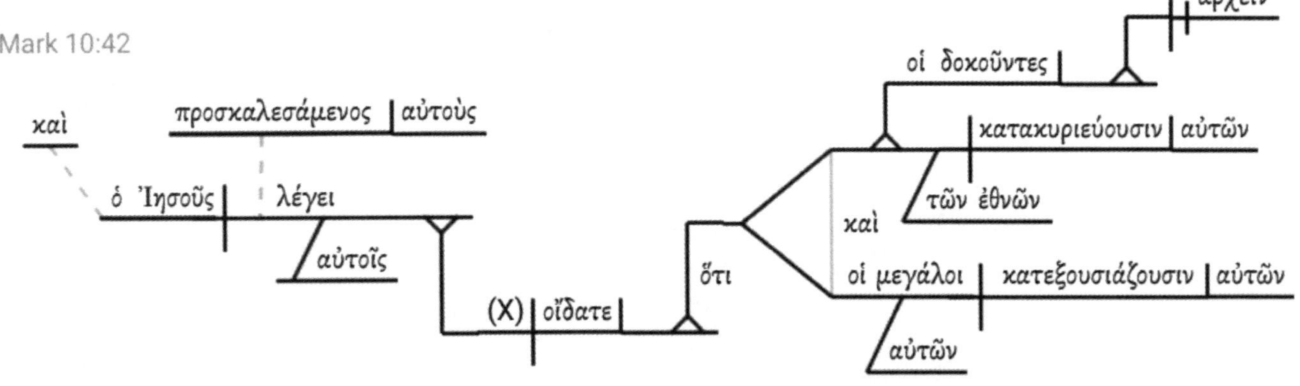

V. Arc diagram of Mark 10:42–45

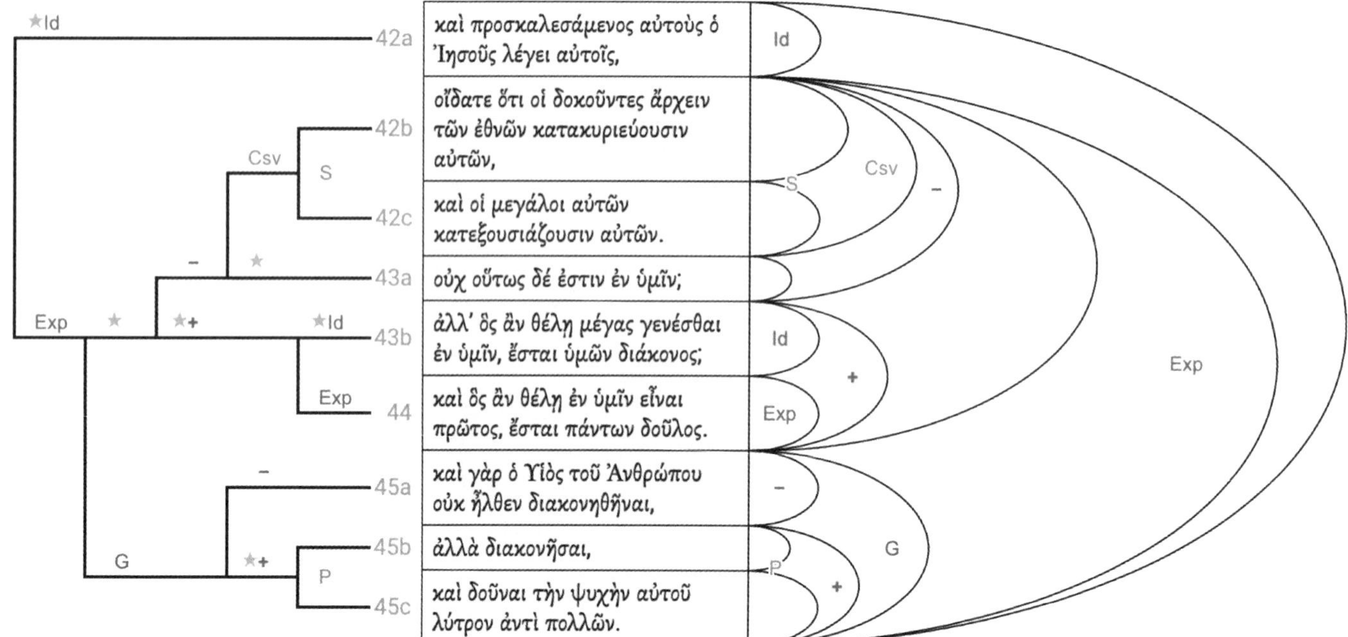

VI. Phrase diagram of Mark 10:42–45

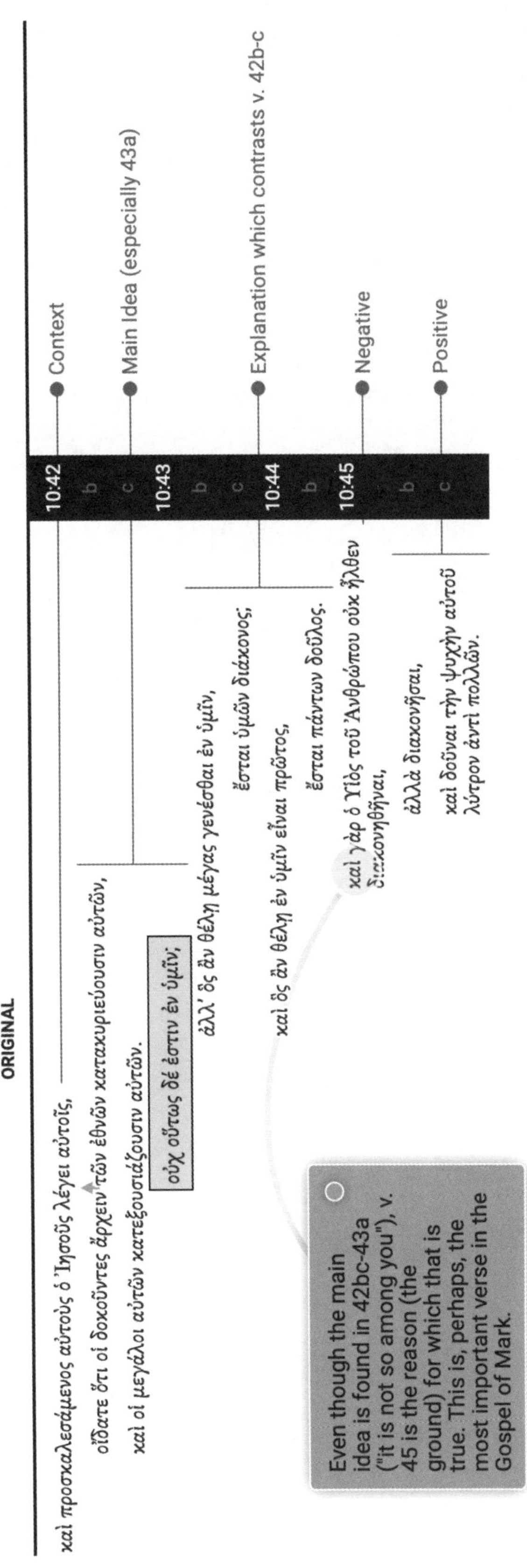

REFERENCES

Bock, Darrell L., and Buist M. Fanning, eds. *Interpreting the New Testament Text: Introduction to the Art and Science of Exegesis*. Wheaton, IL: Crossway, 2006.

Huffman, Douglas S. *The Handy Guide to New Testament Greek: Grammar, Syntax, and Diagramming*. Grand Rapids: Kregel Academic, 2012.

Kantenwein, Lee L. *Diagrammatical Analysis*. Winona Lake, IN: BMH Books, 1979.

Köstenberger, Andreas J., Benjamin L. Merkle, and Robert L. Plummer. *Going Deeper with New Testament Greek: An Intermediate Study of the Grammar and Syntax of the New Testament*. Rev. ed. Nashville: B&H Academic, 2020.

Mounce, William D. *A Graded Reader of Biblical Greek: Exegetical Discussion*. Edited by Verlyn D. Verbrugge. Grand Rapids: Zondervan, 1996.

Naselli, Andrew David. *How to Understand and Apply the New Testament: Twelve Steps from Exegesis to Theology*. Phillipsburg, N.J.: P&R, 2017.

Piper, John. *Reading the Bible Supernaturally: Seeing and Savoring the Glory of God in Scripture*. Wheaton, IL: Crossway, 2017.

Schreiner, Thomas R. *Interpreting the Pauline Epistles*. 2nd ed. Grand Rapids: Baker Academic, 2011.

CHAPTER FOURTEEN

/////////////////

CONCLUSION

Congratulations! Unless you just skipped ahead to read the conclusion (in which case you should go back to chapter 1 and get started!), you are reading this final chapter after having just completed this workbook. We can imagine that you have various thoughts and emotions after putting in all that time and work. You might be thinking, "Is this all really worth it?" "Will I be able to keep up my Greek after I'm no longer taking classes?" "Will Greek really be that important in the ministry that God has called me to?"

Our hope in this brief, final chapter is to remind you that it is worth it. Our goal is to motivate you to keep up your Greek for the rest of your life. Afterall, if you did just complete this workbook, by this time in your overall education you have put in countless hours of vocabulary memorization, paradigm memorization, and syntax review. It would be a shame to let all that hard work go to waste. Most of what follows will not be new to you, but we believe that motivational reminders are helpful when it comes to endurance with the biblical languages.

KEY REASONS TO KEEP YOUR GREEK

With the above in mind, reflect on these reasons to continue studying and keeping your Greek.

1. You should keep your Greek **because you desire to better know God as he has revealed himself in his Word**. Ben Merkle reminds us, "The study of Greek is not an end in itself. The end goal of studying Greek is to know the God who has revealed himself through his Word. God chose to use the Greek language to convey his will for his people through his apostles and prophets. The goal of learning Greek (or Hebrew) is not to parade one's knowledge before others, seeking to impress a congregation or friend. Rather, the goal of learning Greek is first and foremost born out of a desire to behold unhindered the grandest sight: God himself."[1] While there are many reasons to keep your Greek, this one is at the top of the list. What a privilege it is to be able to read God's Word as he inspired it in an effort to grow in our walk with him.
2. You should keep your Greek **because translations are interpretations**. As you should know by now, there is no one-to-one correspondence between words in a different languages. Sure, there is overlap, but no words perfectly correspond in two different languages. When someone translates one language into another, they make a host of interpretive decisions along the way. It is a process to evaluate words and their meanings based on context, and that process is multilayered and laced with interpretive decisions. So, the more we understand the Biblical languages, the more we will be able to think through those interpretive decisions ourselves and the more we will know our Bibles. John Owen says, "Translations contain the word of God, and are the word of God, perfectly or imperfectly, according as they express the words, sense, and

[1] Benjamin L. Merkle and Robert L. Plummer, *Greek for Life: Strategies for Learning, Retaining, and Reviving New Testament Greek* (Grand Rapids: Baker Academic, 2017), 2–3.

meaning of those originals."[2] Looking at this point from a slightly different angle, Scott Hafemann writes that studying the biblical languages

> provides a window through which we can see for ourselves just what decisions have been made by others and why. Instead of being a second-hander, who can only take someone else's word for it, a knowledge of the text allows us to *evaluate*, rather than simply regurgitate. . . . We will be able to *explain* to ourselves and to others why people disagree, what the real issues are, and what are the strengths of our own considered conclusions. It will allow us to have reasons for what we believe and preach, without having to resort to the papacy of scholarship or the papacy of personal experience.[3]

3. You should keep your Greek **because knowing it will help you more faithfully interpret the New Testament**. In Paul's admonition to Timothy in 2 Timothy 2:15, we find a charge to every minister of God's word: "Do your best to present yourself to God as one approved, a worker who has no need to be ashamed, rightly handling the word of truth" (ESV). The more skillful you are with Greek, the more accurate and penetrating you can be in your study of God's Word. As Jason DeRouchie says, "Knowing the original languages helps one observe more accurately and thoroughly, understand more clearly, evaluate more fairly, and interpret more confidently the inspired details of the biblical text."[4]
4. You should keep your Greek **because it will save you time in the long run**. As you are well aware, learning Greek takes time and practice. Some wonder if they will have time to use it with a busy ministry schedule. If you take the time now to work hard and learn Greek as best you can, and keep it up throughout the years, it will save you time in sermon and teaching prep. You will become more proficient in your Bible study, and you will, by looking directly at the Biblical languages, be able to get to the bottom of the matter, or the point of the text, more quickly. Knowing Greek will help you wade through the the sea of biblical commentaries toward the truth of God's Word with precision and speed.
5. You should keep your Greek **because it demonstrates that you value God's Word**. As followers of Jesus, our ultimate authority in everything is God's Word. By taking the time to study and keep our Greek, we are communicating that we value the truth of God's Word rightly. Scott Hafemann is once again helpful on this front. He writes, "Learning the languages affirms the nature of biblical revelation, restores the proper authority of the pastor as teacher, and communicates to our people that the locus of meaning and authority of the Scriptures does not reside in us, but in the text, which we labor so hard to understand. We learn the languages because we are convinced of the inerrancy, sufficiency, and potency of the Word of God."[5] Keeping your Greek, in other words, is an incredible testimony to what you truly believe about God's Word.

THINGS TO REMEMBER AS YOU CONTINUE TO STUDY GREEK

Now that we have considered some reasons to keep your Greek, we also wanted to provide some things to remember as you proceed in that process.

1. First, **keep the big picture in mind**. You likely won't be able to see a vast amount of exegetical gems your first several years of studying Greek. You may see some, but they will probably be pointed out to you by others. It takes time and practice to become proficient with the language. Therefore, don't be discouraged by the pace. Our microwave culture wants things instantaneously; otherwise, those things are not worth doing, or so it's often assumed. Yet, you are studying Greek for a lifetime of faithful interpretation. So, it may be helpful to think of yourself as a bricklayer. Each time you study Greek and work hard at learning

---

[2] John Owen, *The Works of John Owen*, vol. 16, *Div. 3: Controversial: The True Nature of a Gospel Church. Tracts on Excommunication, Church Censures, Baptism, Etc.* (London: Banner of Truth, 1995), 357.
[3] Scott Hafemann, "The *SBJT* Forum: Profiles in Expository Preaching," *SBJT* 3, no 2 (1999), 87–88.
[4] Jason DeRouchie, "The Profit of Employing the Biblical Languages," *Themelios* 37, no 1 (2012), 36.
[5] Hafemann, "The *SBJT* Forum: Profiles in Expository Preaching," 88.

it, you are laying bricks. In time, you will have a large wall before you. Don't let the difficulty discourage you, keep the big picture in mind, and know that the wall is coming.

2. You should set a goal to **study every day, if possible**. Even a little time every day will go a long way in learning and keeping your Greek. We would encourage you to make the original languages a part of your devotional time with the Lord. You can start with easier books like 1 John or the Gospel of John. It can be helpful to pair your reading with a more grammatically focused commentary that might point out things you should be seeing in the Greek text. Consider watching the "Daily Dose of Greek" videos provided by Rob Plummer at https://dailydoseofgreek.com. You will be amazed at how helpful a daily 2-minute video on a verse of the Greek New Testament can be! The more you are in the Greek text the better. It is also helpful to review as you have down time throughout the day. Whether you are waiting for a bus, using the restroom, are in between tasks during your day, etc., take advantage of those small windows to refresh on a paradigm or get into the Greek text.
3. To become proficient in Greek, you must **persevere**. Mastering any language requires hard work and is not for the faint of heart. You may not feel as if language learning comes naturally to you. However, we want to challenge and encourage you to work hard and not to feel sorry for yourself. Keep in mind that the Bible warns us against grumbling or complaining (Phil 2:14) and also reminds us that we are to do all things for the Lord (Col 3:23). Continually remind yourself that this process is worth it. Learning Greek can be hard, but it will pay you back a hundredfold in ministry through your knowledge of God and his Word. So, persevere, persevere, persevere.

Once again, congratulations on completing this workbook. In many ways, your journey to knowing God through the study of the Greek New Testament is never ending (at least in this life!). But we can attest that it is worth it. Don't give up. Don't settle for less. One day soon you will stand before your Lord and Savior, and you will realize that all your labor was not in vain as you sought to rightly divide the Word of Truth (2 Tim 2:15).

/////////////////

APPENDIX

This appendix contains the summary charts from the chapters of *Going Deeper with New Testament Greek* that have not been featured in the current workbook and thus provide a reminder for students to give attention to these components in their further study.

The Greek Language (1)[1]

HISTORY OF THE GREEK LANGUAGE	
FORM OF LANGUAGE	**DATES**
Proto Indo-European	Prior to 1500 BC
Linear B or Mycenaean	1500–1000 BC
Dialects and Classical Greek	1000–300 BC
Koine Greek	300 BC–AD 330
Byzantine Greek	AD 330–AD 1453
Modern Greek	AD 1453–present

COMMON CHANGES IN GREEK FROM CLASSICAL TO KOINE PERIOD	
CHANGE	**EXAMPLE FROM THE GREEK NEW TESTAMENT**
First aorist endings appear on second aorist verb stems	ἐγὼ δὲ **εἶπα·** τίς εἶ, κύριε; ("And I **said**, "Who are You, Lord?" Acts 26:15 NASB).
Less common use of optative mood	Ἐμοὶ δὲ **μὴ γένοιτο** καυχᾶσθαι εἰ μὴ ἐν τῷ σταυρῷ τοῦ κυρίου ἡμῶν Ἰησοῦ Χριστοῦ ("But **may it never be** that I should boast, except in the cross of our Lord Jesus Christ" Gal 6:14 NASB77).
Increased use of prepositions	Εὐλογητὸς ὁ θεὸς καὶ πατὴρ τοῦ κυρίου ἡμῶν Ἰησοῦ Χριστοῦ, ὁ εὐλογήσας ἡμᾶς **ἐν** πάσῃ εὐλογίᾳ πνευματικῇ **ἐν** τοῖς ἐπουρανίοις **ἐν** Χριστῷ ("Blessed is the God and Father of our Lord Jesus Christ, who has blessed us **with** every spiritual blessing **in** the heavens **in** Christ" Eph 1:3).
-μι verbs appear with omega verb endings	τὰ πτώματα αὐτῶν οὐκ **ἀφίουσιν** τεθῆναι εἰς μνῆμα ("[they] did not **permit** their bodies to be put into a tomb" Rev 11:9).

[1] Andreas J. Köstenberger, Benjamin L. Merkle, and Robert L. Plummer, *Going Deeper with New Testament Greek: An Intermediate Study of the Grammar and Syntax of the New Testament*, rev. ed. (Nashville: B&H Academic, 2020), 37.

COMMON CHANGES IN GREEK FROM CLASSICAL TO KOINE PERIOD (CONTINUED)	
CHANGE	**EXAMPLE FROM THE GREEK NEW TESTAMENT**
Disappearance of ϝ and ϙ	**καλέσω** τὸν οὐ λαόν μου λαόν μου καὶ τὴν οὐκ ἠγαπημένην ἠγαπημένην ("Those who were not my people **I will call** 'my people,' and her who was not beloved I will call 'beloved'" Rom 9:25 ESV).
Greater use of paratactic style	Cf. 1 John and James.
Change in meaning of comparative and superlative forms	μετάγεται ὑπὸ **ἐλαχίστου** πηδαλίου ὅπου ἡ ὁρμὴ τοῦ εὐθύνοντος βούλεται ("they are guided by **a very small** rudder wherever the will of the pilot directs" Jas 3:4).
Semantic shifts in specific words	Σὺ δὲ **λάλει** ἃ πρέπει τῇ ὑγιαινούσῃ διδασκαλίᾳ ("But as for you, **speak** the things which are fitting for sound doctrine" Titus 2:1 NASB95).

Discourse Analysis (13)[2]

METHODS FOR ANALYZING A TEXT'S STRUCTURE		
METHOD	**STRENGTH(S)**	**WEAKNESS(ES)**
DISCOURSE ANALYSIS	Using insights from modern linguistics, discourse analysis provides an objective basis for arguing for boundaries, prominence, and cohesion in a text.	Much literature on discourse analysis is overly technical.

Word Studies (14)[3]

PRINCIPLES FOR WORD STUDY
1. Don't make any word mean more than you have to. ("The least meaning is the best meaning.")
2. Prioritize synchrony over diachrony. Study word usage contemporaneous with your text.
3. Do not confuse word and concept.
4. Do not view word study tools as inerrant.

RESOURCES FOR WORD STUDY	
RESOURCE	**DESCRIPTION**
BDAG	Best NT Greek lexicon.
NIDNTTE	5-volume word study tool, excellent linguistically and theologically.
EDNT	3-volume lexicon with focus on theologically significant terms.
Louw & Nida	2-volume work, groups words by "semantic domain" (field of meaning).
TDNT or "Kittel"	10-volume work, extremely detailed diachronic study, some entries have a liberal German bias.
Spicq (Theological Lexicon of the NT)	3-volume work by French linguist.

[2] Köstenberger, Merkle, and Plummer, 469.
[3] Köstenberger, Merkle, and Plummer, 497–98.

RESOURCES FOR WORD STUDY (CONTINUED)	
RESOURCE	**DESCRIPTION**
Liddell-Scott-Jones (LSJ)	Detailed lexicon indispensable for ancient Greek outside the Greek New Testament.
The Brill Dictionary of Ancient Greek (BrillDAG)	Translated from Italian. Heralded by some as "the new LSJ." Criticized by others.
Moulton & Milligan	Lexicon illustrating NT vocabulary through ancient papyri and inscriptions.
NewDocs	10 volumes (as of 2015), continuing the tradition of Moulton & Milligan by illustrating NT vocabulary through Greek papyri and inscriptions.
Thesaurus Linguae Graecae (TLG)	Searchable database of Greek writings from the time of Homer to the fall of Byzantium.
Lust-Eynikel-Hauspie (LEH)	LXX lexicon, concerned with the meaning intended by the translators of the LXX.
Muraoka	LXX lexicon, concerned with how an early reader would have understood the LXX translation.

A STRATEGY FOR WORD STUDY	
1.	Consider the immediate and broader literary context.
2.	Compare English Bible translations.
3.	Consider the same biblical author's other uses of the word.
4.	List the possible definitions of the word according to standard lexicons and word study tools.
5.	Identify other words in the same semantic domain.
6.	Consider uses of the word throughout the NT and LXX.
7.	State clearly and succinctly your discoveries. Beware of theologizing in a reductionistic way.

/////////////////

BIBLIOGRAPHY

Bock, Darrell L., and Buist M. Fanning, eds. *Interpreting the New Testament Text: Introduction to the Art and Science of Exegesis*. Wheaton, IL: Crossway, 2006.

Carson, D. A., and Douglas J. Moo. *An Introduction to the New Testament*. 2nd ed. Grand Rapids: Zondervan, 2005.

Carson, D. A. "Syntactical and Text-Critical Observations on John 20:30–31: One More Round on the Purpose of the Fourth Gospel." *Journal of Biblical Literature* 124, no. 4 (2005): 693–714.

Comfort, Philip W. *Encountering the Manuscripts: An Introduction to New Testament Paleography & Textual Criticism*. Nashville: B&H Academic, 2005.

Black, David A. *Rethinking New Testament Textual Criticism*. Grand Rapids: Baker Academic, 2002.

Byrskog, Samuel. *Story as History—History as Story: The Gospel Tradition in the Context of Ancient Oral History*. Leiden: NL: Brill, 2022.

Decker, Rodney J. *Mark 1–8: A Handbook on the Greek Text*. Ed. Martin M. Culy. Baylor Handbook on the Greek New Testament. Waco: Baylor University Press, 2014.

———. *Mark 9–16: A Handbook on the Greek Text*. Ed. Martin M. Culy. Baylor Handbook on the Greek New Testament. Waco: Baylor University Press, 2014.

———. "The Function of the Imperfect Tense in Mark's Gospel," in *The Language of the New Testament: Context, History, and Development*, ed. Stanley E. Porter and Andrew W. Pitts. Leiden: Brill, 2013. Pages 347–64.

DeRouchie, Jason. "The Profit of Employing the Biblical Languages." *Themelios* 37, no. 1 (2012): 32–50.

Ehrman, Bart D. *Misquoting Jesus: The Story Behind Who Changed the Bible and Why*. New York: HarperOne, 2007.

———. *The Orthodox Corruption of Scripture: The Effect of Early Christological Controversies on the Text of the New Testament*. Updated edition. New York: Oxford University Press, 2011.

Ellis, Edward Earle. "The Date and Provenance of Mark's Gospel." *The Four Gospels*. Ed. Franz van Segbroeck. Leuven: Peeters, 1992.

Epp, Eldon J. "The Multivalence of the Term 'Original Text' in New Testament Textual Criticism." *HTR* 92 (1999): 245–81.

Eusebius. *Eusebius' Ecclesiastical History: Complete and Unabridged*. Translated by C. F. Cruse. Updated Edition. Peabody, MA: Hendrickson, 1998.

Garland, David E. *A Theology of Mark's Gospel: Good News about Jesus the Messiah, the Son of God*. Ed. Andreas J. Köstenberger. Biblical Theology of the New Testament. Grand Rapids: Zondervan, 2015.

Goetchius, Eugene Van Ness. "Review of Toward a Descriptive Analysis of EINAI as a Linking Verb in New Testament Greek by Lane C. McGaughy." *Journal of Biblical Literature* 95 (1976): 147–49.

Gould, Ezra P. *A Critical and Exegetical Commentary on the Gospel according to St. Mark*. International Critical Commentary. New York: Scribner's Sons, 1922.

Guelich, Robert A. *Mark 1–8:26*. Word Biblical Commentary 34A. Dallas: Thomas Nelson, 1989.

Gurry, Peter J. "How Your Greek NT Is Changing: A Simple Introduction to the Coherence-Based Genealogical Method (CBGM)." *JETS* 59, no. 4 (2016): 675–89.

———. "The Number of Variants in the Greek New Testament: A Proposed Estimate." *New Testament Studies* 62, no. 1 (2016): 97–121.

Hafemann, Scott. "The SBJT Forum: Profiles in Expository Preaching." *SBJT* 3, no. 2 (1999): 87–88.

Head, Peter M. "Editio Critica Maior: An Introduction and Assessment." *TynBul* 61 (2010): 131–52.

Hoehner, Harold W. *Ephesians: An Exegetical Commentary*. Grand Rapids: Baker Academic, 2002.

Huffman, Douglas S. *The Handy Guide to New Testament Greek: Grammar, Syntax, and Diagramming*. Grand Rapids: Kregel Academic, 2012.

Instone-Brewer, David. *Divorce and Remarriage in the Bible: The Social and Literary Context*. Grand Rapids: Eerdmans, 2002.

Irenaeus. *Against Heresies*. Pickerington, OH: Beloved, 2015.

Jongkind, Dirk. *An Introduction to the Greek New Testament: Produced at Tyndale House, Cambridge*. Wheaton, IL: Crossway, 2019.

Kähler, Martin. *The So-Called Historical Jesus and the Historic Biblical Christ*. Ed. Carl E. Braaten. Fortress Texts in Modern Theology. Philadelphia, PA: Fortress, 1988.

Kantenwein, Lee L. *Diagrammatical Analysis*. Winona Lake, IN: BMH Books, 1979.

Kennedy, H. A. A. "The Epistle of Paul to the Philippians." In *The Expositor's Greek Testament: Greek Text*, Vol. 3. New York: George H. Doran, 1910.

Köstenberger, Andreas J., Benjamin L. Merkle, and Robert L. Plummer. *Going Deeper with New Testament Greek: An Intermediate Study of the Grammar and Syntax of the New Testament*. Rev. ed. Nashville: B&H Academic, 2020.

Lane, William L. *The Gospel According to Mark*. The New International Commentary on the New Testament. Grand Rapids: Eerdmans, 2008.

Lee, John J. R. *Christological Rereading of the Shema (Deut 6.4) in Mark's Gospel*. Wissenschaftliche Untersuchungen Zum Neuen Testament. 2. Reihe 533. Tübingen: Mohr Siebeck, 2020.

———, and Daniel Brueske. *A Ransom for Many: Mark 10:45 as a Key to the Gospel*. Bellingham, WA: Lexham Academic, 2023.

Leedy, Randy A. *SBL Greek New Testament Sentence Diagrams*. Bellingham, WA: Faithlife, 2020.

Marcus, Joel. *Mark 8–16: A New Translation with Introduction and Commentary*. The Anchor Yale Bible 27A. New Haven, CT: Yale University Press, 2009.

Marshall, Christopher D. *Faith as a Theme in Mark's Narrative*. Society for New Testament Studies 64. Cambridge: Cambridge University Press, 1995.

McGaughy, Lane C. *Toward a Descriptive Analysis of EINAI as a Linking Verb in New Testament Greek*. SBLDS 6. Missoula, MT: Society of Biblical Literature, 1972.

Merkle, Benjamin L., and Robert L. Plummer. *Greek for Life: Strategies for Learning, Retaining, and Reviving New Testament Greek*. Grand Rapids: Baker Academic, 2017.

Metzger, Bruce M. *A Textual Commentary on the Greek New Testament: A Companion Volume to the United Bible Societies' Greek New Testament*. 2nd ed. Peabody, MA: Hendrickson Publishers, 2005.

———, and Bart D. Ehrman. *The Text of the New Testament: Its Transmission, Corruption, and Restoration*. 4th ed. New York: Oxford University Press, 2005.

Mounce, William D. *Basics of Biblical Greek Grammar*. Ed. Verlyn D. Verbrugge and Christopher A. Beetham. 4th ed. Grand Rapids, MI: Zondervan, 2019.

———. *A Graded Reader of Biblical Greek*. Grand Rapids: Zondervan, 1996.

———. *The Morphology of Biblical Greek*. Edited by Verlyn D. Verbrugge. Grand Rapids: Zondervan, 1994.

Naselli, Andrew David. *How to Understand and Apply the New Testament: Twelve Steps from Exegesis to Theology*. Phillipsburg, N.J.: P&R, 2017.

Owen, John. *The Works of John Owen. 16: Div. 3: Controversial: The True Nature of a Gospel Church. Tracts on Excommunication, Church Censures, Baptism, Etc*. London: Banner of Truth, 1995.

Parker, D. C. *The Living Text of the Gospels*. Cambridge: Cambridge University Press, 1997.

Piper, John. *Reading the Bible Supernaturally: Seeing and Savoring the Glory of God in Scripture*. Wheaton, IL: Crossway, 2017.

Porter, Stanley E. *Idioms of the Greek New Testament*. 2nd ed. Biblical Languages: Greek 2. Sheffield, UK: Sheffield Academic Press, 1999.

Robertson, A. T. *The Minister and His Greek New Testament*. Repr. ed. Birmingham, AL: Solid Ground Christian Books, 2008.

Runge, Steven E. *Discourse Grammar of the Greek New Testament: A Practical Introduction for Teaching and Exegesis*. Peabody, MA: Hendrickson, 2010.

Schreiner, Thomas R. *Interpreting the Pauline Epistles*. 2nd ed. Grand Rapids, MI: Baker Academic, 2011.

Sowell, Eric. *An Intermediate Guide to Greek Diagramming*. Koine Works Diagramming. Lexel Software, n.d. https://www.inthebeginning.org/e-diagrams/documents/intermediategreektodiagramming.pdf.

Stein, Robert H. *Mark*. Baker Exegetical Commentary on the New Testament. Grand Rapids, MI: Baker Academic, 2008.

Strauss, Mark L. *Four Portraits, One Jesus: An Introduction to Jesus and the Gospels*. 2nd ed. Grand Rapids: Zondervan, 2020.

———. *Mark*. Zondervan Exegetical Commentary on the New Testament. Grand Rapids: Zondervan, 2014.

Wallace, Daniel B. *Greek Grammar Beyond the Basics: An Exegetical Syntax of the New Testament*. Grand Rapids: Zondervan, 1996.

Wasserman, Tommy, and Peter J. Gurry. *A New Approach to Textual Criticism: An Introduction to the Coherence-Based Genealogical Method*. Resources for Biblical Study, Number 80. Atlanta: SBL Press, 2017.

Williams, Joel. *Mark*. Ed. Andreas J. Köstenberger and Robert W. Yarbrough. Exegetical Guide to the Greek New Testament. Nashville: B&H Academic, 2020.

Zerwick, Maximilian. *Biblical Greek Illustrated by Examples*. English ed., adapted from the fourth Latin ed. Vol. 114 of *Scripta Pontificii Instituti Biblici*. Rome: Pontificio Instituto Biblico, 1963.